praise for *into these hands: wisdom from midwives*

Nothing is more important than how we are born. How we come into this world, how we are ushered in, met and hopefully embraced upon arrival, impacts the whole of our time on earth. It is shocking to realize how few people think of this. This fascinating and informative book will introduce the reader to the astonishing history and world of midwifery, a profession, a calling, a mission that I wholeheartedly support. —ALICE WALKER, Pulitzer Prize winner, poet, author of *The Color Purple, The Temple of My Familiar,* and *Taking the Arrow Out of the Heart*

This book is a prescription for how to fix an ailing system. Midwives are contesting a maternity care industry that leaves women and society in ignorance of the transformation that well-supported birth can bring to new mothers and those around them. — MICHAEL KLEIN, MD, Emeritus Professor Family Practice & Pediatrics, University of British Columbia

Simkins has gathered the remarkable stories of twenty-five extraordinary midwives. They so eloquently remind us of why we must keep working to ensure that every community offers women the option of midwifery care—in the home, birth center, and hospital settings.—JUDY NORSIGIAN, Executive Director of Our Bodies Ourselves, coauthor of *Our Bodies, Ourselves: Pregnancy and Birth*

Into These Hands is an important contribution to the literature on childbirth. Midwives always have and will continue to attend the vast majority of births and have been proven scientifically to be the safest and best birth attendant for most births. Midwives have a vast wisdom about childbirth and this book gives us an opportunity to learn from this wisdom.—MARSDEN WAGNER, MD, Perinatologist and perinatal epidemiologist, author of *Born in the USA: How a Broken Maternity Care System Can Be Fixed to Put Women and Children First*

With the United Nations Population Fund's recent recognition of the importance of strengthening midwifery worldwide to save lives and promote the health of women and newborns, the words of these wise women who birthed modern midwifery couldn't be more timely. This collection is a testament to the skill, dedication, and love with which midwives approach their work. It will undoubtedly be an inspiration to future generations of midwives, who support pregnant women and in doing so, promote social justice.— FARAH DIAZ-TELLO, staff attorney of National Advocates for Pregnant Women

These wise midwives understand an essential truth: when we heal ourselves we also heal our ancestors, our children, and Mother Earth.—RITA PITKA BLUMENSTEIN, Yup'ik Elder, member of the International Council of Thirteen Indigenous Grandmothers

A must read for every woman who has experienced the miracle of birth. A fitting tribute to the legacy of midwifery.—BYLLYE Y. AVERY, Founder of Black Women's Health Imperative

As a medical anthropologist and midwife, specializing in cross-cultural maternal child health, I am convinced that the twenty-five remarkable women chronicled here provide all the key ingredients needed for contemporary North American childbirth reform. Thank you Geradine!—MELISSA CHEYNEY, PhD, CPM, Department of Anthropology, Oregon State University

This thrilling book shows us all why midwifery is not a vestige of our indigenous or pioneer past but rather the vanguard of the best possible future for women, families, birth, and the economy and effectiveness of maternity care.—ROBBIE DAVIS-FLOYD, Author, cultural and medical anthropologist and Senior Research Fellow at University of Texas, Austin

Every woman and baby has the right to a respectful, safe and deeply fulfilling birth experience. *Into These Hands* doesn't just assure us that this can be achieved, it shows us how.— ELAN MCALLISTER, Founder of Choices in Childbirth, co-chair of *The Birth Survey*

During the twentieth century the practice of obstetrics made many advances in the treatment of high-risk pregnancies. As a result, birth moved from the guidance of the hands of midwives assisting women laboring and birthing in their beds at homes, to an institutional event with physicians using technology and instruments to deliver women of their newborns on operating tables in hospitals. This powerful collection of stories is about the reemergence of midwives as the guardians of normal birth in America. At the heart of these stories is the right for women to choose with whom and how they wish to give birth.— BRIDGET LYNCH, Former President of International Confederation of Midwives

Into These Hands offers intimate insight into the world of midwifery and midwives through personal stories that transcend ethnic, cultural and professional boundaries that too often divide us. These stories reflect the personal dedication, sacrifice and challenges of those who have chosen to serve women and children.—MICHAEL E. BIRD, past President of the American Public Association, Vice Chair of Kewa Pueblo Health Board

Birth, power, politics—all of which are inseparable from the story of midwifery— as told by the amazing women who have forged the her-story in *Into These Hands*. Each memoir takes us deeper so that we can witness the insights, wisdom and transformation that these women have experienced becoming and living as midwives. There are lessons for all of us in how to live our passions and make a difference.—DEBRA PASCALI-BONARO, filmmaker, doula, director of documentary films *Orgasmic Birth: The Best Kept Secret* and *Organic Birth: Birth is Natural*

the midwife
matrix

the midwife matrix

reclaiming our bodies, our births, our lives

Geradine Simkins

Editor of *Into These Hands, Wisdom From Midwives*
An Anthology of Memoirs

To the Matriarch Midwives who are the vessels of vintage wisdom.
To the Young Midwives who are the emissaries of new knowledge.
To the People Who Give Birth, each time a precious everyday miracle.
And to the Powers of Lineage and Community that weave us all together.

Every midwife knows
that not until a mother's womb
softens from the pain of labor
will a way unfold
and the infant find that opening to be born.

Oh friend!
There is treasure in your heart,
it is heavy with child.

Listen.
All the awakened ones,
like trusted midwives are saying,
'Welcome this pain.
It opens the dark passage of Grace.'
—RUMI

contents

author's note on language

I recognize that sex and gender are not binary categories, and not everyone who gets pregnant or gives birth identifies as a woman. In order to acknowledge the range of people who give birth—women, transgender men, queer and gender-nonconforming people—I use both of these terms: 'women' and 'people who are pregnant and give birth.' In some descriptions I say 'people who have wombs.' The lived experiences of LGBTQI people, particularly transgender and intersex people, must be recognized. Trans-exclusionary politics and practices are unjust. All people have a right to safe, accessible, respectful, personalized, and appropriate reproductive healthcare.

I also believe we cannot submerge the feminine in gender neutrality until we actualize the 'empowered feminine,' and until woman/feminine has parity and equity with man/masculine. Systemic inequities—social, political, and economic—have been historically stacked against women, resulting in overt attempts to control their reproductive health, rights, and lives. Thus, in most places in this book I use the terms 'woman' and 'women' and the feminine pronouns 'she' and 'her' to denote pregnant and birthing people. I use 'woman' and 'women' to highlight the procreative capacities of people with wombs. This language is intended to be inclusive of trans and two-spirited people who can become pregnant and give birth.

Gender-based mistreatment and violence is a preventable but ubiquitous public health problem. It is born out of culturally created gender roles in which power imbalances exist between men and women, which result in gender-authority. By using the words 'woman' and 'women' I seek to draw the reader's attention to the role of gender dynamics in healthcare relationships and power

XVI | *the midwife matrix*

inequities that do not appropriately prioritize the safety of women, girls, and people with wombs. Cultures of discrimination within some healthcare systems specifically oppress women, girls, and people with wombs, and restrict or deny their autonomy in decision-making through gender-based disrespect, coercion, mistreatment, or abuse.

For all these reasons, it is challenging to avoid using gendered language when talking about reproductive rights and justice. Still, language matters, and words signal inclusion or exclusion. Therefore, when the gender to whom a pronoun refers is unknown or nonspecific—for example, where I might have used 'he or she,' or 'his or her' in the past—I have used the singular 'they' or 'their.' These pronouns avoid male/female binary categories, acknowledge the spectrum of gender identity, and honor gender fluidity. As culture shifts language must also shift. This kind of accommodation is not a lot to ask, but rather, is an essential courtesy and a sign of respect.

Writing a book is always an act of risk taking. As a writer I seek to create an infrastructure of inclusion while crafting a narrative that is navigable and readable.

opening

It was a bright blue summer day in Northern Michigan and the wind was blowing my hair westward as I knelt over my perennial flower garden pulling weeds. I was lost amidst the intoxicating scent of the floral nectars. Lost in the satisfying sensation of plunging my fingers deep into fertile soil. Lost in the soothing warmth of the sun on my bare back. And lost in the rush of bittersweet relief over completing my midwifery career that had spanned more than four decades. I was so captivated by the revelry of the moment that I almost didn't hear the phone ringing.

When I answered it, the voice of my friend and longtime colleague, Judy Luce, said without preamble, "You have to make a small book of the twelve themes you identified in your anthology. Your afterword is the best distillation of essential midwifery wisdom I have ever read, but it gets lost in the dazzling array of memoirs that precedes it." There was urgency in her voice and an earnest insistence that publishing my observations in a stand-alone book was important.

The Backstory

In 2011, I published an anthology called *Into These Hands: Wisdom From Midwives.*[1] It featured 25 memoirs of seasoned midwives, including my own story. All of the midwives were 50 years of age or much older and midwifery was their lifetime career. Each of them was a matriarch in the profession and an exemplar. For this assemblage I intentionally chose a diverse group. The authors lived in a variety of locations, from California to New Jersey, Arkansas to Florida. They were racially and ethnically diverse—Native American, Latina, African-American, South Asian-American, and European-American. They had a variety of religious and spiritual backgrounds—Jewish, Christian, Islam, Hindu, Pagan, Buddhist, and Goddess traditions. They came from diverse ideological and midwifery training backgrounds. They were self-taught, apprentice-trained, graduates of midwifery schools, and recipients of university degrees. They were direct-entry midwives, nurse-midwives, credentialed and non-credentialed midwives, midwifery educators, researchers, and experts in public health and policy.

For more than four years I gathered, edited, and assembled the memoirs into an anthology. Once completed it was a goldmine. The stories represented the accumulated knowledge and wisdom of midwives whose combined efforts represented over 800 years of experience. As a composite they had provided healthcare for thousands of people both in the USA and abroad and had attended over 35,000 births. Once this huge body of work was assembled, I sat back to consider the 25 individual narratives as a totality. I wondered if there was a way to see the distinct pieces as a unified whole or a matrix. And if so, what story did it tell.

In order to decipher the commonality of ideas described by the authors, I conducted a qualitative analysis asking this question: **What matters to these midwives?**

I read and reread every line of over 500 pages of text. Despite differences in class, race, religion, geography, lifestyle, credentials, and midwifery practice styles, 12 themes emerged. The 25 authors from diverse work settings circled through the same network of ideas. When they described their decades-long careers in midwifery, the skills and values that informed their practices, the challenges they faced and triumphs they achieved, the lessons they learned, and finally, the insights they wished to impart, these 12 themes, or qualities, came to light over and over again.

I believe these simple, powerful, and essential qualities are the guiding principles in what we currently call 'the midwifery model of care.' And they are also essential qualities in a much older women-led, women-centered healing system to which modern midwifery is linked.

conceiving the midwife matrix

When I recently reread my anthology I was struck with two things. First, the 25 individual memoirs were powerful and inspiring because midwifery knowledge acquisition gained from lifelong learning can be fluently transferred to others. And second, the commonalities of 'what mattered,' and that which united the midwives' stories, were greater than the sum of their parts. They created a picture of something bigger than the life experiences of 25 individuals.

And I wondered, *what was that 'bigger thing'?*

As I worked to clearly describe the 12 essential qualities for this book, I came to believe my inspiration for the concept of The Midwife Matrix came from the intersection of several places. First, it came from my own thoughts and experiences. Then it came from understanding the lived experiences of other contemporary midwives. And finally it came from a vast sea of collective matriarchal consciousness. I began to think 'the bigger thing' was the flow of consciousness that may be inherited rather than learned; a type of genetic memory, like a survival instinct. If humans are hardwired to survive, perhaps some humans are hardwired to assist the process of surviving birth.

Inherited Knowledge—The Monarch

The monarch butterfly has a migration route that is thousands of miles long, from Mexico to Canada. This distance is much farther than any individual monarch can fly. Therefore the migration is split between four or five generations. Scientists have mapped this multigenerational migration. What this means is when monarchs are born they have an indwelling instinct that compels them to fly to a place their parents, even their grandparents, have never visited or experienced. And yet, their innate complex instincts guide the journey to their precise homeplace, unerringly, across generations.

There are two points I would like to make with the monarch metaphor. First, humans, like other species, have multiple ways of knowing things we have not implicitly learned, which are inborn and instinctual. And second, human cultures enjoy a rich heritage of women-led healing systems that have been active in every region on the planet since time immemorial, and that have been passed from one generation to the next. Modern midwifery knowledge is rooted in these ancient systems, and this knowledge resides in our collective consciousness.

Some scientists say our genes and our cultures coevolve. They say the memory of our inherited biological and cultural knowledge dwells within us.

I wondered, could this 'bigger thing' that the 25 matriarch midwives alluded to, and that I have always felt, be an indwelling instinct that informs and guides our journey as midwives, across generations, unerringly?

I have had the privilege of acquiring academic knowledge that is documented by degrees from several institutions of higher learning. But I also believe there are other ways of 'knowing' that inform my knowledge base. Perhaps the concept for The Midwife Matrix is embedded in my consciousness. It may be cultural knowledge that is etched in my DNA.

After more than 40 years of work in the field of midwifery, I do know this. Modern midwifery is a health science and a health profession that deals with pregnancy, childbirth, and the postpartum period; care of the newborn; and sexual and reproductive healthcare for women throughout their lifespan. Obstetrics, too, has this scope of practice. But midwifery is far older than obstetrics. Midwifery stands on the shoulders of a system of healing that went beyond mere medical care. Its practitioners provided a compendium of broad social medicine to communities, villages and tribes. Modern midwives still 'remember' this.

My concept of The Midwife Matrix is intended to depict a continuum in which the essence of our inherited wisdom is married with the best of contemporary scientific knowledge. Times change, cultures change, knowledge changes. But no matter what, our challenge remains the same: to offer a balanced service so that midwifery continues to be a useful, potent, synergistic blend of art and science in the care of unique pregnant and birthing people.

the midwife matrix is a source pattern

I chose these two words—midwife + matrix—before I knew the details. After looking more closely at their etymology, I was fascinated.

From an Anglocentric perspective, the word 'midwife' comes from Olde English and means 'with woman.' The word 'matrix' is from the Latin word *mater* and literally translated means 'mother' or 'womb.' Matrix is a substance in which something else is embedded.

We can think of The Midwife Matrix as the substance in which all of the knowledge about being 'with woman' is embedded—the mother lode, the wellspring, or the codex. Like a crystal embedded in a rock, or a baby embedded in a womb, **being 'with woman' is embedded in midwifery philosophy and practice.**

In the landscape of complex and rapidly changing modern maternity care, being 'with woman' is the anchoring force of midwifery philosophy and practice, and is the vital feature that marks midwifery as distinct and unique in maternity care—past and present.[2]

Matrix also means a place of origin or a source pattern. In ancient Rome matrix was a 'mother plant' whose original seeds were used for producing other plants.

We can think of The Midwife Matrix as a source pattern, the Mother Plant— the place where the seeds of ancient women's wisdom are used to produce modern midwifery knowledge and practice. Because the environments where the seeds are planted will change, generation-to-generation, locale-to-locale, the plants will also adapt and change across time and place. But the ongoing and ever-evolving expression of the source pattern through the daughter plants of each new generation will always carry the memory and the essence of the Mother Plant.

A Synergistic Exchange of Giving and Receiving

The Midwife Matrix is the interlaced and interdependent circuitry of energy and exchange that is, and always has been, embedded in the art and practice of midwifery. It represents the Mother Tongue that developed in most human cultures eons ago as the first language in which stories were spoken, and rituals were enacted, between a woman giving birth and the people who surrounded and sustained her.

The power of The Midwife Matrix is found when people are in relationship with one another, in a synergistic exchange of giving and receiving, in the continual flow of abundant energy back and forth, and in a dance of ongoing reciprocity.

Twelve Inherent Qualities

Twelve vital qualities are embedded in The Midwife Matrix, and they interact together in a continuous and unending loop, each quality as important as the next. The 12 essential qualities that matter to midwives are: context, content, holism, nature, sacred, relationship, compassion, self-determination, service, activism, courage, and lineage.

Celtic Trinity Knot

Even before my two trips to Ireland where my mother's mother was born, I became fascinated with Celtic knots as a way of understanding my own cultural heritage. When I conceived the idea of The Midwife Matrix I also saw a picture of it in my mind's eye. The triquetra design, also called the trinity design, is a circuitry of loops that has no beginning and no ending.

The triquetra is always a woven unity of three spheres—customarily interpreted as body, mind, and spirit, or earth, sea, and sky—all interrelated and interdependent. In Celtic lore, the triquetra design also represents the birth aperture, or the gateway from the spirit world to the physical world, from the sky-world to the earth-world. The triquetra design is often used to depict the pre-Christian Triple Goddess—Maiden, Mother, and Matriarch.

The reason the Celtic knot design works well to illustrate The Midwife Matrix is because the dynamically interdependent relationships that are shared between midwives and the women they serve are like a grapevine, a braiding of an interlaced trinity of roots, branches, and fruit that feed and support one another. What matters to childbearing women and people with wombs matters to midwives.

The Midwife Matrix: Essence and Intention

Energy exists all around us. Every aspect of our world is infused with the vibration of both positive and negative energy that is constantly moving and changing. Physicists tell us that all natural, human, mechanical, industrial, societal or economic processes are powered by continuous flows of energy, defining and redefining us and everything around us.

Because our minds work well with images, my visualization of The Midwife Matrix is a flow of energy in a continuous loop through a trinity design that represents body, mind and spirit. My image of The Midwife Matrix is a living, breathing, dynamic process of energy transfer among people who are both givers and receivers in an energy exchange. The twelve vital qualities of The Midwife Matrix are indwelling, interactive and synergistic, perpetually woven together in an unending loop of connection and mutuality.

The Midwife Matrix is both *essence* (inherent nature) and *intention* (intended course of action).

interconnecting and evolving

When you use The Midwife Matrix, keep these important aspects and characteristics in mind.

The Midwife Matrix is comprised of 12 interconnected qualities that matter.

- Two external qualities—context and content—are essential in understanding how pregnancy and childbirth practices and protocols differ across the planet, are culturally constructed and reinforced, and are promulgated through differing models of care.
- Three qualities—holism, nature and sacred—are essential as the evolutionary links among the dimensions of life and are the keys to health and wellbeing.
- Three internal qualities—relationship, compassion and self-determination—are essential to the process of humanizing healthcare so that people are treated as unique individuals within the context of their families, values, beliefs and cultures.
- Three qualities—activism, service and courage—are essential to the practice of midwifery, sustaining the midwifery profession, ensuring reproductive justice, and preserving human rights.
- And one immanent quality—lineage—is essential as a source of perpetual, intuitive, practical knowledge and wisdom.

The Midwife Matrix is an evolving design. The Midwife Matrix is a living, breathing, adaptive model for healthcare delivery rooted in an earlier system of holistic, woman-centered, women-led healing. As healthcare continues to change over time, the design may evolve to include other essential qualities.

The Midwife Matrix is personal. When we use this design, clients and patients are placed in the center of a dynamic and empowering healthcare relationship in which they are at the helm of decision-making and they share power with their practitioners. When this happens, people's dignity is respected, their autonomy is honored, their right to make their own healthcare choices is privileged, and they feel more confident. As a result, giving birth and being born become humanized and personalized, and both birth-givers and care providers benefit.

The Midwife Matrix is centered on people not technology. Most people want a birth experience, not a medical experience. While birth technology certainly has its place, every pregnancy is unique and every labor progresses at its own rate. Thus, individualized and supportive care by skilled birth attendants is the key to positive childbirth experiences. Focusing on people rather than technology will increase quality and safety for mothers and infants, while avoiding unnecessary and costly medical interventions.

The Midwife Matrix thrives on collaboration. Just as all life exists in interconnected systems that cooperate with one another to form the web of life, The Midwife Matrix works best when all members of the maternity care team strive to foster harmony, balance, and wellbeing. In this way everyone wins.

The Midwife Matrix is replicable and scalable. This design can be successfully and reliably reproduced. Any type of health or social service giver of care can utilize this approach; any receiver of care can benefit from this approach. It is scalable and adaptable to the needs of the diverse pool of people who use maternity care systems. When practitioners are dedicated enough to learn The Midwife Matrix, and determined enough to advance it, The Midwife Matrix can flourish in any healthcare and human service arena—residences, clinics, birth centers, hospitals, and other care-giving environments.

birth matters

How one gives birth, and how one is born, matters profoundly. This is something I know deep in my bones. But I did not always know this. It took me over four decades of being a midwife, listening to people who were pregnant, giving birth, parenting children, or older people reflecting on their lives, and the publication of my first book to crystallize this knowledge.

It takes only a moment of cruising the Internet to realize how much birth matters. Google 'birth' and you get about 2,850,000,000 hits. Google 'birth stories' and you get 1,100,000,000 hits. Google 'your birth matters' and you get 808,000,000 hits. And that's checking Google, only one of the numerous social media search engines.

Birth Stories Are Origin Stories

Birth stories—good ones and bad ones—nestle in the hearts and souls of people and follow them right into old age. Even when people cannot remember much else, they remember the stories of their births and their babies. That is because birth stories are origin stories. They are stories of how a life began. These stories are important not only to the one giving birth but also to the one being born. They are precious and repeated stories that are consequential to the family and tribe into which a person is born because they impart meaning as well as a cautionary tale.

Every year on their birthdays I call my three children and tell them a piece of their birth story. Each year I focus on a different aspect. This week was my son's thirty-fourth birthday. What I told him was, "Your newborn exam concluded with these words, 'beautiful, mellow baby boy!' " He said, "Not bad for someone who was oxygen deprived." Sean knows the story of his birth and that he was born with a triple-wrapped cord around his neck and needed resuscitation. So I added, "The lesson is that despite adversity you were strong and hardy from the day you were born. That experience could have left you agitated and angry, but you weren't. You were beautiful and mellow."

Sharing my son's birth story reminds him of who he was from the moment he was born. He was vigorous and resilient enough to overcome a trauma right at the onset of life. He can use that knowledge to shape his behavior, over and over again, in dealing with other challenges he will have to face in life.

Birth matters. Not everyone is physically equipped to be pregnant and give birth, and not all who are will choose childbearing. But everyone has experienced gestation and birth. Each person alive today spent a mysteriously spacious time in their mother's body, where they were slowly and meticulously woven cell upon precious cell, and were born.

A mother's womb, as Mohawk midwife Katsi Cook says, is each person's first environment.[3] It is their place of origin. And the sciences of neurobiology, epigenetics, and child psychology advise us that the manner in which the processes of pregnancy, childbirth, and the early postpartum days and months unfold can have an indelible, critical, and lifelong impact on individuals and their families.

Welcoming Spirit Home

I have listened to contemporary young women and men say: "It doesn't matter how you give birth as long as the baby comes out healthy." This comment reflects an underlying reality: sometimes childbirth experiences do happen differently from what we had expected. In fact they almost always do. Birth in its natural state is a rather unpredictable process. And there is no denying the bottom line: we all want a healthy baby.

Nonetheless, it *does matter* how women and birthing people *feel* about their experiences. If this were not so, the Internet would not be rife with stories—both satisfying and unsatisfying, triumphant and tragic—of peoples' birth experiences.

It matters whether a person *gave birth*, or whether birth was *done to them*. It matters how they were treated—regardless of whether they had an uncomplicated vaginal birth or an unanticipated cesarean section. It matters regardless of whether they were at home, in a birth center, or in a hospital. It matters how decisions were made, how much control they had, what choices they were given, and how those choices were supported or denied by healthcare personnel and institutional policies.

It also matters to babies how they are born. They are sensitive, impressionable, and vulnerable creatures, and how they are received and introduced to a strange new world makes an enduring impression on them. In fact, there is compelling evidence that pregnancy, birth, and postpartum factors determine whether a person will get off to a promising or worrisome start in life.[4]

Some cultures understand this fact better than others.

Several years ago I met a wise woman named Sobonfu Somé who brought the rituals and teachings of her home village in Burkina Faso, West Africa, to the industrialized world. One of my favorite teachings is this. Sobonfu's people, the Daraga, believe that the most important moment in any person's life is the moment of birth, because at that moment each newborn baby 'brings spirit home' to the community. Among the Dagara people every new baby is lavishly received and profoundly welcomed because it is understood that they are an important person, a VIP, stepping into a job no one else can do in quite the same way, which will bring goodness to the world.

Sobonfu's people believe that when babies are showered with love and respect from the moment they emerge from their mother's womb, it instills a sense of wellbeing, purpose, trust, and belonging in them that lasts a lifetime. They believe this ritual fosters nonviolent and compassionate societies. Sobonfu calls this birth practice 'welcoming spirit home.'

What Do Women Really Want?

In terms of biology, pregnancy is pregnancy and birth is birth across all cultures. Yet how we humans *perceive* pregnancy and birth, and how we *do* pregnancy and birth, differs. And thus our experiences differ.

In the United States as in other Western countries, under the dominance of the biomedical model, pregnancy and birth are medically managed. And within the *context* of medical management, using the *content* inherent in the biomedical model, pregnancy is goal oriented, product oriented, and at the center is the fetus. In the US the purpose of pregnancy is to make a healthy baby, and the goal of pregnancy management is to accomplish that objective.

Fair enough, you might conclude, that seems reasonable. But what is missing in the biomedical approach, and what is central in the midwifery approach, is attention to women. Attention to their experiences of pregnancy and birth. Attention to the lives they are living while they are pregnant. And attention to what they really want.

Consider this: While pregnancy and birth culminates in the utter transformation of two people's lives—mother and infant—we call it childbirth not motherbirth.

Pregnancy and birth are processes. It takes ten lunar months for the complex processes to unfold. And when we count the fourth trimester—the baby moon— we may as well say the process takes about a year.

Every woman or pregnant person wants a healthy baby. This is a universal desire. But is that really all they want?

It is unfair that some women—a lot of women—are counseled to feel that a healthy baby is adequate compensation for the disappointment or trauma they experience during their pregnancies or childbirths. They are told their regrets or stress will be forgotten amidst the joy of motherhood or parenthood.

You can measure the 'outcome' of a healthy baby—size, weight, reflexes, and responses. But a healthy baby is not the only thing that impacts joyful and healthy outcomes. How do you measure quality of life? Quality of experience?

We know from peoples' birth stories and from scientific literature that safe, satisfying, affirming, and empowering experiences are also fundamentally important to mother/baby/family wellbeing.

What If Our Cultural Beliefs about Childbirth Are Short-changing Us?

What if our relentless quest to control nature, including the most exquisitely uncontrollable process of birth, has resulted in a loss of trust in nature, and thus a loss of something vitally basic, human, and important?

What if we have been seductively captivated by a massively successful marketing campaign that promotes the idea that medical science—as an extension of power over nature—will virtually guarantee the safest and best outcomes for mothers and babies, when in fact it is a belief system that is seriously flawed?

What if by succumbing to the cultural beliefs that birth is unbearably painful and filled with risks there is an inescapable consequence of the pervasive presence of fear? And what if, in turn, fear has a negative impact on a woman's emotional health during pregnancy, and increases the likelihood of her having a less than optimal, even negative, birth experience?

What if the most likely way to get the birth experience you want—one that is both safe and satisfying—is not to rely on the *experts* but to rely on *yourself* by being prepared and informed, and by insisting on being in charge of making your own decisions?

What if our perceptions changed and we all understood that how a person is born—the primal passage that every human being experiences—really matters to the healthy growth and development of each individual, and thus at a profound level, matters to the wellbeing of human societies?

And what if the Dagara tradition of welcoming spirit home with the birth of each new member of society is the wisest ritual we could ever perform?

now or never

After forty-four years of dedicated service, I thought I had finally stepped away from midwifery. I thought I could spend my time gardening, sailing, making art, hanging out with my kids and grandchildren, doing a small amount of consulting, and volunteering in my own community.

What propelled me to get out of my lovely garden—at my friend Judy's urging—and sit at a computer for almost two years and make this book are three intersecting and distressing situations that need our urgent attention.

These three things—needless suffering, biomedicine's impact on maternity care, and medicalized and dehumanized birth—haunt me. I cannot get them out of my mind. After four decades I am encouraged that some things have improved for women and infants. But I am deeply discouraged that some things are worsening.

There is a fourth topic—midwifery—that compelled me to write this book. I am convinced midwifery care offers a significant solution to the serious problems we face with regards to these three disturbing issues.

Further, there is a lens through which the whole milieu must be viewed, and that is reproductive justice.

I realized, like birth, it was now or never. I had to document my concerns, share my insights, and offer some hope for making a difference.

Women and Newborns Are Suffering Needlessly

The US maternity care system is not serving the needs of women and infants.

In spite of our ability to manage complex health problems, for healthy women and their infants the US maternity care environment has increased risks. Despite having significantly higher health spending than comparably wealthy and sizeable countries, the US continues to rank at or near the bottom in indicators of mortality and life expectancy.[5]

The US now has the highest rate of maternal mortality among developed nations, and the rate is three to four times higher for Black women of all socioeconomic levels compared with their white counterparts.[6] While the international rates of maternal mortality have been trending downward in the past two decades, the US rate has been trending upward since 2000.[7] Other women of color, marginalized and vulnerable people, LGBTQI and gender-nonconforming people, and those living in low-income settings also have poorer pregnancy-related outcomes than their nonvulnerable or nonmarginalized counterparts.[8]

Evidence suggests that for a significant number of the 4 million US women who give birth every year, not only is the American maternity care system not providing optimal, safe, high-quality, cost-effective care, it is actually harming many of them.[9] Evidence suggests mistreatment is experienced more frequently by women of color, when birth occurs in hospitals, and among those with social, economic and health challenges.[10] Mistreatment is exacerbated by unexpected obstetric interventions, and by patient-provider disagreements.[11]

Also, in a study of the 28 wealthiest countries in the world, the US had the highest infant mortality rate.[12] A baby born in the US is less likely to see their first birthday than one born in Japan, Finland, Korea, Hungary, Poland, Slovakia, Belarus, Spain and twenty other high-resource countries.[13] Native American and African American infants are three to four times more likely to die before their first birthdays than any other race or ethnicity in the US. A racial division that begins at birth with disparities in access and unequal provision of healthcare characterizes how an infant born in the US will fare.

Poverty also decreases an infant's chances of survival. And when you combine poverty with other serious stressful life events many mother-baby couples in the USA face—such as food insecurity, stress, violence, unsafe living environments, and lack of support, especially for single or teen mothers—the combined factors increase the risk of preterm birth, intrauterine growth restriction, newborn injury, and death.

Research on the topic is convincing. If accessible, equitable, and high-quality maternal-infant healthcare were available to all, a large percentage of maternal and infant deaths and injuries in the US could be avoided each year.[14]

Biomedical Model Undermines Normal Physiologic Birth

Women deserve maternity care that is based on the best evidence about safe and effective practices, and that supports the natural processes of pregnancy and birth. But too often, they do not receive this kind of care.

The US maternity care system is not working well because biomedicine is the model that underpins the delivery of care to healthy women and infants. Biomedicine applied to pregnancy and childbirth patholgizes these normal processes and systematically disempowers women.

Modern Western healthcare, which has only been in existence since the mid-nineteenth century, is a model that focuses on body structures and systems. It concentrates on diagnosis, treatment, and cure. It is a particularly effective model to use for addressing illness and injury, such as broken bones, infections, surgeries, and communicable diseases. Biomedicine is more suited to discovering and treating pathology than focusing on normality.

Within the biomedical model, nonmedical processes and states—such as pregnancy and birth—are viewed as medical conditions with the looming potential for problems, risks, illnesses, or disorders. Western obstetrics uses the biomedical model. This model focuses on the physical plane, and typically excludes psychological, environmental, social, economic, or spiritual influences.

By turning the normally healthy conditions of pregnancy and birth into medical conditions, biomedicine shapes the processes a woman experiences. In addition, the biomedical model transfers control over the reproductive processes from the woman to multiple medical specialists (obstetricians, gynecologists, geneticists, anesthesiologists, immunologists, perinatologists) who focus on multiple subsets of the body.[15]

Social scientists have argued biomedicine makes pregnant and childbearing people passive objects of medical surveillance and management. Thus for many women, the biomedical model results in alienation, separating them from their own bodies, instilling fear, and making them passive recipients of medical care.[16] It can alter a woman's body and mind so significantly that the processes of pregnancy, labor, and birth may also be significantly altered.

In addition, even though most women and infants in the USA are primarily healthy, most babies are born in technology-intensive hospital settings and are routinely subjected to numerous invasive procedures that alter healthy physiologic processes in newborns.[17]

Furthermore, because of the excessive use of technology, the US maternity care system is the most costly in the world while producing some of the worst outcomes and least satisfaction for system users.

Medicalized Birth Has Lead to Dehumanized Birth

In the past century in America, childbirth has shifted from a social model controlled and mediated primarily by women and midwives to an institutional model controlled and mediated primarily by male physicians and institutions. For several decades the World Health Organization, global health agencies, and social scholars have warned that 'institutional birth' has a detrimental effect on birth-givers and their babies, and also on healthcare staff.

Medicalization is the tendency to pathologize otherwise normal bodily processes and states. When that is done, it is believed that these processes and states must, therefore, come under the authority of medical institutions and teams of medical specialists who are uniquely equipped to manage pathologies.

Extensive reports have documented how medicalized birth has precipitated dehumanized birth,[18] which in turn has been documented to cause increases in stress and trauma for women and their infants, even post traumatic stress disorder (PTSD).

Studies have noted that most healthcare providers no longer know what 'non-medicalized birth' is and have never seen a normal physiologic birth.[19] A normal physiologic labor and birth is defined as "one that is powered by the innate human capacity of the woman and fetus."[20] Studies further note that day-to-day maternity care practices are essentially based on observations of medicalized birth, not normal physiologic birth.[21] That being the case, the protocols and practices of a 'medicalized model of childbirth' will differ from those of a 'physiologic model of childbirth.'

In light of the research on dehumanized birth, it is concerning that the biomedical model has been incorporated as the standard maternity care model in the USA. This model has also been exported all across the globe by American agencies and practitioners.

Midwifery Model Is Beneficial to Maternal and Child Health

The status quo need not persist. There is an evidence-based and immediate way to address unnecessary disparities, mortality, morbidity, dissatisfaction, dehumanization, and excessive costs in maternal and infant healthcare. The evidence is clear both in the US and globally: **where women have greater access to midwives, they and their infants fare better.**[22]

Part 2 of this book, Why Midwives Matter, will look more closely at this topic.

While a misperception persists that the highest quality of maternity care must be provided by physician specialists, a vast body of research strongly suggests that midwife-led maternity care is optimal for healthy women and infants. Midwife-led maternity care—when it is integrated into a healthcare structure that promotes team-based collaboration among maternity care professionals when needed—leads to optimal maternal-newborn outcomes and improved health of mothers and infants.[23]

The success of the 'midwifery strategy' has been repeatedly documented in the USA and in countries all across the globe,[24] and supported by international health agencies such as the World Health Organization[25], the United Nations Population Fund[26], and the International Federation of Gynecology and Obstetrics (FIGO).[27]

It is not a question of *"will midwifery work?"* The question is *"why aren't we already implementing it?"*

Reproductive Justice

As you might expect, the answer to *"why aren't we implementing it?"* is big and broad and complex.

Even knowing that midwifery is the magic bullet, and even when there is ample evidence of these three things—needless suffering of women and infants, biomedicine's impact on maternity care, medicalized and dehumanized birth— there is something deeper that we must also confront, because it affects everything. And that is widespread injustice aimed at women and people with wombs.

The concept of reproductive justice as a human rights analysis began to emerge in the mid-1980s. Women across the globe, who met at momentous international summits (in Vienna, Cairo, Beijing, Hong Kong), began to articulate a shared understanding of the lived reality of the health status of women. They defined their reproductive health in light of their reproductive rights (or lack thereof) as a social justice issue.

In the 1990s, Black women and scholars in the USA introduced the term 'reproductive justice' as an intersectional analysis of race, class, and gender politics, stating that these intersections impacted every aspect of a woman's health, including reproductive health.

Black second-wave feminists were dissatisfied with the narrow view of women's liberation that was espoused by most white second-wave feminists, who had a different reality within society—one of privilege, primarily middleclass, straight and college-educated. Thus white feminist attitudes about 'justice' were focused more narrowly than feminists who were women of color, working class women, and queer women. Women shared 'gender'; but 'race' and 'class' separated them.

Activist and movement leader Loretta Ross described the reality of Black, Brown and other marginalized women. She asserted, "Our ability to control what happens to our bodies is constantly challenged by poverty, racism, environmental degradation, sexism, homophobia, and injustice."[28]

Reproductive justice became a framework and a praxis that addressed systemic inequities—social, political, and economic—that affected women's ability to control their reproductive health, rights, and lives.[29]

Twenty-five years after reproductive justice was defined (and over 400 years after reproductive injustices began to be systematically perpetrated upon slave women of African descent and Indigenous women), women in the USA are still experiencing pervasive reproductive injustices on many levels.

As policies that restrict and hinder access to reproductive healthcare persist, and attacks on reproductive rights and justice continue to grow, policies are no longer limited to traditionally targeted and marginalized communities, namely women of color and other vulnerable people who can become pregnant and give birth. However, vulnerable populations are still hit hardest.

Our vision for reproductive justice and birthing rights must not only include improving outcomes for women and their infants, but must also focus on the fundamental right of *all women* to claim control of their bodies, their births and their lives, and to receive healthcare that respects their choices and their dignities. Both survival and dignified care must become the norm for *all women, people with wombs, and their infants* in the USA.

Therefore, the mantra, 'our bodies, our choice' must be viewed through the lens of reproductive justice that does not merely focus on one's gender, but includes one's race, class, nationality, ability, sexual orientation, and social status.

We will explore the topic of reproductive justice throughout this book. However, for an authoritative and comprehensive analysis see the primer *Reproductive Justice* (2017) written by two legendary scholar-activists, Loretta Ross and Ricki Solinger. There is also a preponderance of research on the three key topics highlighted above (needless suffering of women and infants, biomedicine's impact on maternity care, and medicalized and dehumanized birth) and on midwifery as a solution, which I encourage readers to explore in more depth than I am able to provide in this book.

what time is it on the clock of the world?[30]

As a young activist in the 1960s, I had the good fortune of living in Detroit where one of America's premiere and most-beloved advocates for civil, human, and labor rights—Grace Lee Boggs—made her home and focused her work. She lived to be one hundred years old, and since the 1950s she mentored diverse generations of activists through every human rights issue and political movement the USA faced.

Grace famously asked people to consider the context in which they were trying to affect social or political change. Reflecting on the question she posed, "What time is it on the clock of the world?" was not merely a philosophical exercise. Boggs argued, if a person truly hoped to be an agent of change capable of transforming the structures and environments in which they lived, it was the precise question that must be pondered before taking action.

Grace remained a revolutionary thinker to her last breath, constantly encouraging us to be smart, be relevant, be brave. Near the end of the second decade of the twenty-first century, Grace opined that from the long view of her long life spanning a century, she understood that protest strategies and ideological postures that had been used successfully for decades were no longer relevant or effective for this moment in time. She said it was a time for challenging long-held assumptions, a time for reimagining and remaking, a time to "grow our souls."

In the preface of her final book, *The Next American Revolution* (2012), Grace said, "Americans have learned that the tremendous changes we now need and yearn for in our daily lives, and in the direction of our country, cannot come from those in power or from putting pressure on those in power. We ourselves have to foreshadow or prefigure them from the ground up."[31]

Today, the clock of the world is ticking towards imminent collapse of numerous systems amidst major social and political upheavals, both at home and globally.

The vision of constructing a new world radically different from the one our children are on track to inherit depends on a clear understanding of 'what is' and a firm commitment to values and behaviors that assure equity for all people. These values will sustain, rather than destroy, the web of life. It also depends on each one of us doing whatever we can, in whatever sphere we inhabit, using whatever resources are available.

Navigating This Book

In this book, maternal and child health and midwifery are not stand-alone topics. I position them within a configuration of intersecting systems that affect individuals and groups—those pregnant and giving birth, those being born, those who provide healthcare services, those who create and enforce healthcare policies, those who manage healthcare institutions, and those responsible for reimbursement of healthcare services—as a way of understanding the interrelatedness and interdependence of each domain.

Likewise, The Midwife Matrix, as a model for strategic action in maternity care, is a design that recognizes and fosters interconnectedness. It is a relevant strategy that considers 'the time on the clock of the world' and that invests in human relationships rather than increased productivity and profits.

Part 1 of this book clearly defines the concepts and precepts of The Midwife Matrix and the 12 Qualities That Matter. Part 1 also provides personal narratives from my lifelong midwifery career to illustrate the qualities in action, and to demonstrate the diverse ways in which the qualities can be interpreted and manifested.

Part 2 of this book examines 'what is' by reviewing sobering facts about the current state of maternity care in the USA and globally, and the status of maternal and child health. Part 2 examines some ideas that highlight how to conceive and enact a qualitative break from the dominant ideologies and practices of our times, rather than simply reacting rebelliously toward them, or becoming disempowered by despair. The ideologies we will explore are rooted in what Dr. Martin Luther King, Jr. famously called the Beloved Community. It is a vision of a just, equitable, and healthy society rooted in love for one's fellow humans. Part 2 also highlights why midwives matter, and elucidates the work midwives do as change agents to shift the dominant paradigms of our times.

Part 3 of this book explores the wild wisdom of nature and what we can learn from it, as well as the wild wisdom inherent in passionate and unwavering dedication to values that support and sustain all of life. Part 3 is also a definitive 'call to action' for reclaiming our bodies, our births, and our lives on our own terms.

An Offering

This simple book is not a textbook. *The Midwife Matrix* is a tincture, a distillation of the bittersweet nectar gleaned from my own lived experience, from the real-life stories of 25 contemporary matriarch midwives, from my connection to the vast network of midwives that span the globe, and from our ancestor midwives.

I offer this book in order to share a treasury of matriarch consciousness from those who are keepers of women's mysteries, women's stories, and women's wisdom. And through our lineage, as people who receive new life into our hands, we are also connected to the mysteries, stories, and wisdom of the whole human family.

I offer this book as a framework, or a stimulus, for asking the right questions.

I offer this book as a way of affirming the unity of qualities and competencies that matter to midwives—emotional, cognitive, intuitive, and spiritual—and, I assert, matter to the women and people we serve.

And I offer this book as one possible solution, suggesting that, if the 12 qualities that matter are intentionally applied to maternal and child healthcare, these qualities could improve pregnancy and birth outcomes, ameliorate racial and ethnic disparities, reduce costs, and leave people feeling more satisfied. These qualities could create comfort, joy, health, and equity for all members of society—for those who give birth, those who are born, and those who lovingly surround them.

It Happens Only Once

The living processes of conception, gestation, labor, birth, and becoming a newborn human being constitute precious miracles of mythic proportions that happen only once, *ever,* and can never be redone.

Childbirth is the quintessential *now or never* experience.

What Matters

The image I hold for you, the reader, is this. You are gathered around a warm hearth fire after a hard day's work, sitting at the foot of a beloved grandmother who tells you about the things that mattered to her clan. You are listening to stories that connect you to the best of human knowledge and experience, getting a glimpse into the events and elements that have shaped the lives of peoples and cultures. You allow whatever wisdom you may hear from the stories to seep in like a good soaking of the earth in springtime. And then afterward you ask yourself the compelling question: *What matters—truly matters—to me?*

May this small book provide you with inspiration whether you are a person contemplating pregnancy and birth, a partner in the cocreative process, a student midwife or a practicing midwife, a doula, a nurse, a physician, a healthcare service worker, a counselor, an educator, a researcher, a policy maker, a student of life, or a curious soul.

May you be blessed on your life's journey.

Geradine Simkins

March 2020

Maple City, Michigan

the midwife matrix:
12 qualities that matter

context matters

Context is not a neutral aspect of maternity care
and will, to a large degree, determine meaning,
define who is in power, and have a profound effect on
those giving birth, those being born, and birth workers.

Everything in life is experienced within a context. Nothing exists, or can really ever be understood, in isolation from its context.

Yet understanding context in healthcare is actually a slippery idea to define. Some researchers use this analogy. A healthcare intervention (or service) is the 'seed,' and the context of healthcare is the 'soil' or the 'garden' in which the seed is planted. As the analogy goes, a seed tends to flourish in good soil; it will not do well in poor soil.

Because I have been a gardener for almost forty years, this analogy makes sense to me. I live in the northwest part of the Lower Peninsula of Michigan, near the Sleeping Bear Dunes National Park, which is nestled on the shores of Lake Michigan. It is an uncommonly beautiful area of the country, spectacular when seen from the window of an airplane, gorgeous to explore on foot, bike, or snowshoes. The soil near my home is sand, gravel and related deposits that overlie much older limestone and shale. It is not generally loamy or nutrient-rich, and in my neighborhood it takes years of tending and enriching the soil to create a productive garden. Even the heartiest seeds do not grow strong, healthy, resilient plants without the soil being fortified. It requires vigilant attention and diligent cultivation.

More and more healthcare providers and organizations are realizing that context—the soil in which services are sown—has a measurable impact on the experience and the outcome of healthcare.

Context is not a neutral aspect of maternity care and will, to a large degree, determine meaning, define who is in power, and have a profound effect on those giving birth, those being born, and birth workers.[32]

Everything in the context of reproductive healthcare conveys a message. The physical location (clinic, hospital, birth center, or personal residence), the way that physical space is organized, the objects and people in that space, the staff that provides the care and counseling for women and babies, and the liberal or conservative use of technology are all relevant aspects of context that impart meaning.

One of the most significant aspects of context is that it determines who is in power. Each maternity care and birthing environment will clearly define who is in control, and this will impact a woman's sense of safety and trust. Pregnant and birthing people—like most people in their regular lives—feel safer and more trust when they have control over their own experiences.

I once had a client who was deaf from infancy and who had been through years of medical and institutional healthcare that was not always satisfactory to her. She did not trust what was being done to her because healthcare workers who did not speak American Sign Language (ASL) often resorted to touching and manipulating her body without her permission and without any explanation she could understand. They performed tests and applied interventions without her fully understanding the purpose or consenting to them.

When this young woman walked into our birth center for the first time, she went from room to room observing everything, then touching everything, opening cupboards, signing wildly to her mother. The birth center was designed to be homelike and support laboring women with amenities such as a large bathtub and spacious beds in each of the two private suites. All the equipment and medicines were discreetly placed in oak cupboards. The entire place had a welcoming and comfortable feeling. After fully exploring, this young woman broke down crying and simply said, "I feel safe here." Months later, that feeling of safety within this context allowed her to give birth quickly and powerfully, and the empowerment she gained built confidence in her ability to parent her child.

Evidence gleaned from women's own narratives suggests that control has five domains: self-determination, respect, personal security, attachment, and knowledge.[33] Women stated that their ability to make informed choices featured prominently in their sense of 'control.' Curiously, the evidence also suggests that women are keenly aware that they cannot control birth itself, but they expected to have control, step-by-step, over the decisions related to the process.[34]

The subjective and profoundly important sense of 'being in control' is dramatically impacted by the context; namely, where and with whom a person receives maternity care and gives birth.

Yet, within a context, most people may not consciously see how the environment is shaping their experiences, but it most definitely is.

Imagine a woman about to make love. Naked, juicy, open, with all her love hormones flowing freely. Then imagine introducing a group of people into the scene, most of them strangers, who will watch, monitor, poke, prod, and hook her up to a machine to measure the strength of her sexual contractions. Do you imagine that the experience would be altered for the woman and her partner?

Yet there is plentiful documentation in popular culture and social media that affirms the notion that giving birth can be a pleasurable experience, even orgasmic, if the circumstances are suitable.[35] Pregnancy and birth are part of a woman's psychosexual continuum. In the right environment that is private, quiet and safe, a woman can surrender to where her body naturally leads her. While the concept of 'orgasmic birth' conflicts with most people's beliefs, there are many people who have reported birth to be a sensual and powerful experience. This leads us to consider why the context of birth matters, and also to contemplate how environment shapes human behavior.

When we consider context as it relates to pregnancy and birth we must not only think about the environment and people in certain settings where people receive their healthcare, we must also think about the cultural context in which people live. We must consider the dominant beliefs about giving birth and being born that people hear spoken, the 'truths' about birth that are repeated, and the standard practices they see enacted within the birthplace context.

For example, go to the United Kingdom's National Health Service website and search *Where should I give birth?* You will get information on three locations in this order: birth at home with midwives, in a unit or birth center run by midwives, or in a hospital with a collaborative team of midwives and physicians. Each option is weighted equally, meaning, all three birthing locations are stated to be good options. However, the site goes on to say that for healthy, low-risk women, home birth or a birthing center with midwives is recommended; for those with a medical condition, a hospital is best. The default recommended for most people (about 90% of UK women are low risk and healthy) is midwife-led care in an out-of-hospital setting.

Search that same question in the US, *Where should I give birth?* The default answer is in the hospital with a physician, preferably an obstetrician. The 'alternatives' include midwives and out-of-hospital birth settings. And there are many cautionary tales about how home birth can be dangerous and midwives are not as skilled as physicians.

If we assume a low-risk pregnancy is a low-risk pregnancy, then the process is similar person to person. And if we assume childbirth is childbirth, then the process should be similar across cultures and continents. Why does choosing a birthplace result in such different recommendations depending on whether you live in the UK or in the US?

The answer: context.

In the US we believe the safest place to have a baby and to receive high-quality care is in the hospital with obstetric specialists. In the UK they believe the safest place to have a baby and to receive high-quality care—and the most cost-effective option—is out of hospital with midwives.

To what extent do you think living within the context of a for-profit healthcare system versus living within the context of a national healthcare system influences people's beliefs, customs, behaviors, and choices?

The social and political context in which a person lives will influence what they see and think. It is true that each individual sees and experiences their world through the lens of individual perception. But those perceptions are formed by and nested within social consciousness, within a social world.

Another way to think of 'context' is as Russian nested dolls, a set of stacking wooden dolls of increasing size placed one inside the other. At the center is a baby nested within its mother's womb, and she interacts with the natural and social environment. Which is nested within a family that espouses certain beliefs and customs. Which is nested within a community that favors certain social norms. Which is nested within an environment that—depending on its level of purity or pollution—will affect everyone's health and wellbeing. Which is nested within a healthcare system that operates on specific policies, practices, and protocols. Which is nested within a society that has developed a particular structure and model of care for providing health services to its citizens. Which is nested within a nation of social, political and economic regulations that determines how people will utilize the healthcare system, and how service providers will be reimbursed.

We could go on with our nesting metaphor and the influence of being nested within a world, and then within a universe. But the point is, each layer in which a person is nested affects their lives, teaches and reinforces a particular type of social consciousness, and has an influence on their perceptions, behaviors, options and choices.

Here is one poignant way context plays out in maternal infant health in the USA. The Affordable Care Act of 2010 allows states to expand Medicaid eligibility (the process is referred to as 'Medicaid Expansion') to uninsured adults and children whose incomes are at or below 138% of the federal poverty level. Research has found that access to Medicaid services can vastly improve maternal and infant health. Expanded access to Medicaid is associated with fewer maternal deaths compared with states that did not expand their Medicaid program. The infant death rate also fell more dramatically in Medicaid expansion states—by more than 50% from 2010 to 2016. Researchers also found that expansion states saw fewer racial healthcare disparities compared with the seventeen states that have yet to expand Medicaid.[36]

This is a dramatic example of mothers and babies with different outcomes depending on the context in which their healthcare services are located. Statistics are sterile, but stories of real lives saved, stories of real disparities not experienced, resonate with me on a visceral level.

Context matters because the circumstances, people, beliefs, norms, policies, and payment structures that surround a pregnant and birthing woman will significantly influence how she is treated, how she behaves, how she interprets her experiences, how she finds meaning in them, and the outcomes of her healthcare experience.

Birth is birth, but context will influence everything.

Thirty years ago, when we moved onto the land that is now our home, the context was a beautiful canvas of hills, trees, and a tangle of wild native plants. We cleared a portion of the land, built a home, and made a garden where there had never been one. In the beginning my lettuce was bitter, my peas were puny, my tomatoes never ripened, and bugs ate many of my crops. Over the years of cultivating a rich soil bed, giving my garden a lot of attention, having the right tools, making sure my plants received adequate sunlight and regular watering, and being diligent about weeding and protecting my plants from damaging pests, eventually my garden became an Eden. The sustained effort was well worth it. Today, the garden is not only beautiful but it produces nutritious and resilient vegetables, flowers and herbs.

In gardening, practical wisdom tells us a seed sown in rich nourishing soil will blossom and yield a strong and healthy plant. The same is true for the context of healthcare.

When the healthcare organization is receptive, has sustained leadership that values quality improvement, provides training to support staff members, has the tools and systems to implement high-quality services without imposing overly burdensome regulations, the environment that is created is well worth the effort.

The difference between a substandard healthcare context and an environment that is healthy and supportive is palpable. It is more than a matter of adding green plants to a sterile or unfavorable environment. A favorable context goes bone deep and is keenly felt by those receiving care as well as those giving care. Like my deaf client at the birth center, each of us can sense the elements of a setting that make us feel safe and staff we can trust, versus a setting and staff that make us feel unsafe and unsupported.

Midwives are masters at creating a comfortable context in which to provide maternity care because they know how much it matters. But it is not rocket science and it can be replicated in any maternity care setting. But it does take time and intention.

Like flowers and herbs, innovations in context start as seedlings. It's all a matter of understanding how to encourage them to unfold, blossom and grow.

content matters

*The **content** of maternal and child healthcare is defined by
the model of care, and is the substantive and fundamental features
of what health services are delivered to women and babies,
and how those services are delivered.*

In healthcare, context and content are two sides of the same coin, twin sisters who are intricately related though not identical. Simply stated, *context* is 'where' and 'who' and *content* is 'what' and 'how.'

When I was pretty young, just barely into my teens, I began a deep dive into serious reading. Theology, philosophy, and science books scattered the surface of my small mahogany desk. I began to gather more knowledge than I actually had the mental framework or language to understand. So much of the content that fascinated me was seemingly contradictory. I was curious about the contradictions, but I was also confused. I could not get my mind around what 'the truth' was. In my late teens when I came across the word 'cosmovision,' this eleven-letter word, this concept, opened a new world to me.

A cosmovision is a particular way of viewing the world and understanding the universe. A society's cosmovision will significantly influence the way in which it is organized and evolves over time, and will inform all cultural beliefs, behaviors, and practices.

The word cosmovision first came into use by anthropologists to describe how Indigenous peoples think and behave, particularly the peoples of pre-Columbian Mesoamerica whose perception of the universe and how it worked was dramatically different from the worldview of European settlers and colonizers.

Understanding the concept of cosmovison was one of the most important lessons I learned as a teenager. I learned that the family, culture, and nation in which people were raised always underpins their perception of reality and beliefs about what truth is. I learned that there is no right or wrong with regards to a worldview, but worldviews can differ to small or large degrees, and often people are convinced *their worldview* is the only right one. Understanding cosmovision allowed me to comfortably grapple with paradoxes. Later, when I began to work with and for Native American tribes and organizations, I learned firsthand the differences between the cosmovision I was raised with and the cosmovision of the Indigenous peoples I encountered. The differences were striking.

Understanding cosmovision became a very useful tool when I became a midwife. When I transitioned from a direct-entry midwife attending home births to a nurse-midwife attending births in the hospital, I saw these two worldviews—midwifery and medicine—in stark relief. And they differed almost as much as the Indigenous and Western cosmovisions.

In the healthcare realm we call the worldview of practitioners their 'model of care' or their 'healthcare system.' It may be biomedicine, Ayurveda, midwifery, chiropractic, or traditional Chinese medicine.

The content of maternal and child healthcare is defined by the model of care, and is the substantive and fundamental features of *what* health services are delivered to women and babies, and *how* those services are delivered.

The midwifery model of care and the medical model of care each utilize distinct content that practitioners work hard to master and that define their respective models. Content of care includes values, beliefs, perceptions, ethics, skills, tools, interventions, rules, rationalizations, practices, protocols, relationships, politics, and economics.[37]

As we know, there are several ways of caring for the health and wellbeing of women and infants during pregnancy, birth, and the early parenting period. Throughout the world, country-to-country, we can observe different models of maternity care and healthcare systems.

In the US, sometimes the lead professional is an obstetrician or a general practice doctor; sometimes the care is midwife-led. The services midwives offer on a clinical level are similar to obstetrical services, yet there are factors in clinical practice and decision-making that make the content of care very different.[38]

It is fascinating to observe that the enactment of childbirth had been remarkably stable and similar across time and cultures until the twentieth century. Then, curiously, in about one century in the United States, the American way of birth changed dramatically. The prevailing woman-centered model of care (midwifery) that viewed birth as a normal physiological and psychosocial act and gave women the ability to shape, define, and control the events of their own procreative lives was supplanted by a (medical) model defined and dominated by men that emphasized mechanization and interventions to make birth 'better and safer.'[39]

The sweeping changes in the American way of birth—the American worldview of birth—were embodied in a shift in both *context* (location and environment) and *content* (protocols and management) of maternity care.

Birth is a process that is exquisitely designed to work well. The vast majority of births to mothers in the USA have few problems or complications. Yet, depending on what model of care is used there will be differences in content—what services are used (or not used) and how services are delivered (or not delivered).

A few key differences are important to note. A critical philosophical distinction is the perspective of superiority of technology over nature in the medical model, versus the perspective of trusting nature and the body's innate physiologic wisdom in the midwifery model.[40]

Another critical distinction is that the medical model is focused on *assessing risk* by counting adverse outcomes, whereas the midwifery model is focused on *assessing normality* and counting optimal outcomes. This means practitioners of a medical model are focused on anticipating, diagnosing and treating complications that occur in pregnancy with the goal of ensuring the outcome of a healthy baby. Practitioners of a midwifery model are focused on supporting the natural progression of an uncomplicated pregnancy, labor and birth, identifying problems if they arise, and attending to the personal, social, and spiritual aspects that impact women's lives.

Thus, a plethora of evidence suggests midwives specialize in a 'process approach' and in normality; physicians specialize in an 'outcome approach' and in risk management.

Another distinction about content is this. While the medical model is focused on fetal outcome—a healthy baby—midwives are focused on women. Midwives believe that taking care of the needs of women in a holistic approach that addresses their physical, mental, emotional, spiritual, sexual, and environmental needs will not only provide the foundation for a good experience and empower women in the birth year, but in the process will also create the conditions for growing healthy babies. If you ensure the wellbeing of birth-givers, you most likely will ensure the wellbeing of babies.

We cannot predict the type of care a particular practitioner will offer based solely on their training or credentials. Midwives have been known to offer a medical model of care; physicians have been known to offer a midwifery model of care.

What we can say is the model of care by which practitioners were trained does define *how they have been taught* to practice their craft, and *what is considered the customary approach* in their respective professions.

Biomedicine and midwifery's 'take' on the states of pregnancy and birth are fundamentally different.

Biomedicine is speedy and urgent. It is on a quest for *progress*. Biomedicine holds out a hope for a risk-free, disease-free world. Biomedicine tends to consider birth risky and always seeks to find ways to make it better.

Midwifery, by contrast, is slow and considered. It seeks to wait and watch as the innate process unfolds. Midwifery holds out the hope of protecting what nature does best and sees no need to make it better.

Once when I was a student nurse-midwife completing my clinical rounds at a large hospital in Wisconsin, I was written up and reprimanded for insubordination because I would not give a young woman an episiotomy when my preceptor told me to do it.

The laboring woman was a teenager and a single mother who had been accompanied by her own mother to the hospital. Her labor progressed nicely, but as the young woman began to push her mother became frantic because her daughter was not making much progress. She had become overwrought with each attempted push. The teen's mother bellowed, "Can't you do something to help her?"

I suggested that the young woman get off her back and into an upright position more favorable to pushing a baby out. I suggested a number of choices: sitting on a birthing stool, hands-and-knees, or squatting at the edge of the bed. The young woman's contractions were strong, and she was reluctant to change positions. She was also scared. I knew the evidence on birth position suggested that the upright position could benefit the mother and baby for several physiologic reasons, including that gravity could help bring the baby down and out. Lying on one's back was actually an anti-gravity position.

The young mother pushed several times again, on her back, but her efforts were ineffectual. My preceptor, who was standing next to me, leaned over and whispered in my ear, "Cut her."

I looked at her in surprise, and said, "No, she can do this." I knew she could.

I had already been a homebirth midwife for fifteen years before I returned to school to seek my nursing degree and nurse-midwifery certification. Though it seems impossible, I had seen a baby be born over an intact perineum, hundreds of times. My own three children were born that way, and two of them were over nine pounds. I knew that with patience, support, and the right position, babies could be born—were meant to be born—without injuring the mother. But the forces in that room stacked up against me acting in a way I felt was best for this mother and infant.

The teen's mother kept saying, "Would you two do something?" I kept gently saying, "Please, let me help you off your back and into a better position." And my preceptor kept saying to me, each time more emphatically, "Cut her!"

An episiotomy is an incision made with surgical scissors into the perineum—the skin, tissue and muscle between the vaginal opening and the anus. The procedure was once a standard practice in the biomedical model of childbirth. It was used because physicians believed that enlarging the opening would prevent severe perineal tearing. Midwives, on the other hand, did not use episiotomy routinely, believing that the woman's body would adequately stretch, and the infant's head would aid the stretching by massaging the vaginal passage during its decent into the birth canal. In addition, I knew the latest research: the rationale used by obstetricians for conducting routine episiotomies to prevent severe perineal tearing was faulty and was not justified by the evidence. Further, evidence found no benefits of routine episiotomy for the baby or the mother.

My preceptor became increasingly impatient for the delivery to occur. We also had other women in labor. She angrily whispered, and not too quietly, "If you do not cut her *now*, I will."

I couldn't do it. It is not that I was squeamish or recalcitrant. I had previously given episiotomies during emergency deliveries. But as a practitioner, I was weighing the risks and benefits.

My concerns were: the situation was not an emergency; an episiotomy is an assault on a woman's private parts that can cause physical or emotional trauma; an episiotomy was likely to cause more severe perineal tearing and increased postpartum pain; and the young woman would need to be sutured after the birth, which would interfere with immediate post-birth bonding time.

I stood my ground. The preceptor stepped forward, picked up the scissors, cut the young woman, looked at me with smug satisfaction and said, "I'll see you in my office after this is over."

Needless to say, my time working in hospitals under the precepts and practices of the biomedical model did not go that well for me. Had I come to the situation fresh and green, I might have been more malleable and able to fit in better.

But the difference between the midwifery model I had already been successfully practicing, which had produced great outcomes and satisfied customers, and the medical model in which I was being (re)trained were striking. They were actually in direct conflict. The big dichotomies were these. The medical model had little trust or patience for the innate and unique unfolding of the processes of labor and birth, and sought to control women's bodies and their experiences of childbirth. The midwifery model trusted that the process of normal physiologic birth was meant to work well, the less we interfered the better it worked, and the more control the woman had, the more empowered she became.

Yet, as a client or a patient of the complex maternity care system, I believe it is often difficult to actually discern the differences between the biomedical and midwifery models. This is especially true when they occur side by side within an institutional healthcare context, where the majority of US births occur.

Where you can really discern both the glaring differences and the smaller nuances is when you take antepartum, intrapartum and postpartum care out of a medical institution that is immersed in modern technology and medical specialists, and put them into a smaller, less complex structure, like a freestanding birth center or a small homebirth practice with a couple of midwives.

Imagine, if you will, two options in my hometown.

In one setting you drive your car into a behemoth parking structure, enter the hospital, and follow the long winding blue line painted on the hospital floor that leads you to the maternal and infant wing of the hospital where you have an appointment with a physician who is a member of a ten-person OB/GYN team. The room is large, two-tone gray, with several framed posters of landscapes on the wall. After you complete an electronic check-in at a computer, the first question a staff person asks you is, "Can I have your insurance card?" You hand over your card, have a seat, pick up a magazine, and wait for your appointment along with a dozen other women in the large waiting area who sit in rows of chairs. The MA in a white coat calls your name, takes you to an exam room, measures your weight, gives you a urine sample bottle, retrieves it when you are finished, and takes your vital signs and measures your blood pressure. She adds this information to the computer chart, gives you a hospital gown, and instructs you to remove all clothing but your undies. And once again you wait in the small exam room with graphic charts of the stages of labor on the wall until the obstetrician comes in.

After a ten-minute wait, an obstetrician whom you have not met before enters the room reading an iPad in which your history is recorded. She greets you by name and you call her by her title of 'doctor.' She asks how you are feeling, palpates your belly to measure fetal growth, listens for fetal heartones with an ultrasound machine, and says the heartbeat is normal. You feel relief because you have not felt much movement. She recommends that you get prenatal genetic testing, orders an ultrasound screening, checks for swelling of your hands and feet, asks if you have any questions, and writes everything on the iPad. She is professional and businesslike, but she seems a little rushed. You look at your list, ask your questions, and you tell her you are feeling really fatigued. She says that is normal and that her nurse will give you some pamphlets to read. Before you can ask your next question, she concludes your visit. The visit with the OB lasted eight minutes. On the next visit you see a different OB and are told that they want you to meet all of the ten doctors because they cannot predict who will be on call when you got into labor.

In another setting you drive onto a tree-lined street in a neighborhood to a modest house that has been converted into a freestanding birth center, park your car at the front door, and enter through a series of gardens and edible flowers to see one of the three midwives. The walls are colorful and decorated with homemade quilts and birth photography. The first question a staff person asks you is, "Would you prefer a cup of tea or a glass of water?" You get your cup of tea, you are handed your medical chart, and you sit on a cozy couch in what used to be a living room. After you finish your tea, you weigh yourself, do a urine sample, take it to the lab room and test it, then record your findings in your own chart. You wait for your appointment in your street clothes, you browse the lending library and select a few books, and you chat with the other person in the room who is there for her six-week postpartum checkup.

After five minutes the midwife you saw last month calls your name and takes you into a small exam room that had been a bedroom at one time and still has a homey feeling. The midwife has an iPad in her hand, she has greeted you by your name, and you call her by her first name. She asks how you are feeling and for the next ten minutes you tell her about your physical complaints, the challenges you are having being pregnant, working, and caring for your toddler, and that you feel really fatigued. You spend another ten minutes talking about diet and nutrition, exercise and rest, relaxation techniques and meditation, and strategies for juggling all the demands of your busy life. Then she asks you to tell her what your weight and urine were this week, and what you have decided about prenatal testing. She tells you the results of your bloodwork, which she hands to you to put into your chart. You discuss your options for prenatal testing for about five minutes, and she asks if you have any further questions. She seems professional, relaxed, and unrushed. Then she has you lay back on the daybed that doubles as an exam table, lifts your shirt, palpates your belly to measure fetal growth, and she takes your hands to feel little body parts so you can visualize how your baby is lying. Then she listens for fetal heartones with a handheld Doppler and you laugh with relief when she says the heartbeat is normal. You tell her that you feel really relieved because you haven't felt much movement, and she explains how to stimulate your baby to elicit movement. She asks if you have any further questions, and you tell her all your questions have been answered. Your appointment lasted forty-five minutes. On your next visit you meet with the third and final midwife. Two of the three midwives in this practice will be with you when you go into labor.

These are generic but real-life scenes of two prenatal care options in my town or any-town America. The scenes describe both context and content. The context (location and environment) will be determined by the content (model of care or healthcare system) under which a particular practitioner operates.

But if you do not look closely, you might miss the differences. Content matters not simply because of the clinical services that are provided (as you can see, they are similar in both settings) and not because of the outcomes of care (they are similar too). Content matters because of *how* services are provided, *who* has the power and is considered in charge, *what* practices and protocols are customary, *what* gets attention or does not, and *how* clients or patients feel about and experience their care. These factors can be different model-to-model.

Prenatal care sets the stage for participation in a certain model of maternity care. But things get even clearer when you view the experience of childbirth through the lens of different models of care.

I once had a client who was an obstetrician and her husband was a pediatrician. She was pregnant with her sixth child and she had been contemplating a birth that was significantly different from the previous five. She chose our freestanding birth center. One Friday night at 5 P.M. she called and said, "Start running the water in the birth tub." Fifteen minutes later she arrived followed by a gaggle of kids. Over her shoulder she gave instructions to the nanny, walked into the birthing room and closed the door, unbuckled her overalls, and slipped into the birthing tub. She immediately sank into hot water and into a tranquil meditative state. Her husband arrived and he knew his job was to be a supportive partner and take photos and *not* be a pediatrician.

Less than an hour later, in a quiet candlelit room, she pushed several times, birthed her beautiful daughter into her own hands, and lifted her newborn onto her chest. She exhaled the most enormous and satisfied sigh of relief and said, "This is the birth I've always dreamed about. It could never have happened this way in my world." She said the peace, wonder, and intimacy of this way of giving birth—the same act she had performed five other times—was compellingly different.

Curiously, just last week I ran into this woman at the memorial service of my midwife partner and dear friend, Clarice Winkler, who attended that birth with me. I told her that I was making reference to her birth in my book. She became very emotional. This physician is a rare breed. As a practicing obstetrician she

strives to offer a midwifery model of care. But she told me she continues to struggle within the context of the hospital setting that specializes in the medical model
of childbirth. She wants to offer her patients a taste of the kind of birth she had with
her last child. Her colleagues consider her radical. Some think she is misguided.
But she knows what she knows and can never unknow it. She called her daughter
on the spot, now sixteen, and asked her to come over to the memorial so that I
could share her birth story with her. The mother said, "I want my daughter to
hear firsthand what is possible for her." It was a joyful teary reunion.

The unfortunate truth is that the dramatic cultural shift in our perceptions
about how we think about and experience pregnancy and childbirth has imposed
significant restrictions. It requires women and their infants to conform more to a
series of mechanized routines in the birthplace than to the instinctual unfolding
of processes that involve body, mind, and spirit. This transformation has resulted
in a dominant childbirth paradigm (biomedicine) that focuses more on production than reproduction, more on emergency than emergence.

There are so many aspects to consider that this entire book could be about
the content of maternity care. The conversation about how the model of care that
is used will shape both the experience and the outcome of pregnancy and birth,
for both the giver and receiver of care, is extensive and complex. This is because
we tend to believe what we are told about the inherent value of the content of
the dominant US childbirth paradigm. We are taught and tend to believe that it
is the right way, and perhaps the only one way, and that other ways are unsafe or
unsound. But this is not 'a truth,' it is 'a viewpoint.'

When I learned about the concept of cosmovision in my late teens, it helped
me to understand how two cultures living side by side—the Indigenous peoples
in the region in which I lived and the descendents of Europeans settlers, the white
people—could see the world so differently.

For example, something as simple as their beliefs about fishing, which each
group perceived from its own concept of how the universe worked, were not only
contradictory but were in conflict.

The Indigenous peoples looked at fishing from the worldview of 'a gift
economy.' To their mind, they were in a relationship of reciprocity with the land
and lakes, the fish were their relatives, and were considered a gift. They believe if
the fish sacrificed its life for the humans, it was the human's moral responsibility
to keep the environment in which the fish lived healthy and safe, and to do so
with a grateful heart. They believe a relationship of reciprocity and responsibility
builds sustainable ecosystems. They believe gratitude begets abundance.

The white people looked at fishing from the worldview of 'a market economy'. They had a settler mentality that viewed land and lakes as property, real estate, and capital, and natural resources as commodities they could control and dominate, and sell for a profit, without feeling a moral responsibility to keep the fishing grounds healthy and safe for the fish. A commodity relationship is built on taking not giving, on yield, profit, and net worth.

So what is the truth?

Culture-to-culture, a fish is a fish, and people have to eat. But is the fish a gift or is the fish a commodity?

As I understand it, built into the language of the Indigenous peoples of my region through which they express their worldview is a sense of kinship and reciprocity with the animate world. And as I also understand it, built into the language that expresses the worldview of the white people in my region is a sense of mastery and privilege to dominate the natural world.

From these two perspectives, birth—as a wild force of nature as observable as a galloping horse or a rushing waterfall—either has a life of its own that we can respect and dance with, or is a series of contractions and documentable stages that we can master and control.

I often think of a woman or a person with a womb—who is pregnant with new life and laboring feverishly and instinctually to get that new life born—as the last wild, free, untamed, undomesticated human frontier. And from the Western worldview, which tends to think in terms of dominating and conquering, it appears as though that wild, frenzied, fiercely uncultivated frontier must be managed and controlled.

Is it a gift or is it a commodity? If you think about it philosophically from differing worldviews, this is the question that probes the heart of the matter, makes us think, and asks us to dig deep for answers.

Birth is birth, but content—the model of care or the healthcare system in which it occurs and which has been shaped by a particular worldview—will determine the degree to which birth is a gift or a commodity.

holism matters

Holism recognizes that what
affects one part affects all parts because everything
is intimately connected—body, mind, and spirit.

I am old enough to remember the days when doctors still made home visits.

In the late 1950s, one of my brothers had such a bad case of chickenpox that my mom called our doctor to say he was so sick and listless he could barely talk. And this was the most loquacious of the three boys. Our doctor fit my brother into his busy schedule that day. The doctor examined him, suggested a pain reliever and an antihistamine, and gave my mom instructions on how to care for him, including some old fashioned remedies like an oatmeal bath and calamine lotion. Two days later, on Saturday afternoon, my mom looked out the window to see a man dressed in a black overcoat carrying a black bag walking up the sidewalk. He rang our doorbell. When my mother opened the door, it was our doctor. He said he had been worried about my brother, that he had never seen a worse case of chickenpox, and he thought he'd stop by to check on him.

This doctor was a general practitioner. He did not specialize in a particular area of medicine, but rather took care of our entire family, and most of the families in our neighborhood, from birth to death.

He cared for my mother when she was pregnant, delivered her babies, did all the newborn and childhood exams for growth and development, gave immunizations, treated us for throat and ear infections, dealt with allergies, provided school physicals when we got older, set broken bones, and did minor surgeries. Our doctor did physicals for those entering the military, attended to old people like my grandmother who had muscular dystrophy, and provided care for sick and dying elders. He also provided education and counseling to his patients in-person and over the phone. Over the years he came to know our entire family by providing healthcare services for all of us.

This doctor, and those like him, did it all. Growing up we did not see any other doctor, except when my father was in a near-fatal car accident and needed the kind of emergency care and immediate surgery only specialists could provide. But when my dad recovered, he went back to our old doc for his regular healthcare.

Today, I do not know a single doctor who makes home visits. Nor do I know a single physician who has as wide a range of expertise and experience as our old family doctor had. Those were simpler times. In the intervening decades between my childhood and my adulthood, the contemporary system of healthcare in America has changed dramatically.

Today, we might say our doctor provided holistic healthcare.

Holistic medicine is actually an ancient system that dates back thousands of years. Aristotle, born in the third century BCE, was said to have described the concept of holism. Indigenous peoples the world over have had models of holistic healthcare. However, the most recent vintage surfaced in the early twentieth century when a South African statesman, soldier, and philosopher named Jan Christiaan Smuts defined holism as "the tendency in nature to form wholes that are greater than the sum of the parts through creative evolution."[41] In 1926, Einstein predicted two mental constructs would direct human thinking in the twenty-first millennium: his own description of relativity, and Smuts' concept of holism.

And indeed, by the late twentieth century the concept of holism had become well integrated into many social, political, economic, spiritual, and philosophical spheres. Each sphere has interpreted the central concept—the whole is greater than the sum of its parts—including holistic medicine.

There are four essential elements to holism as it relates to holistic medicine.

First, it takes the whole person into consideration within the context of the life they are living. Second, it focuses on primary care and treatment, beginning first with natural healing, lifestyle changes, noninvasive remedies, and the body's own ability to heal itself before moving to more invasive therapies, like drugs or surgery. Third, it is empowering, guiding clients or patients to take responsibility for their own health and wellbeing. And fourth, its goal is to bring balance to all aspects—body, mind and spirit—and create a sense of equilibrium within the whole person.

The simple formula: whole person + natural remedies and the body's innate ability for healing + empowerment + balance = holism.

Midwifery theories and practices are based upon the best scientific evidence available. And midwifery philosophy is holistic in nature.

The midwifery model is a holistic model that uses the least amount of intervention from the midwife to achieve an optimal outcome for mother and baby. The totality of the pregnant person is taken into account, not just the physical factors, but also mental, emotional, spiritual, social, cultural, relational, and environmental factors.

Pregnancy and childbearing are complex and multilayered experiences of tremendous importance. They carry significant meaning for the woman, her family, and the community. That is why in human history and across cultures it has been unusual for pregnancy and birth to be defined and treated as if they were merely biological functions.[42] Instead, most societies have integrated a range of social and cultural traditions into the care of mothers, babies, and families during the auspicious birth year.

A modern holistic framework for maternity care recognizes the importance of this broader approach. Rather than focusing on specific parts of the body or the patient's physical needs, such as lab work, vital signs, and baby checks, a holistic approach intentionally encompasses multiple aspects of care for a mother and infant that address their needs within the context of their family and culture.

A holistic approach considers the lived experiences of the whole person—values, beliefs, home environment, relationships, nutrition, support systems, mental health, stress level, and safety.

In the middle of my midwifery career—when I transitioned from direct-entry midwifery to nurse-midwifery and shifted my focus from homebirth to public health and equity issues—I worked at a bilingual migrant health center. Our town in Northern Michigan was a destination on the Midwest stream of farm laborers coming from Mexico and Central America. The migrant clinic was the medical home for many Latino families. As one of two nurse-midwives at the clinic I cared for 75-100 pregnant women each season, as well as their entire families. Many of our clients came to the clinic for care, but many lacked transportation and worked long hours that prevented them from getting to town. So we also made home visits to over two dozen rural migrant camps in our region.

One particular year, a young girl I had cared for as a child was a teenager and arrived at the clinic eight months pregnant. She had no prenatal care prior to her arrival. She worked full days in the field with her family members harvesting fruits and vegetables, which required strenuous physical exertion. She earned $5.94 per hour, which went into the family coffer. Although she was young, a single mother, and healthy, she was very tired. Her nutritional needs were not being fully met, and she had very little time for rest. On one occasion she came to her prenatal visit with a black eye. In her ninth month, at term, she gave birth quickly to a healthy seven-pound baby girl and returned to the migrant camp twenty-four hours later.

Typically, I made postpartum home visits on day one, three, seven, ten, and at two weeks. The condition of the run-down cinder block building in which she lived had six housing units that were very poor. Actually, they were despicable. Government officials usually turned a blind eye to the migrant camp conditions. It was summer, and it was hot inside. The 8' x 12' room had a Coleman stove in the corner, a mini refrigerator, and a makeshift shelf for food. Several mattresses covered the cement floor. Six people, now seven with the baby, lived in this unit. The family ate outside at an old beat-up table with a selection of folding chairs and plastic lawn chairs. They kept duffle bags with their clothes in the pickup truck. There was a bank of four portable toilets on site. The yard area was strewn with old farm implements.

When I arrived for a visit on day three, my client was sitting on one of the mattresses against the far wall with her baby bundled and in her lap. Her little sister had been allowed to stay home and take care of her, but the other family members were needed to work in the fields. My client looked exhausted, listless, and scared. She had been crying.

I had brought some food and cold juice with me and the first thing I asked her was if she was hungry. She was. I fed her and her sister, and then began to do the normal baby checks. I did a physical exam, including listening to heart and lungs, inspecting the umbilical cord, checking the baby's hips, eyes, and newborn reflexes. I did a hearing screening. I asked the new mama questions about feeding, the baby's peeing and pooping, and sleeping. We talked about immunizations, bathing, dressing, and newborn safety. When the new mama had finished eating and drinking a full glass of water and some juice, I did a postpartum exam on her. She told me her father wanted her to go back to work in a week, and she began to cry. She wasn't sure how she would manage. Then I asked if she would like me to hold the baby so that she could take a nap. She felt a bit embarrassed and did not want to impose, but quickly, she agreed. I asked if it would be okay if her little sister and I did some dishes. Again, reluctantly but gratefully, she agreed.

In my subsequent postpartum visits that became our routine—I'd bring food, check the baby and the mama, hold the baby and let the young mother take a nap, and straighten up the room. She got stronger, healthier, happier, and her father agreed (with the insistence of her mother and my advocacy) that the young mother be able to stay out of the fields for a full three weeks.

This type of story was common among the migrant farmworker population. Some might say what I provided to this young woman was part midwifery care and part babysitting and housecleaning. I thought of it as holistic care.

When I was in nursing school and spent my first day on the floor in a hospital, I was told this. Each patient is unique, and pain is whatever the patient tells you it is. What is clear about treating each individual as unique within a holistic framework is that you come to understand that wellbeing, like pain, is whatever the patient says it is.

For one person pregnancy will be a breeze, and for another, a burden. Labor and birth will be quick and easy for the client who births on Monday, and for the client who births on Wednesday it will be hard, horrid, and overwhelming.

In order to improve the delivery of healthcare and the experience of those receiving our services, midwives take the whole person into consideration. Midwifery care is grounded in an understanding of the social, environmental and cultural experiences that impact the health and wellbeing of our clients.

Holism recognizes that what affects one part affects all parts because everything is intimately connected—body, mind and spirit.

I think back to healthcare encounters I have had as a patient that have been both satisfying and unsatisfying to me. The most unsatisfying were those in which I felt the physician was rushed, distracted, not really acknowledging or understanding what I was saying, and focused on the computer. This happened to me just last week. I had my annual exam and I was allocated forty-five minutes. But the vast majority of the time was spent discussing questions required for Medicare and my Part B insurance plan, and entering data into a computer. The doctor rarely looked at me. The hands-on portion of the visit took five minutes—skin check, breast exam, ear and throat exam, listen to heart and lungs. I had three concerns on my list. First, I had some moles, for which I was referred to a dermatologist. Second, recurring shoulder and neck pain from injuries, for which I was referred to an orthopedic specialist and a physical therapist. And third, generalized fatigue that prompted a brief discussion, for which I was referred to an internist. My family doctor said she felt bad that she did not have time to address these issues other than superficially. She said she would like to see me in six months and we could delve into them more deeply. Six months? I was stunned, but this scenario is not uncommon.

My doctor is immersed in a model of care and a healthcare system that has clear parameters. For her to deviate significantly from the standard of care would put her business in jeopardy. But for me, the patient, the encounter was unsatisfying. And even though I am quite healthy I was directed to see three or four specialists in order to address the concerns on my list.

By and large the most satisfying encounters I have had as a patient were those in which I felt that I was truly seen, heard, listened to, and that my needs and expressed concerns were not only considered important but were actually addressed. But that level of satisfaction is a rarity in most of the healthcare encounters I have had in recent years. And it is the same for most other people who seek healthcare services in the USA.

It is not only disheartening it is actually heartbreaking because I know there is a better way. I know it when I see it. I can feel it when I experience it. But the standard of care in the USA is not it.

We have shifted from healthcare that was decidedly holistic in my childhood, to healthcare that is very specialized in my adulthood. The result is that many advances in modern medicine have improved our quality of health, and thus, our sense of wellbeing. But simultaneously, many aspects of modern medicine have not only diminished our quality of life but have also weakened our sense of wellbeing.

In the US we have a system of allopathy, or biomedicine, where medical doctors and other healthcare professionals treat symptoms and diseases using drugs, radiation, surgery, and medical technologies. But it is not done in an integrated manner. The vast majority of healthcare is divided into specialty areas—from the start of life to the end of life, and everything in between. Nowadays, very few physicians 'do it all' to provide healthcare to an average healthy family over the lifespan of all its members.

Numerous practitioners in the US healthcare system possess a piece of the puzzle. And depending on a patient's condition, they must seek care from separate specialties: obstetrics, gynecology, pediatrics, adolescent medicine, allergy and immunology, gastroenterology, oncology, cardiology, endocrinology, genetics, hematology, neurology, psychiatry, radiology, surgical specialties of all kinds, respiratory medicine, sports medicine, occupational medicine, nuclear medicine, maternal-fetal medicine, infectious disease medicine, internal medicine, geriatric medicine, and the list, literally, goes on and on.

Specialization allows physicians to have an in-depth knowledge of their specialty area, which is great in treating conditions such as communicable diseases, serious injuries, and life-threatening illnesses, like cancer and cardiac disorders. And patients benefit from the physicians who have high-level expertise.

Because of the range of expertise available, we sometimes make the mistake in thinking that a comprehensive approach such as modern biomedicine will ensure a patient's healthcare needs are being met. But in fact comprehensive care from numerous specialists often leads to fractured, uncoordinated care. A patient's real needs may slip through the cracks in a comprehensive healthcare approach.

The majority of women in the US are low-risk during their pregnancies, and for them holism is the preferred framework, as opposed to highly specialized but fragmented care.

A key feature of holistic care is that it is patient-centered. The totality of the person is taken into account, not just the physical factors. Because the Affordable Care Act of 2010 (ACA) defines how healthcare services are to be delivered in the USA, and because patient-centered care is favored, patients are acknowledged as being key players in determining which healthcare outcomes they value. Through guidelines in the ACA, healthcare practitioners are directed to use a holistic framework and shared decision-making in order to partner with patients to achieve health and wellness goals.

Health is a multidimensional state of being. Understanding health will always be dependent on our understanding of life.

What this means in practical terms for maternity care providers is, first and foremost, *determine what women want by listening to them*. If you listen, they will tell you what they want and need.

Numerous studies suggest women want three things from maternity care. They want freedom to exercise choice in decision-making, including the use of complementary therapies and culturally based traditions. They want their concerns and fears addressed. And they want continuity of care.

Midwives believe that working with the trinity of body-mind-spirit inherent in holism is where the real power and satisfaction lie, both for clients and for health service workers.

When you think of holism think of my old family doctor who had multiple skills and who knew our whole family's health status, and attended to our healthcare, over many decades. And think of the young migrant woman and the overlapping services she was given to address the whole range of her needs.

And then imagine all the possibilities—endless, really—for the time when our healthcare systems and practitioners finally acknowledge the concept that *we are whole beings, more than the sum of our parts*. And imagine an era when we truly live by the understanding that *everything is connected and interrelated,* and it all matters.

nature matters

Nature has masterfully designed the elegantly complex
processes of pregnancy, birth, lactation,
and mother-infant attachment, and in most cases,
no amount of tampering can improve them.

Nature is the rhythm, breath, and heartbeat of life, and the epicenter of the 12 qualities that matter.

A few years ago I went on my first long-distance sailing adventure. After months of preparation the day for departure finally arrived. My husband and I left our safe homeport in Grand Traverse Bay for a month-long journey. We headed north into Lake Michigan passing port after port until we could no longer see land. The feeling of being in a very small vessel on very big water was both frightening and exhilarating. On our third day we traveled all through the night so that we could reach the Georgian Bay in Canada. It was a murky, challenging, tiring sail. We traveled through many lightless hours cruising deep, dark waters, riding wave after wave, with pouring rain stinging our faces and drenching our clothes. It was miserable.

Finally we entered the North Channel of Lake Huron in Southern Ontario. We arrived at our destination in the dark of the night. But as the sun rose and the fog lifted, I began to see the shapes and colors of the land around us. Clouds of lavender and gold in the sky overhead highlighted the pink granite, the glacier-smoothed black basalt, and the windswept pines. The rock formations were prehistoric and geologically distinct from anything I had ever seen. The crystal-clear water was a striking color of turquoise, still and smooth. We were in a fascinatingly new land, discernibly less civilized than my home territory. It was peaceful, timeless, and achingly beautiful. I called this place a water wilderness, a nature paradise in its purest form.

It had been a struggle to cast off our lines and make the ambitious trip. But I will never forget the intoxicating feeling of being on an unknown shore and taking in the magic of this geographical jewel of Ontario for the first time. All of my senses felt more invigorated, my spirit was lifted, and joy ran bone deep.

In teaching expectant parents about labor and birth, the sea as a force of nature is often used as a metaphor. Learning how to handle the rough waters a sailor encounters while navigating a sea voyage, we midwives say, is akin to the ebb and flow of contractions a woman must learn to navigate during the birth journey. In the past decade I have come to understand, firsthand, why this metaphor is so fitting.

In the latter part of my sojourn on the planet, I married a man named Fred who came into my life with a sailboat. In the past decade I have been learning to sail. It involves a new language that is often hard for me to discern. I am mastering new skills as nuanced and as tricky to learn as the competencies of midwifery were. But I get better at it every year.

We live near the shores of Lake Michigan, one of the widest and deepest freshwater seas in the world. Learning to be *in* big water not *on the shores* of big water has taught me how to live in the world in ways I could not have learned on land. There are lessons I have learned as a sailor that have been very poignant and have informed my way of being in the world almost as much as being a midwife has. And many of these lessons are applicable to birth. Here are a few.

Control is an illusion. The world is not safe and it cannot be made to be safe, even though we humans fervently wish it to be so. But as it turns out, safety is a relative term, always subject to individual interpretation. The sea is a vast and unbelievably powerful force of nature. I came face to face with this reality, especially when sailing in storms out of sight of land. I cannot conform the sea to my will. Rather, I must surrender to its power and do my very best to pay attention, be in the moment, ride the waves, make good choices, and learn how to survive. Patience, as it turns out, is truly a virtue, and when it fails me, I make mistakes. A compass is my friend. It keeps me from getting lost. Following the inner compass of my heart also keeps me from losing my way. When something strange or disconcerting happens on the wild open sea and appears to be the whim of fate, in retrospect I often recognize it as something in which I could have influenced the outcome. It could have been different had I made other choices.

Sailing might sound crazy (we are land beings after all) and maybe it is. But it is also thrilling. Being out on big water away from the busyness and frantic pace of life on land brings me into a slowed-down pace that soothes my soul. It's refreshing, freeing. It's not about doing and accomplishing; it's about *being*.

On the big water I have learned that nothing lasts forever. If I wait and watch, everything changes. A mighty storm, scary and roaring, often precedes an incredible moment of peace embellished by the most gorgeous and colorful sunset.

The power of nature, especially a storm, sometimes scares sailors and afterward they choose to stay on land. Yet other sailors realize life is full of storms—small and large—and they learn to navigate and are rewarded by encountering distant horizons and amazing places they have never been before.

In sailing, the force of nature is all about the wind. The key to survival is a total paradox. You must give up trying to control nature in order to be in control of your small vessel within nature. I have learned that directing the wind is impossible, but adjusting our sails is well within our control. When I start the journey in the morning, even with a destination in mind, I never know where I will end up by nightfall. Out on the boat I can usually (not always) grasp the notion that I can adapt to whatever life throws at me, and that the forces of nature are not adversarial. They don't care much about my little desires and fears. They simply are what they are.

One of my very favorite times on the boat is twilight. It's quiet and magical. I tend to think of twilight as occurring at the day's end, but there are actually two times of twilight. Morning twilight is *dawn*, and evening twilight is *dusk*, and both times of day share unique qualities. Twilight time is the liminal space between worlds, the space between 'what was' and 'what will come next.'

It seems as though nature purposely programs the labors of most women to begin in twilight.

Twilight is a contemplative moment when the busy noise in a woman's mind becomes dim so the beacon in her body can become brighter. Whether it is a few minutes or a few hours, and whether it is literal or figurative twilight, this time is a necessary part of preparation for the long and arduous journey ahead.

Twilight is a place of transition where a woman stands on both sides of a threshold, not knowing, waiting.

It's almost like being in dreamtime. We think of 'transition' as occurring at the very end of labor when the woman's body changes gears and prepares to push the baby out. But there is another transition, one that occurs at the very beginning of labor, when the woman leaves the known world of her normal daily activities and enters a world of the unknown. Expectant.

At her own pace and in her own time, a woman makes the transition from the liminality of her quiet time, private time, dark time. Then she enters into an active state, shedding layers of clothing, ego, and proper behavior to take on her free, wild, undomesticated self and ride the wave of contractions with rhythmic fervor. It is not a common or familiar state of reality; it is a decidedly altered state.

When a woman lets go of consensual reality and opens to this state of altered reality the force of labor can flow freely through her. It is exquisitely, frighteningly, amazingly different from any other state of being.

Flooded by a force of nature—hormones, blood, oxygen, heat, and energy—a laboring woman becomes transformed.

And there are also other forces of nature at play. The lunar effect—the gravitational pull of the moon—is widely believed to have an influence on initiating labor. Just as the moon's pull affects the earth's waters in the form of tides, the moon's pull can also affect the amniotic water in a pregnant woman's womb. Or a storm—a change in barometric pressure—can influence the internal pressure of the mother-baby universe. The influence of external forces is less provable, but the internal forces of nature are a certainty.

Labor and birth offer an extraordinary one-time opportunity to experience a natural altered state of reality. You might think "Magical Mystery Tour" was written by Lennon and McCartney, but I think it was inspired by the Goddess of Birth who sings " ... *the magical mystery tour is coming to take you away, coming to take you away.*"

In this altered state of consciousness we teeter at the threshold of the infinite. We get to this territory through surrender, by giving up conventional control and allowing innate control—our body's natural wisdom—to emerge and take over.

Watching my daughter meet the challenges of her labor, and seeing my granddaughter born into the hands of midwives was one of the greatest privileges and joys of my life. I was astounded at Leah's strength and persistence in the face of a very tough first labor.

Afterward her doula told her, "I have never before seen a woman so strong, so much like a goddess, a lioness. You were panting, pushing, roaring in your primal power as you gave birth."

Though I have seen hundreds of women in labor and giving birth, I had never seen my own daughter so transformed. It was truly a phenomenal sight to behold.

Contrary to the pervasive messages with which today's generation of women and birthing people are constantly bombarded—particularly in social media, popular culture and movies—**birth is a fundamental human process that is meant to work well.**

We seem to have lost sight of the fact that, like other mammals, we are exquisitely designed to reproduce and provide sustenance for our species. Women's bodies know how to conceive, birth, and nurture human infants. Babies know how to grow in utero, be born, and suckle at their mother's breast.

A central theme of the midwifery model is an essential trust in the body's innate ability for conception, gestation, birthing, lactation, and early parenting. But because this essential belief is obscured by ongoing cultural messages of how hard and perilous these processes are, many people are confused and lack confidence in nature.

On so many levels, we humans are in a gridlock of culture versus nature.

Culture encodes our shared learning through a system of agreed-upon perceptions, values, and beliefs. We discussed this concept earlier—cosmovision or worldview. These systems are human-made.

Our American 'cultural directives' influence women to think of labor pain as unbearable, birth as frightening, and breastfeeding as inconvenient. These are not the beliefs in every culture, not even in the USA.

For years I was a practicing midwife in northern Michigan and I had a group of clients who were Amish. Almost all of them gave birth at home unless there was a medical risk. Their reasons were religious, financial, comfort, and control. The Amish were different from my other clients regarding their beliefs about childbirth. The Amish use medical services when they feel it is medically necessary, but they typically do not believe pregnancy and birth constitute 'medical necessities.'

Because most Amish people do not use birth control, pregnancy and birth are an ongoing part of everyday life. They have large families. Children hear, and often see, the natural process of human birth, and animal births, as they grow up. Amish girls are not exposed to the culture of fear to which most other girls and young women in the US are constantly exposed. Amish girls do not fear that their bodies will fail them. Their mothers model how the reproductive processes are meant to work well.

Amish women are not tied to due dates and they typically have no anxiety about when it will happen. They believe their infants will be born "when they are supposed to be born." When labor starts the woman continues with her daily chores until things 'get hard.' She is not preoccupied with every contraction; in fact it is just the opposite. The Amish only call the midwife when the woman is well into her labor, when she has to stop her chores, when she says "it's time."

Most Amish women give birth quietly, quickly, surrounded by women from the community, and often their husbands and older daughters. They usually get into the positions most favorable to the mechanics of childbirth such as semi-sitting, squatting, or kneeling at the edge of the bed. They rarely thrash and cry out in pain. The room is usually quiet and peaceful. The loudest sounds besides hushed whispers are rhythmic breathing and soft sighs.

From the outside looking in Amish women appear to have less pain in childbirth than other women. It's a remarkable phenomenon I would not have believed (since my own three childbirths hurt a lot and I yowled and thrashed) if I had not seen it, repeatedly, with my own eyes. Amish people strongly believe 'nature will take its course,' and indeed it almost always does take its course in the way they expect.

It may be that simple: we get what we expect.

For most women who are not raised like Amish girls, who are exposed to a different type of cultural conditioning about how women are supposed to behave, labor and birth is a different kind of experience. Typically it is wilder, longer, louder, and women are more fearful.

I remember a client from years ago. She lived in a cherry orchard in a picker's shack. She was having her first baby. Her mother, an OB nurse, did not approve of her daughter's choice to have a homebirth. During the young woman's labor her mother was continually trying to calm her down, subdue her, and kept requesting pain medication for her daughter. The young woman, however, wanted a natural unmedicated birth. She dilated to six centimeters and then 'got stuck' for several hours. The midwives said the baby was in a posterior position and it would simply take time. The grandmother became very vocal and said, "You need to take my daughter to the hospital." Tensions rose, it turned into quite a scene.

The young woman finally stood, kicked everyone out of her bedroom, and bellowed, "I need to be by myself and do it my way." And she closed the door.

She got on her hands and knees. She rocked and she swayed. She moaned and she yelled. She became fierce. She became clear. She became wild—an unstoppable, roaring force of nature, as wild as a raging storm, guided by an ancient, dependable, overwhelming rush of pure energy. Within an hour her baby moved into a more favorable position. Within the next half hour she dilated fully and began to push. She called for my midwife partner, Nancy Curley, and she called for me. Then she called for her mother, and smooth as a summer rain, her chubby nine-and-a-half-pound baby girl was born into the waiting hands of her midwives.

The winning combination was this: the context (out of hospital), plus the content (the midwifery model), plus honoring the woman's right to choose her own path (self-determination), plus trusting the process (nature) to take its course.

Afterwards, this woman's birth story was one of empowerment, confidence, accomplishment, and joy. The extraordinary paradox is that she was in control even as she surrendered to an uncontrollable process. And that made all the difference.

I had a very similar situation with another woman, who also had her overbearing mother at the birth, who also got stuck at six centimeters. This young woman was overcome with fear, and her mother prevailed. We went to the hospital.

In this context (hospital), using a different model of care (biomedicine), where 'next-step decisions' were made by medical specialists not the woman (lack of self-determination), and 'nature's course' was perceived to be potentially dangerous, the outcome for this woman and baby was a cesarean section.

Her story was something like this: *My cervix would not dilate and my baby got stuck. My pelvis was too small and my baby was too big. My baby was in distress and they had to do emergency surgery or she might have died.*

From a clinical perspective, her baby did get stuck but not for the reasons she was told. Her pelvis was of a normal size and shape. At seven pounds her baby was not too big. (Her second baby was born vaginally and weighed nearly eight pounds.) But yes indeed, her baby became stressed, which resulted in the need for an emergency c-section.

This type of birth story can be laced with undercurrents of inadequacy, confusion, disappointment, failure, and regret. The stories of women who feel they have had cesarean surgery unnecessarily are ubiquitous on the Internet. Women tell about how they were misled into thinking a c-section was quick, manageable and somewhat pain-free. Check out the website of the International Cesarean Awareness Network (ICAN) and read the stories posted there.[43] They are both heartbreaking and inspiring. As a result of their dissatisfactory experiences, these women are some of the fiercest warriors I know for normal physiologic birth.

I have attended numerous births in the hospitals that have become 'stuck', typically at six centimeters. At the request of my clients I have used synthetic oxytocin, called Pitocin, to induce or augment labor contractions. And it works amazingly well. Except for when it doesn't work.

When the baby is not ready to be born, or the mother is not ready to give birth but is forced to have contractions, 'a cascade of intervention' ensues.[44] A small intervention is introduced that leads to a bigger intervention, then a cascade of interventions follow. And unintended consequences tumble forth like an overflowing and unstoppable river in springtime that busts through a dam.

A cascade of intervention stems from the belief that the normal physiologic processes of labor and birth can be improved. And here is how it works.

A woman is not progressing in labor and she is struggling with pain and fear. She chooses IV medication to cope with pain. She is limited to laboring in bed because the IV pain meds make her a fall risk. Because she is less mobile and cannot use gravity to help the baby move deeply into her pelvis, her labor is slowed down. She is given Pitocin to speed up labor. Due to the intensity of the induced contractions, sometimes coming one on top of the other, pain and fear overwhelm her, and she is given epidural analgesia for increased pain relief. This requires her to labor on her back in bed so that she can be properly monitored. She begins to feel feverish and her temperature spikes. An infection is suspected. When she is completely dilated she might be given an episiotomy to hasten the birth because she cannot feel the urge to push, and use of forceps might become necessary to forcefully pull the baby out. Because of that she might have greater vaginal and perineal tearing that requires more extensive repair and results in more afterbirth pain and longer recovery.

In another scenario, after epidural analgesia is inserted into the mothers back via a long needle, often delivered in combination with opioids or narcotics, the woman's blood pressure drops, or the baby's heartbeat plummets, or both. Because of the change in vital signs, an emergency cesarean surgery becomes necessary. After the cesarean birth, antibiotics and numerous blood tests are required for both mother and newborn. The baby is taken to the NICU for observation because they may have experienced respiratory distress due to the narcotics. The separation may also interfere with mother-infant bonding and breastfeeding. A longer hospital stay is required after surgery than for a vaginal birth. Breastfeeding is more challenging for the mother who is dealing with an abdominal incision. The baby may have a hard time 'latching on' due to the narcotics. And the normal postpartum physio-logic responses in both mother and newborn may become depressed due to the effect of pharmacological agents used in labor.

Afterward, the woman is told that she experienced an emergency, a cesar-ean was necessary, and her baby would have died without the c-section, which might be true. She is left feeling confused but grateful that the specialists came to the rescue.

What she is not told is that the cascade of interventions to get her body to do what it was not ready to do in the first place is what precipitated the emergency.

Do not misinterpret what I am saying. There are certain cases when everyone would agree a c-section is necessary. In a true emergency a c-section is lifesaving, and we are grateful for skilled surgeons, pharmacological agents, and compe-tent surgical staff. However, the World Health Organization recommends that surgical birth be used sparingly, and that only ten to fifteen percent of all births medically require cesarean surgery.[45]

But have you ever considered this? In this day and age, cesarean surgery has become a national as well as a global epidemic, and a large percentage of newborns spend time in neonatal intensive care. One in every three labors (nearly 33%) in the US ends in a surgical birth. And newborns at all birth weights are increasingly admitted to a neonatal intensive care unit, totaling over half a million American newborns each year.[46]

What is failing here? The bodies of women and infants, or the system in which women and infants are situated?

I grew up in Detroit where, in 1903, Henry Ford stirred a quiet revolution by building his first gasoline-powered horseless carriage. But several years later Ford rocked the world when he introduced mass-production methods and created the world's first moving assembly line for automobile manufacturing. The assembly line proved to be a brilliant model for creating finished products much faster than with individual handcrafted methods, improving affordability, and increasing profits. Ford's innovation became the template for the entire auto industry. He was a smart man who changed the world.

Detroit is also where Henry Ford's innovations inspired the first hospital in the country with a mother-baby assembly line featured in the maternity ward. Ford's concept spread like wildfire all across the nation and became the template for modern maternity care.

The brilliance of an assembly line is that it produces 'sameness': the same processes, creating the same products, for the same purposes. When we shifted to this model and mentality in 'the new maternity care,' there was no place for a wild card like nature, which produces a similar but never 'the same' process, even in the same woman.

Researchers note there has been a direct link between the rise of the assembly line and mass production and the rise of standardized, mechanized, assembly line obstetrics.[47] These innovations, during the Industrial Revolution in the twentieth century, marked a turning point for American birth. The goals of the new methods were to tame nature, control the natural process of childbirth, and 'make birth better.'

But better for whom?

The shift from a low-tech, social, individualized, midwifery model of childbirth to a high-tech, impersonal, assembly line, medical model was a significant trend in the early twentieth century. It heralded the **industrialization of childbirth**.

But a further development, the gradual and insidious **corporatization and medicalization of childbirth** that took hold in the latter half of the twentieth century is quite another development. And it *did not make birth better* for most low-risk, healthy women and infants. Just the opposite.

Getting clear about the influence of the *corporate business model* that evolved in the mid-to-late twentieth century—the model that has come to dominate maternity care and the entire US healthcare system today—is essential to understanding the big picture.

Once again, as with the advent of assembly-line obstetrics, the introduction of corporatization and medicalization of maternity care changed everything. It changed the workplace, the nature and organization of birth work, the division of labor, the standardization of roles and tasks defining what products birth workers were to produce in the industry, the rise of a managerial superstructure, and how the subjects or raw material of the industry—mothers and babies—were to be managed and processed.[48]

When childbirth was made to fit into a routine system, there was no longer an emphasis on the fluid (if sometimes messy) process of an individual woman's labor and birth, her specific needs or unique situation, or continuity of care from a single practitioner.

Rather, the corporate business model emphasized standard, efficient, procedure-oriented tasks to be completed on all patients across the board at various antepartum, intrapartum and postpartum stages. Who would administer each procedure depended on the technical complexity of the task and the skill level of the staff member. But everything was done to ensure a "continuous operational flow of patients"[49] inspired by Henry Ford's continuous moving assembly line.

To ensure that women would be willing to buy the products and submit to the procedures of the new corporate maternity care industry, persuasive marketing of the goals of a corporate and medical model of birth had to be undertaken. To (re)shape women's thinking about the fundamental experience of giving birth there had to be a hook.

The biggest lure in the marketing scheme was the promise of painless childbirth.

A featured product was a narcotic called Twilight Sleep that boasted painless childbirth. It was a concoction of morphine (an opioid drug that reduces pain) and scopolamine (a drug that reduces memory of pain). While 'Twilight Sleep' was a comforting sounding name, it did not always work as well as it was touted. It often caused hallucinations, delirium, and combative behavior, and many women had to be restrained and padded, tied to their beds, sometimes blindfolded with padded hoods, due to violent thrashing. Women typically labored and gave birth in darkness and isolation. One-on-one supervision could not be provided due to the way hospitals were set up.

At the time of birth, a groggy baby who may have suffered respiratory distress due to central nervous system depression from opioids was thrust into the arms of a confused and groggy mother. The mothers often had no recollection of giving birth. Mother-infant bonding was inhibited due to the hazy fog they were both in. My own mother told me she did not remember giving birth to most of her children, except the one for whom they did not get the drugs administered "in time."

And that is why many women loved Twilight Sleep—no pain, no remembering.

Advocates of Twilight Sleep said the problem with the pain of childbirth was not only the *experience* of pain itself, but also the *memory* of the pain. If the memory could be eradicated then the debilitating fear and anguish would disappear.

But at what cost? Is experiencing pain but remembering nothing ultimately good for people?

Detractors of Twilight Sleep said pain became a phantom, an unvoiced thing that haunted their bodies forever.[50] Their bodies had very much experienced pain, but their minds could not remember it. There remained a bizarre and troubling blank slate where their births should have been.

But continually sensing phantom pain is just one of the documented consequences of trying to subdue or obliterate the natural processes of labor and birth.

There were fierce advocates and equally as fierce detractors, but this practice persisted for several decades. From 1915 through the early 1970s it was common practice, in part because women all across the nation pushed their doctors to implement Twilight Sleep.

It was also popular because obstetricians, overwhelming male, often had disdain for women's bodies and the body's "abnormal functions" in childbirth. Women could be better controlled when Twilight Sleep was used.

In an early volume of the *American Journal of Obstetrics and Gynecology*, published in the 1920s, it stated, "Labor is pathogenic, disease producing, and anything pathogenic is pathologic and abnormal. In fact only a small minority of women escape damage during labor, while 4 percent of babies are killed and a large indeterminable number are more or less injured by the direct action of the natural process itself. So frequent are these bad effects, that I have often wondered if Nature did not deliberately intend for women to be used up in the process of reproduction."[51]

From the prevailing medical authorities at the time, *nature* was described as the culprit, the cause of damage, dysfunction, pathology, and even death.

But in 1958, at the insistence of a letter to the editor of the *Ladies Home Journal* from an anonymous labor and delivery nurse who described delivery practices as "torture," the magazine, which was known as a champion of women's rights, published an investigative article called "Cruelty in Maternity Wards." A floodgate was opened.

Letters from women all across the country poured into the magazine for months detailing treatment that was distressing, and in some cases inhumane, at the hands of modern obstetric practitioners and within standard hospital protocols.

Inhumane practices included shackling women, ostensibly to protect them as they writhed in pain, and some women retained scars from where the straps cut into their wrists. Sterilizations were imposed on some women without their consent, targeting women of color, and often without their knowledge due to the insidious fog of Twilight Sleep. And some women were later called "crazy" because of persistent nightmares, and eventually committed to insane asylums.

In retrospect, Twilight Sleep has been considered one of the worst obstetrical interventions (experiments) of the twentieth century. But it took until the end of the 1970s before Twilight Sleep faded into the night and into obscurity. Also at that time, people like me and other warriors for reproductive rights came onto the scene to champion a revolution to take birth back.

Here are some of the questions I propose we need to contemplate. *What is it about nature that we feel we must control? What is it about the reproductive processes of women's bodies that frighten us so much? What is it about significant but temporary pain that we feel we cannot—or should not—endure?* These are ethical and human dilemmas for which we do not seem to have definitive answers.

Midwives do not suggest that 'natural childbirth' is for everyone. First of all, the topic can be fraught with diverse interpretations. And more importantly, each person has the right to chart her own course and find her own way using her own internal compass.

Rather, midwives prefer to take a slightly different tack. If we assume that nature's plan for birth makes sense, how do we work *with* and not *against* nature?

Nature's plan for birth is simple, has perpetual longevity, and is designed to work well. But just as every sailing adventure is unique with particular weather and wind patterns never to be duplicated, with unique storms that will arise and then abate, so too each woman-baby birth journey happens the way it happens one and only time.

Most woman-baby dyads are capable of crossing the birth threshold together successfully. It is true that nature can make mistakes, things can go wrong, and not everyone is able to conceive, birth, breastfeed, or thrive.

Nonetheless, nature has masterfully designed the elegantly complex processes of pregnancy, birth, lactation, and mother-infant attachment, and in most cases, no amount of tampering can improve them. The dependability of these processes working well has kept our species alive and dominant on the planet for millennia.

Nature is not personal. It is neither out to get us nor is it going to save us.

Nature is universal, an inexplicable force. Humans, like all of life, belong to a whole web in which we are never apart from nature. We can learn to live in harmony, or we can fight against the forces of nature. But either way, we cannot escape nature. Nature is an ever-present companion whose moods we can learn to love, just as we can learn to love the waves on an open sea.

I have been on sea journeys and I have been on birth journeys. And in both cases, even when it seemed impossible, working with and not against nature was the only sensible thing to do.

When we stand at the threshold of giving birth, we could make a vow to let the wild force of nature move through our bodies unfettered.

We may experience nature in the hushed but strong way of the Amish women, or untamed and raucous like the woman who gave birth in the picker's shack.

Either way, when we let it flow, we open to the elemental gift of nature, which is the powerful, trustworthy, innate force of life.

Working in concert with nature—rather than against it—matters. It may be our key to survival not just in the realm of women's procreative lives but also in our communities and in our world.

We could make the conscious choice to honor nature, work with nature, and trust nature at the very beginning of every human life. What a difference that one simple act could make in the world.

sacred matters

There is a **sacred** and invisible domain
through which women and infants
must pass to give birth and be born.
Birth is not just physiologic;
it is a soul journey.

My mother's mother, Mary Helen Donnelly Daly, was just a girl of eighteen when she left home. In 1905 she traveled from rural County Tyrone in Northern Ireland to the bustling city of Belfast and boarded a ship, alone, for America. Like many other Irish immigrants fleeing to 'the promised land' in order to escape the aftermath of the deadly potato famine, she landed on the shores of New York. She settled in a cheap boarding house and worked as a maid. She was penniless, frightened, and determined to succeed in the new land. Like all immigrants it was a struggle for my grandmother to adapt and assimilate to her new life. Among the things my grandmother did was to try to 'act American.' She could not lose her thick Irish brogue but she could disguise her native beliefs.

Much like the Indigenous peoples of North America, the Irish are known for their belief that everything in life is imbued with spirit. Everything—the land, wind, water, trees, animals, rocks, sky, thunder. Irish people believe everything the eye can see and the senses can perceive, from the infinitesimal to the infinite, is vibrant and sentient and has spirit.

Just as the Irish believe that the wild, raw, geographical phenomena of the outer landscape is alive, they also believe humans have a rich inner landscape of spirit. The invisible world is forever interfacing and entwining with the outer spirit-filled world.

The Irish believe the unseen world is as real as the seen world. The Irish myths and songs are filled with stories of how the physical and metaphysical worlds are connected in a continual and mutual cycle of unfolding and becoming. It is a magical, multidimensional way to view one's existence, which is embedded in the Irish language and lifeways, and which my grandmother brought with her from Ireland to North America.

I believe this way of seeing the world is instinctive in young children of any culture who seem to have no problem accepting the potential of alternative realities, like Narnia and Hogwarts and Oz.

But imagine my grandmother's shock when she realized that to live in America you must believe that the world is rigid and dense. Mountains are mountains, trees are trees, and stars are stars. They are not living breathing beings alive with energy and spirit, perhaps even relatives with kinfolk of their own.

The other notion my grandmother had to give up was her belief that the Creator had three faces—one was the father, one was the mother, and one was the spirit that united them. Irish Catholics are very curious in that they follow the dictates of Rome but they also created a spirituality that is uniquely Irish, one that is more amorphous than Roman Catholicism, one that does not separate humans from the forces of nature nor place them in dominion over those forces. It is a spirituality that is an explicit declaration of the unity and merit of all things. But my grandmother's notion of 'Mother-Father God' had to be suppressed as she strove to think like an American Catholic.

I was raised as a typical Catholic, but in my teens my mother reclaimed the moniker and notion of Mother-Father God. At the same time I began to study theology and philosophy and I learned that historically across our planet, in the last two millennia, women and nature have both been cast as 'unsacred' by patriarchal religions and structures. These constructs are permeated with beliefs and rules that seek to control and diminish women and their bodies, and also seek to control nature.

Today in most world religions the feminine face of God is blurry, often nonexistent. Spirituality with a feminine presence is a vague and distant memory.

In contrast, I often hear midwives describe 'woman' in a way the ancient Irish myths once did, and many Indigenous cultures still do, as a reflection of the Divine Feminine.

Often you will hear midwives bearing witness to how a woman is perfectly and elegantly designed for biological functions of mythic proportions. Midwives see woman as a doorway from the spirit realm to the physical realm. Woman is a sacred living environment, the first environment,[52] and the chalice in which all human life gestates. Woman is the sacred portal through which human life emerges, and the sustenance by which newborn human life thrives.

Those of us who have been privileged to work in the field of midwifery for decades, even many of us who are just starting out, know that something else is happening in the shadows of the biologic processes. There is an unseen realm occurring simultaneously in the presence of the visible world. Any ordinary person who has ever watched an episode of the British TV series *Call the Midwife* has also witnessed this phenomenon.

There is a sacred and invisible domain through which women and infants must pass to give birth and be born. Birth is not just physiologic; it is a soul journey.

The invisible sacred cannot be underestimated in its importance in the birthing process. I have witnessed the wonders of the child-making and child-bearing year, again and again, and as a midwife I have been immersed in those miracles. Over the years, caring for pregnant women and their babies and going to births became a kind of spiritual practice for me. More than in any church, when I sat at the altar of birth, God walked in.

I was once at a retreat where an athletically fit young man told his story of climbing Mt. Everest. He said, "That trek and reaching the summit was the closest I can ever imagine coming face to face with the Source of it all." The teacher, a Tibetan monk, smiled and acknowledged the young man's revelation and enthusiasm. Then he chuckled softly and said, "Yes, that is what we men have to do in order to *feel* the Source. For women, they give birth and they *are* the Source."

Sadly, the sacred is not intentionally incorporated into the biomedical model of childbirth in the USA. However, that does not mean people do not recognize the sacred. It does not mean people do not crave the sacred. And it does not mean people birthing in any environment cannot bring the sacred with them.

I once had a Native American client who chose to birth in the hospital. She discussed her birth plan with her nurse-midwife team who agreed that she should invite members of her extended family to the birth in order to create a sacred space and conduct spiritual ceremonies. The woman and her family, including her uncle who was an Ojibwe medicine man, set up an altar of sacred objects and herbs. During labor, only her female relatives were allowed to sit and kneel by her side, and they comforted and fortified her with traditional remedies. In a corner of the room her uncles and other men drummed and sang throughout the labor. The mother was in a squatting position as she gave birth, and an auntie held her up on either side. The birthing baby glided through a tangle of hands—those of the young mother, her mother, and the midwife—as he gently descended onto the handmade birthing blanket on the floor.

Soon after the baby was born the woman's uncle was invited to the bedside where he blessed the mother and infant, said grateful words about the placenta, the honorable organ that had kept the baby alive, and then welcomed the baby into the family clan with a traditional ceremony. Songs were sung and prayers were said. The family was immensely satisfied that their sacred traditions could be brought into the hospital birthing suite. It made the experience all the more precious to the entire family.

Another time I was attending a hospital birth of a young Hmong woman. Her mother, aunties, and other female relatives surrounded and comforted her throughout the labor process. Even though the baby was born calmly and peacefully, I noticed the older women became very agitated after the birth. They talked amongst themselves in hushed but obviously distressed tones, which I could not understand because I did not speak their language.

I asked the new mom what the problem was. She explained that among her people there is an important spiritual practice of burying the placenta at home so the ancestors will know where to come for the person when they are ready to return to the spirit world. They were upset because every time they came to the hospital for a birth of one of their people, the placenta was taken away and their sacred tradition could not be performed. I knew the problem would be very simple to remedy. I carefully and reverently wrapped up the placenta and gave it to the grandmother. She burst into tears and so did the other women. Then they stood and bowed to me repeatedly, laughing and gesturing, cherishing the placenta, and saying prayers of gratitude. It was such a pleasure to be able to accommodate something so simple and yet so monumentally significant to them.

Every midwife has a story about the spiritual realm of birth and how people have found ways to bring their most sacred traditions into their birth experiences.

Birth creates a literal opening in our bodies, but birth also creates an energetic opening to the sacred. It is a rite of passage that enlivens every layer of body, mind, and spirit, which creates an internal, soulful unity.

Each of us walks in two worlds—an inner world that we carry around with us, and the outer world that we share with others. Walking in these two worlds leaves some of us feeling unified and some of us feeling fractured. In order to live compatibly in a new country, my grandmother had to compartmentalize her life. She had to set aside essential and beloved internal values and traditions so that she would fit into the external world.

Paradoxically, reclaiming my grandmother's beliefs became a beacon for me. It reoriented me to what we, as humans, seem to have forgotten; everything in the world is connected, everything is imbued with spirit.

What my grandmother had to forget I was able to remember.

There are plenty of naysayers for a world bursting with spirit. At times this orientation to the world may seem impractical, chaotic, and uncontrollable. But therein lies its power. When we open our judgment-oriented minds to this notion, a barrier is removed from a gateway to our passion-filled hearts that clarifies just exactly how the material and spiritual realms intertwine in human experience. To feel the merging of a strong sense of mystery with an ardent embrace of the world, inside and out, is sublime.

When we sacrifice the mystery of birth to the mechanized and often soulless modern birthplace, we humans suffer a profound loss of something that truly matters.

Reclaiming the sacred in the ordinary miracle of birth is deeply satisfying to the souls of all whom the childbirth experience touches—those giving birth, those being born, and those supporting and celebrating the journey.

relationship matters

*It is an essential longing of humans to be
in **relationship** with one another.*

What does it mean to be human?

This question is at the heart of one of the most fundamental inquires about our existence. Artists, philosophers, scientists, and theologians have attempted answers, but the question has puzzled, inspired, tormented, and challenged humanity for centuries. The multitude of perspectives is so diverse it has made finding a singular answer remarkably elusive.

From a biological perspective, here are the basics of the genesis of being human. A male germ cell, or sperm, and a female germ cell, or ovum, unite to form one single cell, called a zygote. Typically (not always) the act of creating a human life is an enjoyable if not an ecstatic act of union between people. The zygote undergoes millions of divisions and a dazzling flurry of activities. There are 75 trillion cells in the human body. Yet this huge conglomerate of disparate cells, which is called upon to create different organs and systems, develops and functions remarkably as a coherent whole. Ultimately, what began as a relationship between two separate beings results in the birth of a third (and sometimes a fourth or fifth) completely new human being. Becoming human means integrating nearly infinite parts into a unified whole through continual patterns of connection and integration.

From an evolutionary biology perspective, scientists say there have been many versions of the *Homo* species, but *homo sapiens* are the only ones that have not ended in extinction. What is distinct in the evolution of modern humans is an urge toward mutual cooperation in order to survive. Even the work of Charles Darwin, the premier evolutionary biologist credited with the theory of 'survival of the fittest,' on closer inspection actually proposed 'survival of the kindest' as the more likely strategy that enabled humans to survive effectively and efficiently. From that perspective, what it means to be human implies an emphasis on compassion, kindness, and behaviors that are mutually beneficial to all.

From a neurobiological perspective, scientists have documented that our need to connect—each of us—is hardwired into our brains before birth and is the primary driver behind human behavior. Our nervous systems want us to connect with other humans beings. An example is mirror neurons that enable humans to mindread each other and to harmonize with one another. Scientists say that our primary imprinting is connection, and that being human means being in relationship with one another. It is what (most) humans do; we connect.

Among the many theories of what it means to be human, there are significant overlaps. It involves continual patterns of comingling and integration; survival of the species based on instincts and behaviors that are mutually beneficial to all; and innate neurobiological hardwiring that compels humans to connect with one another.

It is an essential longing of humans to be in relationship with one another. Our existence is dependant upon connectedness—body, blood, and bone. It starts at the very beginning, arguably even before consciousness arises, when we are merely sentient beings floating in a saltwater sanctum. And that longing to be in relationship with one another continues until the moment we die.

Perhaps the fact of our integral connectedness makes people intuitively seek relationships and belonging. Perhaps our desire for connectedness also makes women seek maternity care providers who are willing to create and nurture relationships during the extraordinary baby-growing, baby-birthing year.

Some people interpret being in relationship quite broadly.

For much of my midwifery career I have worked for and with Indigenous peoples. In the late 1990s and all of the 2000s, I was a comanager of the Michigan Inter-Tribal Healthy Start Project. One year we joined with all of the other Healthy Start projects that primarily served Indigenous peoples—six out of one hundred projects nationwide—and we gathered in Hawai'i for a summit of the Native People's Council. It was designed to address maternal and child issues unique to Indigenous, tribal, and urban Indian peoples. Our gathering also included federal government representatives who were project officers. I was privileged to be among the minority of non-Native people present.

Every meeting of Indigenous peoples that I have ever attended—whether formal or informal, regional or national—begins with a call to prayer and thanksgiving. Thus, on day one of our summit in Hawai'i, we began with an intertribal ceremony at the volcano Kilauea, a very sacred site to Native Hawaiians. It is the most active of the five volcanoes on the Big Island, and is believed to be 210,000 to 280,000 years old. In 2018, flowing lava devastatingly claimed the habitat around this magnificent natural wonder. But in 2003 we were blessed to be at this site for our opening ceremony.

We formed a large circle standing shoulder to shoulder at the edge of the volcano. The Native Hawaiian people offered a traditional water ceremony, and the Native Americans offered a traditional smudge ceremony, which has similar qualities. The water or smudge was infused with sacred herbs of the respective peoples. In turn, each person in the circle was anointed with water and smudge. Medicine people spoke words of supplication, instruction and gratitude, and prayers were spoken to Creator, the Earth spirits, and the ancestors. Dances were enacted as teaching stories. Blessings for the upcoming summit were bestowed on the entire group as well as on those who were not physically present but were 'holding the space' for the gathering. And afterward, offerings were left as gifts at the threshold of the volcano.

In that very first ceremony and throughout the week of meetings, a particular Indigenous teaching kept being repeated and revisited. In fact, it permeated every conversation we had. It was about relationship, connectivity, and kinship.

Though I am not Native, I will tell you what I was privileged to learn in Hawai'i and continue to learn today from Indigenous peoples.

The worldview of Indigenous versus Western people is very different. And of course there are hundreds of different Indigenous peoples and worldviews, hundreds of Western cultures, and each is unique. As I understand it however, there is consensus among Indigenous peoples on the broad strokes. Central to their beliefs, and since time immemorial, Indigenous peoples have had a respectful, spiritually and physically dependent, intricate, intimate, grateful connection to the land and all the beings that inhabit the land, and to the spirits of places and things.

The nature of their tie to the land and sea is not one of ownership but of stewardship. The connection to people and other beings is as relatives. In my region, prayers begin and end with the phrase, 'Mitakuye Oyasin,' 'all my relations.' I was taught that 'all my relations' does not simply refer to blood relatives. It implies an intrinsic kinship to the spirit of everything—animate and inanimate, living people and long-gone ancestors. It extends to family, nations, Mother Earth, Father Sun, Grandfather Sky, Grandmother Moon, the stars, the rocks, the clouds, the bones, all the two-leggeds, the four-leggeds, those that swim, those that fly, the root nations, and the crawling beings who share the world with us.[53] And everything is imbued with intelligence and wisdom.

To begin and end gatherings with the phrase Mitakuye Oyasin reminds us of our interconnectedness to all beings, all things, and to Creator. It reminds us that I cannot exist without you; you cannot exist without me. 'I live in the sea, and the sea lives in me' is not a metaphor; it is our reality. Likewise, 'You in me, and me in you' is also our reality. I was taught that if this intrinsic connectivity were severed—just as if an umbilical cord were severed—the physical and spiritual wellbeing of the People would be in danger.

The Native peoples stress that being 'out of right relationship' with people, the land, and other beings is considered a state of serious imbalance and disharmony that requires intervention to fix.

Growing up, I was not taught this way. It was because of the generosity and kindness of people who believed I could understand and respect their Indigenous knowledge that I learned. And then later I discovered that my own Irish ancestors, also tribal people and practitioners of earth-based spirituality, held similar beliefs.

Many observe that in these postmodern times humans are not only becoming more severely alienated from nature but also detached from one another. We no longer feel the responsibility for protecting the needs of the human family and sustaining all of life. And many observe that our lifeline, our connection to what it means to be human within a species and within the world that holds us, is in danger.

There is a frightening theory that we are dramatically altering what it means to be human. With technological acceleration, gene editing, and artificial intelligence looming large, we seem to be in the midst of an existential crisis unparalleled in human history.

It is not difficult for a non-Native person to sense the wisdom and importance of the Indigenous worldview. At some point, way back when, all people were Indigenous to place. Some place. And they knew their lives and livelihood depended on intimate connections to people, places, and things.

We are conceived and born and imprinted with the longing for connection, and as human communities we have survived and thrived best within the integral web of cooperative relationships. It is no wonder, at the time of pregnancy and birth, amidst the most vital and vulnerable of human experiences, we desire intimate connections with one another that nourish, protect, and sustain us.

Connection continues to be what humans crave.

This is what the birthing people from Gen X, the Millennials, and the Centennials tell midwives: even though they rely on their handheld computers a hundred times per day, and even though they are comfortable with the technological wizardry of the contemporary American birthplace, it is the way they are treated in their healthcare relationships that most impresses, pleases, or disturbs them.

What clients like about working with midwives is a mutual investment in building relationships that involve time, energy, and heart.

Time is a precious commodity in establishing and nurturing relationships. Adequate time is rarely accorded women in conventional maternity care settings. The average allotted prenatal encounter with an obstetrician is six minutes.[54] With midwives in almost all settings, healthcare visits run from twenty to sixty minutes. Without an extended investment of time, trust is difficult to achieve, and building meaningful relationships is less likely to occur.

Pregnant people—in the midst of a life-altering situation—need to be listened to. Their fears need to be addressed. Their questions need to be answered. Their intuitions need to be supported. Their birth plans need to be privileged. Their unique emotions need to be honored.

For relationships to really work, connections have to exist and develop on multiple levels. In a relationship as short-lived as the birth year, but which is supremely important to the wellbeing of birth-givers and their partners, the key components are an investment of time and genuine caring paired with clinical skills and technological interventions. Part of the relationship loop involves linking the care delivered by practitioners with patient-perceived value.

The vital question is: **Are patients getting their needs met in the healthcare relationship?**

This question so caught the attention of national healthcare reformers that in 2008 the Centers for Medicare and Medicaid Services (CMS)—one of the biggest payers of healthcare services in the US—defined **value-based care.** They devised a framework to reward healthcare providers with incentive payments based on the quality of care they gave people with Medicare.[55]

More than ten years later these programs are still part of CMS's broad strategy to reform how healthcare in the US is delivered and paid for. Value-based programs have a three-part aim: better care for individuals; better health for populations; and lower cost. As the healthcare industry transitions toward this value-based model, hospitals, health facilities, and providers have to change their approach to provider-patient relationships.

What has developed from this dialogue (and the monetary incentives that led to practitioner buy-in) is a **patient-centric approach**. This model aligns healthcare decisions with patient's wants, needs, and preferences, and includes more education so that patients understand their own health status better and can take charge of their health and wellbeing.

A patient-centric approach is a humanized approach. Research shows this approach leads to decreased overall expenses, improved care, and greater satisfaction for both givers and receivers of care.[56] This approach is a radical departure from the commonplace 'doctor-as-God' and 'I know best what you need' model of healthcare that most people in the US have experienced as routine.

Value-based, high-quality healthcare with a patient-centric approach implies a commitment to getting to know people, connecting with them, understanding their unique needs, and building relationships.

And curiously enough—this approach is what midwifery care is built on.

Take the case of Jennie Joseph, a British-trained midwife who upon arriving in the USA was horrified by the maternal and child outcomes, particularly the rate of mortality for Black women. She learned they were three to four times more likely to die in the childbearing year than their white counterparts. Jennie's pioneering work in Florida provides human connection, empowering education, an evidence-based approach, and prenatal care for all regardless of ability to pay. She provides woman-centered, family-centered care. She and her patients use shared decision-making. The maternal-infant outcomes among the patients in the population Jennie serves—mostly vulnerable and marginalized folks and people of color—have shifted from deplorable to exemplary.

Jennie insists that, next to access to care, the most important thing she offers is connection. Jennie says, "Once you can connect a woman to her baby, to her situation, to your staff, to yourself, once she feels safe to connect, a whole world opens up."[57]

Jennie can document what Indigenous peoples have always known. Relationships matter because they are as fundamental to our survival as food and water, as important to our wellbeing as sunshine and fresh air.[58]

Yet in Florida where Jennie's model is producing outstanding results, the same population of Black women that are cared for by obstetricians still suffer a three to four times greater chance of dying during or shortly after birth than white women. This devastating disparity can be remediated through care measures taken before and during pregnancy as proven by midwife Jennie Joseph.

When we talk about the shortcomings of the medical model, we are talking about the 'system', not about individual people who have generously dedicated their lives to medicine and healthcare. But it is critically important to acknowledge that how a healthcare system is designed (context and content) makes it more or less conducive to acting on the human instinct towards caring. How a model of care (midwifery or medicine) is designed also makes it more or less conducive to intentionally fostering human relationship building.

Honoring relationships extends to newborn babies as well. They have an extraordinary capacity for social behavior immediately at the time of their births. Mediated by the limbic brain, a mother and infant couplet continues their synchronistic relationship with one another after the birth.[59] Scientists confirm that human brains are physically wired to develop in tandem with another person through emotional communication, beginning before words are spoken.[60]

One need only observe an undisturbed mother and newborn who are lost in enchantment of one another to see the resonance built into the design of human relationships.

Midwives continue to assert that it is optimal for mothers and infants to be in environments and among people where there is an understanding of the biologically innate yearning to be in relationship, which is built into the mother-baby couple.

Midwives and many other care providers believe that caring relationships may be the linchpin that is vital to the whole enterprise of improving maternal-infant health in the USA. This may be true regardless of *who* provides care (physician, nurse, or midwife), and regardless of *where* that care is provided (home, birth center, clinic, or hospital.)

The essence of midwifery care is woman-centered. For midwives and the women they serve, relationships are at the heart of satisfying maternity care.

Midwives strive to meet the needs of pregnant and birthing people above those of institutions, cultural norms, colleagues, and personal agendas. They do this by creating partnerships with those they serve, fostering authentic relationships, and sharing power to achieve a common goal…confident, empowered mothers and healthy babies.

When we contemplate how to make childbirth experiences better, or how to provide value-based maternity care, it is not the birth environment that needs our focus. We need to focus on the relationships between women and maternity care providers, because ignoring these vital relationships comes at a cost to everyone—women, infants, and care providers.

A good relationship can create a positive experience for even the most challenging birth, while a negative one can leave emotional scars, and physical ones too, which can last for years.

From four decades of working in the field, I have learned that the midwife-woman relationship is rather unique. It is not quite like a friendship, but it is more than a typical professional-to-patient relationship. It goes deep into very sensitive and private realms, and it gets very personal. It also thrives on reciprocity, give and take, and the very things that make us human: connection to one another, trust, and rapport.

We are wired to be social creatures. We are wired to connect and to care about one another. We are exquisitely designed to seek participation in relationships for our mutual wellbeing. For people, life is all about seeking satisfying and supportive relationships. That is what it means to be human.

compassion matters

Compassion *is not a luxury,*
it is a biological imperative because
our brains are hardwired to care about one another.

Small hands are good. All of my life I have heard this comment intoned by my clients, part praise, part gratitude.

Those who have been pregnant, given birth, or simply had a gynecological exam have also told me, small hands that move with the grace of tenderness are a double blessing.

I look at my hands today and think of all the ways in which they have touched people. On the outside, they are golden brown from being in the sun, speckled with age spots, adorned with a ring on each hand. On the inside they are smooth and soft, a unique pattern etched by my life line, marriage line, health line, fate line, crisscrossing to reveal what has been in me since birth and what may yet lie ahead.

My hands are a repository for a special kind of knowledge, a unique wisdom one gathers into one's body after years of touching people's lives so intimately, both the joys and sorrows of human existence.

My hands have been placed on either side of voluptuous pregnant bellies to feel the wriggling vibrancy of new life and measure its growth. My hands have been used to manipulate breech babies into a head-down position, to determine cervical dilation, to free infants whose shoulders were stuck behind bony maternal passageways, to untangle umbilical cords, and to guide babies into the light of a new day.

My hands have been baptized, over and over, with the fluid of life's messiest and most precious sacrament. They have caught and caressed luscious naked wet babies and lifted them into their mother's arms. My hands have felt tiny spines vertebra by vertebra, probed soft spots at the crest of little round heads, and tested newborn reflexes while teeny toes curled around my fingers.

My hands have held the hands of a woman as she endured her fourth IVF procedure, steadying her shaking body with my touch as the gynecologist completed the transfer of three fertilized embryos into her uterus.

My hands have wrapped around the full body of a new mother, stroking her back as she cried out in grief for lost dreams, for her baby born with a genetic malformation incompatible with life.

My hands have rested lightly on the shoulders of a father sitting in the NICU in front of an isolette, watching his daughter sleeping, born prematurely, willing her to open her eyes and breathe on her own.

My hands have stroked the hair of a woman lying on her bed, facing her newborn, memorizing every feature of his tiny face, examining every part of his little body, as she prepared to lovingly relinquish him for adoption.

My hands have been enduring ambassadors of compassion. Touching, consoling, encouraging, comforting, reassuring, year after year, time and time again, season after season of life experiences.

Hands, I believe, are a midwife's most reliable agent of compassion.

What is compassion?

Compassion is defined as having three aspects: noticing another person's pain; experiencing an emotional reaction to their pain; and acting in some way to help ease or alleviate the pain.[61] **Noticing, feeling,** and **responding** are interrelated characteristics that each contribute to the process of compassion.

You might wonder if everyone is naturally compassionate. Definitely yes, and sometimes, not so much.

A plethora of scientific research confirms that compassion is deeply rooted in our basic neurological patterning. When we see someone in pain an area in our own brain fires mirror neurons that activate tactile and emotional regions as if we ourselves were in pain. As a result, we experience an authentic longing not only to assist but also to alleviate the suffering of another.[62]

Compassion, as it turns out, is a primal, inherent human trait built into our brains, spiraled into our genes, and pulsating through our nerves. The Golden Rule is actually a codex for what exists as an inherent human attribute. The principle of treating others as we would like to be treated originates from impulses coming from our brain and consciousness, which have evolved and persisted over time to the benefit of humanity.

Compassion is not a luxury, it is a biological imperative because our brains are hardwired to care about one another.[63] This innate neurobiological mechanism promotes interdependence. Without compassion for others the survival and flourishing of our species would have been unlikely.

We see evidence of how compassion unfolds everyday in the lives of ordinary people, from random acts of kindness to enormous outpourings of care and concern when disasters hit. In our troubled world, we also see the opposite of compassion unfolding with alarming speed and intensity. When people experience trauma or abuse their capacity to express compassionate behavior takes one of two paradoxical twists: their ability to notice, feel and respond to the pain of others either accelerates or diminishes dramatically.

Research also asserts that compassionate behavior is individualized. It is significantly influenced by temperament, upbringing, and culture. Some research suggests people are more or less compassionate based on a sliding scale between living in their heads and living in their hearts.[64] Apparently, it is a wide continuum.

It is common to think of compassion as something individuals possess (or do not possess). But compassion is actually a quality that is found in collectives as well. Thus, an organization will be designed to encourage or discourage a greater or lesser amount of compassion among its members. For example, generally speaking, large hospitals are known to be more impersonal and less compassionate than smaller community-based clinics.

Researchers at Stanford University's Center for Compassion and Altruism Research and Education designed a simple model to teach compassion to healthcare providers. The model was particularly helpful in addressing the tendency for healthcare institutions to provide less compassionate care the larger they became. Here is the three-step framework of what compassion looks like.[65]

First, compassion involves **listening with the whole body**. This means turning your whole body toward the speaker, not just your head. In involves using body language that conveys you are listening (arms uncrossed and relaxed with no distractions in your hands, like cell phones or iPads). It involves body signals that indicate you are engaged, like leaning toward not away from the speaker.

Second, compassion involves **soft eye contact**. This means not gazing deeply into another person's eyes, or staring them down, but rather, focusing on the triangle created by the person's eyes and mouth. Eyes are the mirrors to the soul, and tender eyes, soft eyes, teary eyes speak volumes about caring. Compassion occasionally involves looking away in order to regroup or break the intensity that ongoing eye contact can provoke.

Third, compassion relies on **connecting gestures**. These are things that let the other person know you are connecting to what they are expressing, such as smiles and head nods, without interrupting the speaker. Connecting gestures are signals that encourage the person to continue speaking. And when appropriate, touch is the ultimate connecting gesture. Some research has found that people more readily recognize touch as an indication of compassion than voice or facial expressions.

Thus, even if temperament, upbringing, or living more dominantly in your head than your heart limits your ability to be compassionate, the skills of compassionate communication can be learned or enhanced.

In the same time period that value-based care and a patient-centered approach have been formally introduced and incorporated as best practices in healthcare delivery, researchers have also identified the mysterious substance that could reduce pain, lessen anxiety, promote faster healing, boost immune system functioning, and leave patients feeling more satisfied.[66]

It is compassion, loving-kindness, directed toward patients but also toward oneself, to alleviate human suffering and promote healing and wellbeing.

What if we understood that in terms of optimum health, compassion may be the best medicine for our troubled times?[67]

What if care providers understood that the statistical significance of compassion-oriented healthcare on improved health outcomes is greater than the effect of aspirin on lessening the chance of a heart attack?[68]

Research suggests that extending compassion to pregnant and birthing people could result in reducing the rates of preterm birth, low birth weight, infant mortality, maternal mortality and morbidity, postpartum depression, and mental illness. And what if we knew that giving compassion could also increase the rates of breastfeeding, mother-infant attachment, and successful early parenting?

Research also found that compassion, as an exquisitely crafted dance of mutuality, also confers benefits to caregivers. Extending compassion floods the caregiver's brain with chemicals that promote mental and physical wellbeing. Thus, the 'act of giving' has built-in rewards; it is pleasurable. Bringing compassion to the workplace also results in more engagement in work, less exhaustion, increased resilience to stress, a sense of more meaningful work, and more resistance to burnout.[69]

These revelations may unsettle certain people, especially physicians who have been trained to maintain a professional distance from patients, or who feel the most important things they offer are specialized skills and proficient delivery of clinical services and technological interventions. Healthcare administrators may be skeptical, assuming that extending compassion by healthcare staff takes extra time and negatively impacts the monetary bottom line.

But actually, research suggests that compassion improves caregiver productivity and morale while reducing preventable medical complications, reducing the number of return trips patients make to hospitals, and reducing unnecessary interventions and surgeries. All of these factors lead to an overall decrease in healthcare expenditures, less strain on the existing financial resources, and reduced costs from wasteful overuse of drugs and technologies.

Why, therefore, have we in the USA been slow to get on the compassion bandwagon?

There is a powerful force for change in the American healthcare system, but powerful forces oppose it. It is a battle that is as much philosophical as it is financial; as much spiritual as it is political. And it brings us back to the quintessential question we keep asking: **Is our priority people or profits?**

Yet, a new healthcare system is struggling to be born in the USA.

This system will offer high-quality care to every individual regardless of race, ethnicity, gender identity, faith, or culture. This system will not tolerate discrimination and racism that causes detrimental affects on people. This system will not impose trauma on people as a result of medical treatment. This system will not jeopardize people's financial security in order to access the care they need.

Each one of us is called to serve as midwives to this birth. Each one of us is called to usher in this new era of comprehensive change that is beginning to take shape. We are called to honor each and every life as important, sacred, and worthy, and to advocate for the kind of skillful and compassionate healthcare all people desire and deserve.

Compassion—that healing, loving, magic potion embedded in the soul of kindness—as it turns out, matters a great deal not only to individuals, but also to the work of midwifing changes in our healthcare system, changes that hover on the horizon of possibility. Training our innate 'compassion equipment' can relieve suffering, improve health, empower self-confidence, and change our world.

It's in our hands. Small hands, large hands, calloused hands, soft hands. Your hands, my hands, our hands.

self-determination matters

At the core of **self-determination** is a critical question:
Are women in charge of their bodies, their births, their babies,
their decisions, and their lives, or not?

The older I get the more I believe the old adage: your health is your prized possession.

It's hard to stay healthy. It takes work and discipline. I slip up, everyone does. But generally I watch what I eat. My food is lean and green mixed with a modicum of the good kind of fats. I take vitamins and herbal supplements. I go to aerobics class three days a week, lifting, bending, stretching, and sweating. I bike, hike, kayak, and garden. I am judicious about my intake of alcohol. I try to get eight hours of sleep at night. I meditate and reflect. And I do my best to cultivate joy and live in gratitude. And of course, I have white privilege that has provided me with an unearned but measurable dose of protective health advantage.

As I grow older, I have been sticking more consciously to my formula for staying healthy. I believe I am slightly ahead of the curve in health, strength, and flexibility for a woman my age. Still, I am not an athlete or a yogini, and I sometimes wonder what it would be like to be extraordinary in my physical prowess.

When I watch a true athlete like Serena Williams, she looks like a goddess in action—powerful, sleek, beautiful, and fierce. She demands attention and she commands the tennis court. She has won more Grand Slam singles than any other man or woman. She is the only tennis player to ever accomplish a golden career grand slam in singles and doubles. She has broken records, captured titles, and reinvented the game like no other tennis player. She has consistently dominated the field.

She is widely regarded by most sports analysts as the undisputed greatest tennis player of all time. And some analysts say she is the best athlete, man or woman, in modern history.

Serena is powerful, famous, college educated, and wealthy. But all those things, her health, strength, fame, and fortune, could not keep her from almost dying right after the birth of her first child.

In the cover story of *Vogue* (February 2018) Serena told her own story. She had an enviably easy pregnancy. She went into labor. Then she had an emergency cesarean section, which reportedly concluded without a hitch. The newborn's daddy cut the cord and the healthy baby girl was placed on Serena's chest. All was well, everyone was happy.

The next day, while still recovering in the hospital, Serena began to have breathing difficulty. So as not to worry her mother, Serena walked out of the room to the nurse's station to get help. Between gasps she told them exactly what she needed—a CT scan with contrast and IV heparin (a blood thinner) right away. The nurse, however, thought that the pain medicine Serena was taking might have been making her confused. Serena knew what she needed, insisted on what she needed, but her plea was ignored.

A doctor was summoned who began to do an ultrasound on her legs. Serena said very emphatically that she needed a CT scan and a heparin drip, not an ultrasound. Again, her request was not honored. When the ultrasound showed nothing, the medical team finally acquiesced, took her for a CT scan, and just as Serena has suspected, several small blood clots had settled in her lungs. Minutes later she was on the IV drip.

Serena had a medical history that included clotting problems. The medical team could have, should have, been prepared for the possibility of life-threatening clots. But they weren't.

This emergency precipitated a cascade of additional health complications. Her c-section wound burst due to intense coughing as a result of the pulmonary embolism. She had to return to surgery for the wound to be repaired. Her doctors found a large hematoma, a swelling of clotted blood, in her abdomen. She had more surgery and a procedure to prevent additional clots.

When Serena finally made it home to her family—after three major surgeries when she merely entered the hospital to have a baby—she had to spend the first six weeks of motherhood unable to get out of bed.

Evidence shows that Black women are often dismissed or ignored in the healthcare system. Serena's near-miss experience places her among the 50,000 women a year in America who experience life-threatening complications. And some researchers say that number may be even higher. Black women are three to four times more likely than white women to die from pregnancy-related complications.

Even one of our greatest and most celebrated American athletes like Serena Williams, a woman who can command the tennis court like no other athlete, and can raise TV network viewing higher than any other tennis player ever has, could not get a team of medical providers to listen to her.

Black women assert the medical community does not take their pain seriously and that discrimination and systemic racism are the culprits. This is one reason why Black women are statistically at the greatest risk for pregnancy-related deaths and childbirth-related injuries. According to Alliance for Innovation on Maternal Health (AIM) the main cause of complications that kill women in the childbearing year is "denial and delayed response from the healthcare team."[70]

All people have the right to self-determination. In healthcare this right is encoded in the bioethical principle of autonomy, which refers to the inherent right of individuals to hold views, to make knowledgeable, noncoerced, voluntary, well-considered decisions, and to take actions based on what they believe and value. **In essence, self-determination means to have control over one's own life.**

Serena Williams knew her medical history and knew what she needed. But not all people do. Typically, in the complicated world of modern obstetrics, women and birthing people are not given enough information to make informed decisions about the use of technology and obstetrical interventions. They often lack knowledge and feel powerless to influence their own care. And when women refuse certain standard interventions, they can encounter troublesome consequences, which range from annoyance on the part of staff to threats, bullying, coercion, use of physical force, and even arrest.[71]

Established evidence demonstrates that in low-, middle-, and high-resource countries women have experienced mistreatment during labor and childbirth and their fundamental human rights have been violated.[72]

Mistreatment and abuse of human rights begin when patients are not respected, when their choices are not privileged, and when the patient-provider relationship lacks the informed consent process, which can result in women being coerced (mildly or forcefully) into undergoing interventions for which they have not given their consent.[73]

While the term obstetric violence may not be fully recognized in the US or its laws, scholars and legal practitioners in the US, and jurisdictions in other parts of the world, have defined and documented it. The Declaration on the Elimination of Violence Against Women was adopted in December 1993 by the United Nations General Assembly, which included violence during healthcare encounters.[74] In 2014, the World Health Organization identified disrespect and abuse during childbirth in medical facilities as a priority for evaluation, prevention, and elimination.[75] And the rights of women and newborns have been delineated in international and regional laws and are widely accepted as fundamental rights inherent to all people regardless of age, nationality, place of residence, national or ethnic origin, religion, language, gender, sexual orientation, or any other status.[76]

Obstetric violence—mistreatment and crimes against pregnant women and those giving birth—is documented by legal scholars in the USA as being on the continuum of gender-based violence. Examples are verbal abuse, nonconsensual procedures such as vaginal cutting (episiotomies), physical manipulation and restraint, hitting and slapping, involuntary sterilization, forced cesarean surgery, sexual violation, physical abuse, and arbitrary detention.[77]

Not all American women are victims of obstetric violence, although Black, Brown, and low-income women experience it to a larger degree. However, in a national survey in the USA, women across a wide spectrum of class, race, and education reported they felt coerced by obstetrical care providers.[78] The most vulnerable women were most at risk. These same women—low income women, teenagers, women of color, women who use drugs, gender nonbinary people, immigrants, women in prison, and homeless women—also have the most to gain when they are treated with dignity and are able to gain mastery over their own lives.

Research studies note that over-medicalization that pathologizes the processes of labor and birth, coupled with a high-tech patriarchal approach that puts specialized physicians in charge of complicated decision-making, and that often isolates women from social support, may play a significant part.[79]

It is noteworthy that, unlike patients in almost any other realm of healthcare, the right to autonomy and self-determination is uniquely threatened for women and people with a womb who are pregnant, in labor, and giving birth.

At the core of self-determination is a critical question: *Are women in charge of their bodies, their births, their babies, their decisions, and their lives, or not?*

Most birth attendants have good intentions with regard to the care of their patients and clients. The root of the problem is typically not with the individual practitioner, but rather with the standards, attitudes, and protocols inherent in the model of care, and the policies institutionalized in the healthcare system in which people provide that care.

Researcher and midwife, Saraswathi Vedam, and colleagues have developed a patient-informed tool (Mothers on Respect Index, MORi) to measure autonomy, respect, and the quality of maternal healthcare.[80] Among the key findings were these. Women under the care of midwives had higher (better) MORi scores. Women from vulnerable populations and women with medical and social risk factors during pregnancy had lower (worse) MORi scores.

Midwives advocate fiercely for women's ascendancy and right to take owner-ship of their pregnancies and births. They assert that women are the primary caretakers of their pregnancies and the primary actors in the childbirth drama, not healthcare providers, hospital administrators, or any other agencies.

Midwives encourage women to be informed, articulate, and proactive regarding their individual needs, including understanding the characteristics of the context (environment and personnel) and content (protocols and policies) of their own healthcare.

At the center of the midwife-client relationship is the practice of shared decision-making, which fosters self-determination.[81] It offers the opportunity for clients to receive complete and accurate information, clarify values, explore preferences, set goals, create a personalized plan of care, and receive decisional support from their midwives.[82]

With shared decision-making, the woman and her family have the opportu-nity to weigh the evidence against their tolerance for risk and perception of health and safety, and then make the decision that is best for them. In this way a woman and her partner become committed to the choices they have made and are better equipped to face the challenges of labor and birth with self-confidence. Thus, shared decision-making is both collaborative and an empowerment process.

A recent study found that confidence *before* labor was the strongest predic-tor of confidence *during* birth.[83] Women whose self-determination had been strengthened felt more confident, had a greater sense of control, felt more informed in making decisions, perceived labor contractions as less painful, and rated their overall experiences as more positive.[84]

Conversely, lack of confidence, fear, and anxiety during labor were associated with increased perception of pain, increased requests for pain relief medication, prolonged labors, and increased obstetrical interventions, including emergency surgical births.[85] Consequently, the role of the birth attendant—doctor, midwife, doula, or nurse—in cultivating confidence and positive experiences cannot be underscored enough.

Another discussion in the realm of self-determination is about choice. The maze of choices, the amount of choices, and the sophisticated clinical language used to explain choices to clients and patients make the concept of informed consent almost impossible to achieve in most medical institutions. Further, the idea that pregnant and birthing women can be empowered by giving them the freedom to make choices is a ruse if people do not understand their choices, or do not have the freedom to exercise choice-making.

The overwhelming consensus is this: women rarely have *real choice* in institutional maternity care settings. There is only an *illusion of choice*. Essentially, all but the rarest of women in the rarest of circumstances will not be *required* to follow hospital rules. Most women will be *expected,* or *coerced,* to do what their doctor wants them to do.

The heart of the matter is this. A minimum of three critical factors must be viable for self-determination to mean anything in the birthplace: **knowledge of choices, freedom to make choices**, and **access to the services those choices guarantee**.

But none of these factors is systematically embedded in the American healthcare system, particularly for people of color and marginalized and vulnerable people.

Reproductive justice expert, Loretta Ross, says "What good is a right if you cannot access the services that right protects?" This is why **the conversation about self-determination must be expanded from a quest for reproductive rights to a demand for reproductive justice**.[86] The road to fully implement this new paradigm will be arduous and complicated.

If Serena-mega-famous-powerful-superstar-Williams did not have the freedom to make choices, even when she was fully informed of what she needed, how can we expect that anyone else will have true freedom of choice? Especially if they are Black, Brown, queer or poor, if English is not their first language, or if they have mental or physical disabilities. It is not likely to happen.

If a national treasure like Serena Williams, a World Champion tennis player who the hospital staff must have known was an international celebrity, could not command the attention of nurses and doctors when she pleaded, "I need help, I know what I need, please listen to me," how can we expect that the concerns or requests of the average person will be listened to and respected?

If you think, *we've come a long way, baby,* think again. Women have to fight to be heard, fight for what they want, even fight for what they need in emergency situations.

What will it take for the purveyors of the American way of birth to honor the ethical principle of autonomy? It is one of the principles adopted by the American Medical Association, ostensibly to define "the essentials of honorable behavior for a physician," which the profession of medicine purports to uphold.

What will it take to allow women control over the choices that impact their lives, their newborns, and their families?

What will it take for our maternity care system to truly empower women in the processes of pregnancy, birth, lactation, and parenting?

These are the questions that haunt me, anger me, sadden me, baffle me, and keep me up at night.

The question is... *what will it take?* The answer is... *a revolution.*

Over forty years ago a French obstetrician sparked a radical and revolutionary childbirth movement. He was a man trying to change the way women gave birth and the way babies experienced being born. He created the most famous maternity clinic in the world, Pithiviers Hospital in France, became an internationally acclaimed 'birth guru,' and changed global birthing practices.

At the center of Michel Odent's philosophy and practice was this: ensuring that each woman decided how she would give birth, and supporting her to do it in her own way and with full control over her own body. When Odent first introduced his method, it was revolutionary thinking inside a hospital setting. It still is revolutionary today, forty years later.

Odent initiated childbirth practices such as birthing pools and labor without drugs. He declared that these basics must be in place: the woman-infant couplet must be the central figure in the childbirth event; the birthing environment must be proper and private for nature to take its course; and midwives, the most qualified attendant for most births, must be the primary birth attendants.

As for himself, the obstetrician, he insisted his role was to be available but far in the background, preferably outside the birthing room, being patient, standing by, absent unless he was truly needed.

Odent is a surgeon, author, and founder of a research center. He is steeped in scientific acumen, respected for insightful narratives about culture, and acknowledged as being a step ahead of the game. In his book called *Childbirth and the Future of Homo Sapiens* (2013), Odent identified "cultural blindness" as a primary barrier in understanding the importance of the childbirth experience as it relates to the survival of the human race. He warned about the consequences of millennia of evolution juxtaposed with modern childbirth practices, which have caused women to lose the ability to give birth as nature intended.

The ideal, in Odent's view, would be for women to labor and birth alone except for one "knitting midwife."

It was Odent who first observed this unremarkable sight—a knitting midwife—and then actually made a scientific study of the phenomenon. He concluded that the repetitive nature of knitting imparted an unmistakable air of reassurance, and created a platform for the ethical principle of self-determination in childbirth to be realized.

Imagine the scene I will describe; it is what a revolution in childbirth looks like.

My friend Clarice Winkler was the lead midwife at the Greenhouse Birth Center, and she was the epitome of the knitting midwife. I have numerous photos of her at the birth center we cofounded, sitting quietly in the background with a pregnant woman, head bowed over her work, needles in her hands, yarn in her lap, hot coffee with cream and honey at her side.

Throughout a woman's labor, Clarice sat in the birth room and knitted. A gentle rhythmic activity—*in, round, through, and off, in, round, through, and off*—calming her, and in turn, calming those around her. Unlike reading, using a computer, or looking at a smartphone, when Clarice knitted, the laboring woman felt her presence. She saw that Clarice's eyes were not fixed on something else and that her mind was not consumed elsewhere.

That is the winning equation of a knitting midwife; to be still but not absent, to be present but not predominant.

From this place of quiet presence without obviously watching, Clarice noticed everything, monitored everything, and yet her offstage position gave the woman and her partner a sense of privacy.

Clarice encouraged the laboring woman and her partner to discover their own unique path through the maze of contractions and sensations, and to find their own ways of coping. She knew, and they knew, they had worked hard together for nearly a year to be ready for this moment in time. Everyone had confidence they were as prepared as they could be.

The knitting midwife sends a lot of messages into the birthing environment. As the needles click and clack she lets the woman know, *I am not rushed. I do not need to be anywhere else. We have all the time in the world. You just do what you need to do. I am here with you.*

If Clarice was needed for anticipatory guidance or immediate hands-on assistance, she was close by and quick to accommodate. Otherwise, thread-by-thread, stitch-by-stitch, she rhythmically and calmly knitted a simple project that did not require a lot of attention—a hat for the baby about to be born. All the while she imparted a contagious, conspicuous, unmistakable sense of wellbeing to everyone in the room. Her presence was an unspoken and powerful message that said, "You got this," while at the same time assuring, "And I got your back."

I had the privilege of working side-by-side with Clarice, one of the most brilliant and compassionate midwives I have ever known. I have seen this way of childbirth with my own eyes, I have experienced it and stood witness to it hundreds of times for real-life, real-time people.

That is what transformational change in childbirth looks like. Simple but revolutionary. And it's attainable, a place to start. It is more likely to work outside of an institutional setting like a hospital than inside, but still, it is a snapshot of what is possible.

The quest to reclaim our bodies, our births, and our lives is so crucial that hundreds of templates and guidelines have been created as roadmaps for this revolution. One of my favorites is the groundbreaking and powerful toolkit called Respectful Maternity Care Charter: Universal Rights of Women and Newborns. This toolkit was organized by the White Ribbon Alliance (WRA), in partnership with a wide range of stakeholders, and based on established international and regional laws.[87] WRA is a people-led, globally connected grassroots movement for the health and rights of women and newborns, connecting partners and professionals from diverse sectors. It puts average citizens at the center of global, national, and local efforts to create transformational change. It is visionary and practical human rights and advocacy charter.

Just as this book was going to press, I discovered another excellent tool. The Black Birthing Bill of Rights, copyright (2020) by the National Association to Advance Black Birth (NAABB), is a resource for every Black person that engages in maternity care. It states, "We want each Black woman and birthing person to know their rights and to have the tools to confidently exercise these rights. The Bill of Rights also serves as guidance for government programs, hospitals, maternity providers, and others as they transform their policies, procedures, and practices to meet the needs of Black birthing people." It is a comprehensive guide to equitable, high-quality, respectful maternity care that fosters self-determination. (See https://thenaabb.org/index.php/black-birthing-bill-of-rights/.)

What if every woman and birthing person had the experience of feeling safe, being in control, feeling confident, and being in the protective presence of a midwife while surrounded by loved ones who cherished them as they delivered a new being into the world?

What if every woman and birthing person was in a place that was warm, safe, private, quiet, and dark so that their mind could relax, their body could release birth hormones naturally and easily, and their spirit could become attuned to the vigorous work at hand?

What if women, birthing people, and their partners actually had undisturbed and empowering pregnancy, childbirth, and postpartum parenting experiences, and babies were born gently and safely?

If you begin to hear the famed whisper in your ears from the film *Field of Dreams… If you build it, they will come…* Do not ignore it.

This revolution is still possible.

service matters

*Committing oneself to **service** contributes to actualizing
the attainable vision of the Beloved Community,
a society based on justice, equity, inclusiveness,
and love of one's fellow human beings.*

One late night after a marathon five-day meeting of the board of directors of the Midwives Alliance of North America (MANA), held at the home of beloved Ohio midwife Abby Kinne who now walks in the Spirit World, my colleague Tamara Taitt and I conceived a brilliant brainchild. Amazingly enough, we were able to bring our vision to fruition with the help of a talented documentary filmmaker from Maine, Nicolle Littrell, owner of Woman in the Moon Films.

On May 5, 2012, International Day of the Midwife, MANA launched our brainchild, a public education campaign called I Am A Midwife. It was a series of short, edgy, informative interviews profiling midwives across the country, using social media to create social change. It appeared on the YouTube channel for the Midwives Alliance, and each quarter for over a year, a new series of video interviews was launched. I Am A Midwife campaign provided a glimpse into the lives of everyday midwives. It answered questions about what a midwife is and does by profiling the diversity of midwives practicing in a wide range of settings. The interviewees practiced in urban, rural and tribal areas, hospitals, birth centers, homes, academia, research institutes, and public health arenas.

Recently, I watched the YouTube videos again. I was struck with the language with which the individuals described what being a midwife meant to them. They used an array of words and concepts, like compassion, love, approachability, safety, empowerment, freedom, feminism, revolutionary, skillful, women caring for women. But service was a concept that each and every midwife spoke about in their interview.

When you watch and listen to midwives talk about their work, you come to understand it is more than a job, more than a profession. For many, midwifery is 'a calling.' And midwives say they are called to serve life.

Service is one of the qualities in The Midwife Matrix that demonstrates how our lives are connected by thousands of invisible silver threads, binding us one to another. Service is a quality that continuously runs through the stories and the lived experiences of midwives, and the tales that people tell when talking about midwives.

I will share a few stories about midwives in service to life.

Elizabeth Moore, a midwife from Colorado, did lots of interesting work in the for-profit world before becoming a midwife. She changed professional gears dramatically because she said, "I wanted to do service work in the world that had long meaning." Elizabeth traded a much bigger paycheck for more meaningful work because she said, "I wanted to accompany women at the heart of a transitional time in their lives. I wanted to walk with them when they crossed the bridge to motherhood. I wanted to bear witness, and stand with them, because I believe that bearing witness to the experiences of women can deeply change lives, many lives, forever."

Sister Angela Murdaugh, a Franciscan Sister of Mary, established Holy Family Services and Birth Center near the Texas-Mexican border, in order to bring high-quality midwifery care to a population of underserved and impoverished women and their families.

Shafia Monroe served Black communities by creating initiatives to prevent maternal and infant mortality, increase breastfeeding, and train Black doulas and midwives to serve people in their own communities.

Diane Holzer traveled to remote and impoverished areas of the Ecuadorian Amazon several times a year to support Indigenous peoples in creating a sustainable future for their communities.

Rondi Anderson worked for Doctors Without Borders in India, Somalia, Sierra Leon, and other countries in order to implement reproductive health programs for some of the world's poorest people.

Midwives are committed to serving humanity through acceptance of the full range of human experiences—birth and death, joy and sorrow, abundance and loss, triumphs and tragedies. We do this despite the difficulties, and precisely because we are willing to grapple with the difficulties.

Many midwives in the I Am A Midwife videos said they came to midwifery through roundabout ways, but typically through doorways of service-related activities.

Sherry DeVries served as a Peace Corps volunteer in Micronesia. She accidentally found herself in a hut where a birth was underway, and when she tried to leave the midwife, said, "Stay, sit by me." Sherry said, "The experience of being immersed in a culture that valued the community midwife changed my perspective on birth and what it means to be a mother." She returned stateside, became a midwife and worked for many years as a practitioner, and then became the cofounder of a midwifery education program at a community college in Wisconsin. She was program director and trained direct-entry midwives to qualify for certification and licensure. After that program was running successfully, Sherry returned for another stint in the Peace Corp.

Patrice Bobier is a farmer. She and her husband operate a 200-acre farm in rural northern Michigan, raising cattle and growing food for themselves and their community. Patrice is also an experienced midwife, and she often sends her clients home with the nourishing fresh food harvested from her garden.

Nancy Gallagher, also a midwife from Michigan, initially used her midwifery skills to receive new life, and now uses those same skills to help people peacefully depart on the leaving end of life. Nancy generously gives to her community by accompanying people on their death walk, supporting family members, and helping people have a high-quality transition into the Spirit World.

Deb Kaley spent her entire midwifery career in El Paso on the border of Texas and Mexico, in service to the famed *Maternidad La Luz*. She operated a midwifery practice with a community birth center to care for underserved Mexican and Mexican-American families, trained direct-entry midwives on site, and thus created a dynamic partnership-based service that benefited birthing women as well as midwifery students.

Sheila Simms-Watson from Florida said having her second baby at home with a midwife changed her life. "It planted a seed," she said, "and I knew every woman needed to have this choice." She concluded, "I was called to serve, and I became a midwife."

Umm Salaamah Sondra Abdulla-Zaimah is a formidable force for service to humanity. Her motivation stemmed from her own experience as a young teenage mother who was badly treated in the US maternity care system. Consequently, she vowed to take better care of other women. She started out as a police officer in New York City where she had emergency childbirth training, and inadvertently delivered some babies. She later became a nurse-midwife. She worked for decades delivering babies in Georgia, Kentucky, Mississippi, Florida, Texas, Tennessee, and Honduras. She helped launch international public health programs, including a midwifery training program in Ghana and a maternal health clinic in Senegal. Umm Salaamah said, "I think every community should have their own midwife. If you go in with an attitude of love and respect, as if they are your sister, your daughter, your mother, you will see that people love their children, they want the best for their children, and they want the same things you want."

Committing oneself to service contributes to actualizing the attainable vision of the Beloved Community, a society based on justice, equity, inclusiveness, and love of one's fellow human beings.[88]

Placing service to humanity at the center of our lives means several things. It is a spirit that infuses our actions. It is a purpose that we bring to our endeavors. It is an intention to serve the needs and best interests of all people we encounter.

Midwives do not have a corner on the market for giving. However, from time immemorial, the ethic of serving humanity has been central to the work of midwives. There are only a handful of other professions where its practitioners are on call 24/7, will drop everything in their lives for an unspecified amount of time, often for days on end, to be in service to humanity.

Midwives have always done more than just deliver babies. We have tried to wrap our arms around the whole community. We have been committed to the health of all the people. And we have tried to assure the conditions in which people can stay healthy.

I cannot think of a time in my life more trying on the soul than now, when things have drifted so far away from attaining the Beloved Community. The challenges we face are interconnected, complex, and demanding. And while it is definitely harder on some groups, it affects everyone, regardless of race, ethnicity, class, creed, gender identity, sexual orientation, ability, or national origin. All of the values and institutions of our society are being challenged, everyone feels the tension, and everyone senses the discord and disconnection among people.

In our communities—where the self meets the world—when we find ourselves in the acts of giving and serving, we discover who we are and what unique and valuable contributions we can make. Each of us, in our own way and within our unique situations, can hear and respond to the calling to serve.

One of the most fundamental truths is this. We are dependent on inter-connection with one another for our daily existence and the necessities of life. We cannot live without the goods, services, and kindness of others. Dr. Martin Luther King, Jr. called it "a network of mutuality."[89] Interdependence defines us as individuals, nations, and globally as never before.

Now more than ever, it matters that we work together in our communities, side by side, to advance our shared humanity. Following our passions, guided by our innate urge for kindness, feeds our hungry spirits in ways we cannot know until we become involved in giving of ourselves and serving others.

As I watched the final interview of the I Am A Midwife videos, I was struck with another component of service: bringing healing and wellness to a world of pain.

The video featured a young midwife from San Francisco named Nile Nash. She said, "If we take care of our women and children around those moments of birth, the primal time; if we help them achieve true maternal and child health that includes physical as well as spiritual wellness; and if we truly empower our women and safeguard our babies, everything else will fall into place."

Believing in the Beloved Community is not enough. It takes commitment. It takes participation. It takes service. It takes generously giving from your heart.

activism matters

Activism is about ordinary citizens standing up to preserve
human values and behaviors of integrity, standing firm
for what will benefit humanity and all living beings,
especially amidst disorder and degradation.

Service and activism are different qualities in The Midwife Matrix. Service is generously giving from the heart. Activism is intentionally fighting to change what is inadequate or unjust.

The mantras for service might be, "*When I give, I give myself*" (Whitman), or *I give back what is given to me* (Law of Reciprocity). The mantras for activism might be, *Speak truth to power*, or *Nothing about us without us*, both of which imply being an active defender of human rights.

Activists disrupt the status quo and are committed to crafting a better way.

I became a political activist in the 1960s. I was a white, Catholic teen living in the suburbs of Detroit. Because of the family in which I grew up, and the progressive Catholics with whom we associated, I was deeply influenced by and motivated to take action in the civil rights movement. I was amongst a substantial cadre of white, suburban, middleclass American people who were filled with hope for prosperity, harmony, equality, and an interracial society in which all people enjoyed the benefits and resources of our country.

In 1969, when I moved to the central city to attend Wayne State University, I also accelerated my work as an antiwar activist, a member of the New Left, and a radical feminist. I moved from my parent's home in a white suburb to a poor black urban neighborhood. The radical Catholics with whom my parents and I had been working conceived a place where a group of eight would live in a big old house, one side of which would be living quarters and the other side would be a peace and justice center. The eight people chosen from a group of two dozen interested people would live communally and work at the center. Four men and four women were chosen, and to my surprise and delight I was one of them. I was still a teen; the others were in their mid- to late-twenties. Two of the eight people, including my roommate, were awaiting controversial trials for antiwar political protests.

We chose the name Detroit Peace Action Center. We provided draft counseling for those conscripted into the army for the Vietnam War who were unwilling to serve; organized antiracism teach-ins and actions in the city, particularly related to police brutality in black communities; and built bridges between working class folks in the community and folks from the suburbs who were committed to making life better for citizens of Detroit.

Growing up in Detroit, and becoming part of 'the movement' in the 1960s was unique, because Detroit was one of the few large cities in the USA in which black and white people were actually, and intentionally, working together in the movement. In the aftermath of the 1967 Detroit Rebellion—a multilayered, complex and dramatic upheaval caused by a long and deep seated history of oppression of black people in Detroit, which became deadly, riotous and destructive—people were eager to remediate injustices and build coalitions of activists. Many initiatives had already taken root, and dozens more emerged to deal with multiple problems.

Detroit, as the world's auto manufacturing capital at the time, was the undisputed labor union center of the country. Southern blacks that migrated north to work in the industry joined with Northern whites to organize workers and articulate labor rights. Grassroots Black Power groups flourished in Detroit and were aided by allies in white groups willing to support them. Antiwar groups, often undergirded by faith-based groups, wove webs of ecumenical solidarity. Women organized consciousness-raising groups focused on women's liberation.

I was fortunate to be mentored by some exceptional movement leaders— black and white, clergy and laity, young and old. It was an extraordinary learning curve for me, a time that imprinted me with the soul of an activist.

When I moved to Northern Michigan in the 1970s I was able to take my insights and experiences with me. I focused on the peace movement as well as social and environmental justice. The area was predominantly white with two minority populations—Hispanic migrant farmworkers and Native Americans. I gravitated to projects and programs that would serve the needs of these populations.

But honestly, I did not expect for activism to become such a prominent part of my midwifery practice. I thought of midwifery as a calling, a profession, not activism, per se. In retrospect that notion was naïve.

When I got to know other modern midwives I realized we had this in common: we never intended to become activists just because we wanted to catch babies. We never thought we'd be so involved with navigating politics, crafting legislation, creating precedents in case law, affecting civic decisions, developing policy, and organizing grassroots support.

We did not know that becoming midwives would open the door to confronting racism in healthcare and in our own organizations, ameliorating racial and ethnic disparities, and addressing power imbalances and discrimination caused by race, class and gender. But in order to practice our craft, in order to effectively serve our clientele, in order to preserve our profession, we had to engage in activism.

In the 1960s and 1970s when my cadre of midwives entered the scene, most of us did not start out having knowledge, skills, or advocacy acumen in the realm of maternal and child health. We just simply started. We were part of a wave of people of all races, classes, and genders—mostly young—that began a lifelong fight to secure a more equitable place for women in American society.

At this time, the context in which we began our work was one of severe oppression of midwifery. Midwives in Europe survived the professionalization of obstetrics and gynecology and the resultant usurpation of the field of women's healthcare. Medical specialists became dominant in Europe but midwives and physicians learned to work collaboratively. But by the mid-twentieth century in the USA, midwifery had been nearly annihilated in the wake of 'new medicine' and the corporatization of the healthcare industry.

It was a time of significant oppression of women in general. Millennials and Post-Millennials may find this fact surprising: the idea that women should have a voice and rights equal to men was considered preposterous. The concept was far too radical. Yet against all odds, we successfully toppled accepted norms, and we set into motion many groundbreaking social and legal transformations.

Activism built a sense of identity. Activism allowed us to have greater control over our lives. Activism decreased powerlessness and increased resilience. Activism taught us how to adapt and become stronger in the face of adversity.

We each found our own pathway to activism.

Take Kate Bowland, a midwife in Santa Cruz. One sunny day in 1973 she opened her clinic door to police who said, "You are under arrest." Her case went all the way to the California Supreme Court, which ultimately defined direct-entry midwifery as the illegal practice of medicine and a potential danger to unborn babies. This event set a new legal precedent and changed Kate's life. She came to believe, "When laws are unjust or immoral, it is our responsibility to disobey."[90] For Kate and many others, midwifery became an act of civil disobedience.

Or consider Ida Darragh, Debbie Pulley, and Carol Nelson who (with others) have worked nonstop since the 1980s to develop and implement standards for competency-based certification of the Certified Professional Midwife (CPM), advised citizens at the state level in the arduous challenge of getting CPMs regulated and licensed, and served on advisory committees to advocate for state and federal recognition of the CPM.

More recently, Nicolle Gonzales, a Navajo midwife from New Mexico who identifies herself as Diné, found there was no room within modern obstetrical care for a culture of birthing that had existed for generations among her Indigenous peoples. Nicolle, one of just fourteen Native American certified nurse-midwives in the United States, is taking action to change that. She is establishing the first Native American birth center in the USA in northern New Mexico. Not only will people be able to incorporate cultural practices into their birthing experiences, but Nicolle and her colleagues will also directly tackle many of the health issues that disproportionately affect mothers, mothers-to-be, infants, and families in her community. The birth center will be holistic, taking into consideration social determinants of health that may otherwise be overlooked.

Today—at the beginning of the third decade of the twenty-first century— much has been accomplished to advance midwifery and maternal-child health. But there is much more work to be done. Midwife as Activist is still a necessary component in The Midwife Matrix.

Direct-entry midwives are regulated in thirty-five states, with licensing bills on the horizon in ten more states. But the work to get CPMs regulated in all fifty states requires ongoing activism. Nurse-midwifery is legal and regulated in fifty states. But it takes dedicated activism to get CNMs salaries on par with physicians who provide similar services in clinics and hospitals all across the USA.

The work to get midwifery care integrated into all healthcare systems requires ongoing activism. In order to secure third-party insurance reimbursement so that all birth-givers have access to the high-quality care of midwives, regardless of where and with whom they choose to give birth, requires continual effort.

Midwifery is recognized as a key solution to improving maternal-infant health while decreasing healthcare costs. Yet healthcare in the USA is primarily a for-profit system. Evidence shows that for-profit institutions offer relatively profitable medical services. In all healthcare specialties, including maternal-infant care, profits depend on generating revenue. Midwives are not the biggest revenue generators, obstetricians are, and OBs order far more tests and utilize more costly interventions than midwives. More interventions result in more revenue for institutions. One of the biggest revenue boosters in maternal-infant care is cesarean surgery. While ample evidence suggests that cesarean surgery is often performed for nonmedical reasons and carries increased risks for women and their infants, there is also a provable connection between cesarean births and increased profits for providers and institutions.[91] Many midwives consider their primary activist enterprise to decrease the rate of unnecessary cesarean surgery.

Over the long careers of the twenty-five midwives who inspired The Midwife Matrix, they found themselves advocating not only for their profession but also for the rights of the people they served.

Californian midwife Arisika Razak said, "My belief in the essential worthiness of all human beings and in the right of women to be treated with respect and dignity—especially when they are engaged in bearing the future of humanity—is at the core of my beliefs."[92] As an African-American woman, her own experience of substandard and dehumanized care mandated that as a midwife she become a proponent for those who were poor, helpless, female, and alone, and advocate for their right to respectful and dignified care.

There are many factors that impede access to high-quality maternal-infant care for certain birth-givers. Foremost is the intersection of race, class, sovereignty, and gender.[93] Therefore, activism is necessary to ensure that optimal birth conditions are guaranteed, and reproductive rights are protected, especially for Indigenous, Black, and Brown people, low-income and vulnerable people of all races and ethnicities, people with disabilities, LGBTQI people, immigrants, people in prison, and other marginalized people whose reproductive and human rights are challenged everyday in the USA.[94]

My entry into the ranks of national midwifery leadership forced me to confront another kind of activism. It has to do with addressing and redressing inequities *within our midwifery organizations*, which privilege some of us while disempowering others of us.

From my perspective as a leader I have come to see why, in essential ways, we have been unable to build a truly interracial midwifery profession, and inclusive midwifery organizations, in the USA. The genesis of this reality parallels the growth and development of the Second Wave of American Feminism—a period of feminist activity and philosophy that first began in the early 1960s in the USA, and eventually spread throughout the Western world and beyond. The full history is too complex to cover here; the literature is robust and I encourage readers to explore it. And while feminist ideas from the mid-twentieth century were transnational, thus there existed multiple *feminisms*, I will only provide a very brief overview of some of the key points with regards to how black and white feminism developed and differed in the mid-twentieth century in the USA.

'Why' black and white feminism developed differently is this: black women lived at the triply dangerous and oppressive intersection of race, class and gender; white women did not experience injustices in all three categories of identity.

'How' black and white feminism developed differently is a bigger story.

White, young, radical '60s women, members of the New Left, antiwar, and civil rights movements, and primarily middleclass, college educated and straight, joined with other women to create their own women-centered movement: feminism. Their early theory and praxis of feminism consistently emphasized the central theme of women's liberation in terms of gender, namely, freedom from sexism, patriarchy and structural inequities between males and females embedded in the fabric of America society.[95] And while they were sincere in their struggle to understand the divisive power of race in America, the destructive power that racial divides perpetrated on people of color, and the consequences of class exploitation, either through naïveté or arrogance they neglected to understand a critical analysis: race and class perpetuated inequities as much as gender did.[96]

White feminists envisioned a radical, integrated, egalitarian feminist movement that would be the foundation for building a peaceful, equitable, just and racially integrated society.[97] They naïvely or idealistically worked to create conditions for interracial integration, believing that coming together in the same spaces, in the same neighborhoods, in the same organizations would ensure equal access to the resources of American society. I contend they were idealistic because while they held visions of egalitarianism, they did not have the practical framework or strategies to make their vision a reality. Also, many radical white feminists did not look beyond 'integration' to the broader social changes that would be required for their vision to become manifested as real-life transformational change for marginalized populations. And many white feminists were unwilling to give up their power and privilege, unwilling to truly share power and resources with others, such as people of color and people who were not heterosexual.

In the 1960s and 1970s, the black liberation movement, the centerpiece of which was Black Power, became a transformational force. Many black women were deeply influenced by Black Nationalism and the emerging strong, proud, black identity and culture. Black feminism grew out of black liberation ideology and the women's movement.[98] However, black movements were often identified along gender lines (black men), and white women often dominated the women's liberation movement. The needs and voices of black women, and their multidimensional experiences regarding both race and gender discrimination, were ignored.[99] Therefore, they created a black feminist movement.

Although black feminists were not disinterested in the issues of gender and inequality between males and females that captured white feminists attention, they were more interested in issues of broad-based equality, full inclusion in the benefits of society, addressing the effects of slavery and racism, and social justice. They were, in fact, suspicious of white women's gender politics, which focused on freedom of sexual expression, abortion rights, quality of personal life, and breaking the corporate glass ceiling.[100] Many black feminists felt that white women's lives were already far easier than theirs. While black women paradoxically felt strong within their families and communities, and had embraced a 'black is beautiful' ethic, they nonetheless felt vulnerable in the larger world due to significant issues of economic survival, class oppression, racial discrimination, and violence perpetrated against their communities. Black feminists, from the beginning, saw these major systems of oppression as intersectional.[101]

While white feminists desperately sought to create a unified American feminism, black feminists increasingly felt the need to separate from their white counterparts due to ideological differences.[102]

Thus in the era of the '60s and '70s—sparked by black freedom enterprises as well as the women's liberation movement—'identity politics' was born and spread throughout the USA, Canada and Europe. Identity politics was based on multiculturalism and 'the politics of differences.'[103]

Identity politics became an organizing model that prioritized the concerns most relevant to a group of people that shared an affiliation, such as racial, ethnic, religious, sexual orientation, cultural, or any other identity. Identity politics encouraged people to form an exclusive allegiance to the group(s) with which they identified. Black feminists designed theories and strategies—and organizations—around the social and political identities that, when combined, created unique modes of discrimination and oppression for them.

With identity politics the dream of integration among groups diminished, or disappeared, as the oppressed groups segregated themselves in order to develop their own identities, power, philosophies, and safe spaces.

And this is exactly what happened in the midwifery world. Modern midwives sought to create a unified, interracial and multicultural American midwifery. Even though a united midwifery profession, ideologically, would have been the strongest way to promote a profession that was struggling—and still struggles—against a male-dominated patriarchal healthcare machine that fights to keep midwifery subservient to medicine, white midwives and midwifery organizations failed to recognize two central components for unity: shared power and cultural humility.

I regret that as a midwifery leader I was not fully aware of the racial story of American feminism and the impact identity politics were having on our midwifery organizations and workforce. I regret that the profession of midwifery and our organizations had become embedded with the same kinds of racism and oppressive mechanisms as institutions in the larger society. Even though I was the first president of the Midwives Alliance of North America to advocate for and adopt social justice as a formal, significant, strategic organizational goal, and even though I worked passionately to move my colleagues and the organization in that direction, my efforts fell short of the outcomes I had envisioned. I also made mistakes that I wish could be undone. I am saddened and disappointed that my colleagues and I experienced some of the same pitfalls early feminists had in our attempts to bring unity to our profession.

It has been sobering and humbling to find that oppressive forces are not only on the 'outside' but also on the 'inside.' White privilege and embedded racism remain glaring issues that must continue to be addressed in the midwifery profession, as in the larger world. I know this for sure: when Black and Brown women win, humankind wins.

Here is one of my quintessential life lessons: "You don't know what you don't know until you know you don't know it." Until then, you go along blithely thinking you have it 'all right.'

The central lesson I learned as a leader is simple but profound: *leaders must lead.* An activist leader must envision a path for making the world a better place, create consensus around your vision, chose a broad base of partners to work together to manifest the vision, and make decisions to enact the strategic goals you have chosen. And then you must use your power, voice and influence to lead.

Yet, once an action is set in motion, intended outcomes are not guaranteed. Unforeseen forces, out of your control, will impact the course a strategic action will take. Sometimes you will be spectacularly successful beyond what you imagined. Other times you will fail spectacularly beyond what you feared could happen.

Leadership is not for the faint of heart. Certainty and security are illusions. The trick is to learn from both successes and failures and try again in new and innovative ways without losing heart.

As Helen Keller wisely observed: "Security is mostly a superstition. It does not exist in nature, nor do the children of men as a whole experience it. Avoiding danger is no safer in the long run than outright exposure. The fearful are caught as often as the bold. Life is either a daring adventure or nothing. To keep our faces toward change and behave like free spirits in the presence of fate is strength undefeatable."

The other lesson I learned as a midwifery activist is that oppressed people need to be the leaders of freedom movements for the oppressed. They are smarter, wiser and savvier about what they need than those from the outside. Informed activism requires that people of privilege—whether that is gender, race or class privilege—learn to be good allies, advocates, listeners and followers.

People like myself, who are white activists determined to be good allies to marginalized people, have some key competencies to master in order to avoid time-wasting, body-hurting, soul-draining conflict that makes empowerment that much harder to attain.

Good allies get educated and get clear on the conditions under which marginalized and vulnerable people live. Allies are willing to use their privilege to fight with and for marginalized people and causes. Allies uplift the voices of marginalized people, which are typically discounted and ignored. Allies listen more than they speak. Allies use their sphere of influence to call out and confront racist and discriminatory actions and ideologies, including acknowledging their own participation in racist systems, or collusion with systems of injustice that perpetuate white privilege and white supremacy. And allies learn to lean into their own discomfort about assumptions they have lived with their whole lives that may inadvertently cause harm to others. White allies could explore Dr. Robin DiAngelo's recent book (2018) called *White fragility: Why it's so hard for white people to talk about racism*. It details the counterproductive reactions white people have when their assumptions about race are challenged, and how these reactions maintain racial inequality.

Allyship is hard activist work that gets easier with practice. The truth is, allies must be willing to pay the price, and to practice, practice, practice.

Today, American midwifery is splintered along several lines: educational requirements, credential preferences, organizational affiliations, differing perceptions about place of birth and models of care, race, culture, and philosophical differences, among other things.

In today's world, the far-reaching goals of unity that were envisioned in the second-wave of feminism seem utopian. As women, we have suffered the loss of each other by segregating ourselves from one another, as do other Americans who segregate themselves and push 'others' away.

One of the most important undertakings of activism for midwives, therefore, is never giving up on reaching across racial lines, or across other lines that separate midwives, in order that we may one day forge a unified, multiracial and multicultural midwifery workforce and profession to serve our diverse and multicultural country.

Activism teaches us that no matter what—we must keep sowing the seeds of change.

I eagerly look to the younger generations for new and workable solutions to the issues that segregate midwives into separate camps. I am hopeful that my younger colleagues will ensure that people of all races and ethnicities are able to secure the resources they need to become midwives, and feel supported professionally, in order to serve their communities. And I still believe in the unifying mantra that captured our collective imaginations when I began my activism journey so many decades ago: "we shall overcome!"

We have such big work to do. Together, midwives must engage in masterful activism in order to address the social determinants that perpetuate inequities and produce disparities for women, people with wombs, and their infants.

Together, we must conduct sweeping activism to make services available that have been proven to make a difference, like midwifery,[95] and institute maternal and child healthcare policies that are equitable for all.

Activism is about ordinary citizens standing up to preserve human values and behaviors of integrity, standing firm for what will benefit humanity and all living beings, especially amidst disorder and degradation.

We stand at the threshold of one of the most radical times in human history. And the signs are everywhere that it is about to get more radical, more chaotic. Each of us is here to share our intelligence and generosity. We are each encoded with goodness and kindness. We are designed to cooperate with one another. It is incumbent upon each of us to remember who and what we are, as individuals and as a family of humans, woven as one cloth, destined to live together, with a magnificent capacity for caring.

We have a big road ahead of us. Fortunately, a defining characteristic of activism is that we are in it for the long haul. Once activism gets inside of you it becomes a part of who you are, part of your life journey.

Because there is so much work yet to be done to manifest the Beloved Community, one of the biggest risks of being an activist is over-giving, and the inevitable burnout that comes from that unhealthy pattern of behavior. In healthcare, we have become aware of the concept of 'care for the caregiver.' As activists, we must be vigilant about protecting ourselves, setting boundaries, caring for ourselves, and taking a break for rest and recuperation when necessary. We must learn when to say yes and when to say no.

Activism requires us to learn the competencies of resilience, reflection and renewal so that we will continue to be able to work for the betterment of the planet, the uplifting of all humankind, and the survival of the web of life.

There is a world I often dream about.

Imagine a world in which all-encompassing priority is given to the social, environmental, economic, educational, and physical factors that have been linked to better maternal, infant, and child health and wellbeing.

Imagine a world in which unnecessary healthcare spending is replaced with cost-effective alternatives, evidence-based and promising practices are the norm, practitioners are paid based on competency, quality, outcomes, and cost, and high-quality healthcare is an inalienable human right for all citizens.

Imagine a world in which politicians and policy makers are engaged together to design and fund better healthcare systems based on humane, skillful, compassionate, respectful, and equitable care for all people across the lifespan.

Imagine a world in which midwifery is an independent and united profession that works in collaboration with other medical professions, is a fully reimbursable service, and is returned to its honorable place as an accepted and respected cultural norm.

Activism matters because it is a key ingredient in transforming a vision into a reality, for this generation and for generations to come.

courage matters

Courage is the willingness, no matter how afraid a person might be, to walk through life with an attitude of fearlessness.

When I was a baby, just eighteen months old, I managed to get the screen door in our living room open to the outside world. I walked onto the porch, down the stairs, onto the sidewalk, and headed towards Telegraph Road, one of the busiest highways in the metropolitan Detroit area. And then I walked across four lanes of traffic.

Each of my parents, both at home, thought the other one was watching me. When they looked for me throughout the house and discovered I was missing, my frantic father burst out the front door, took the porch steps two at a time, and ran towards his biggest fear: Telegraph Road.

He looked past the cars whizzing by to the grassy median in the middle of eight lanes of traffic, and saw a woman holding a baby. When the traffic cleared he ran across the road to where I was wrapped in the protective arms of a stranger. As the story goes, the woman was reluctant to hand me over to my father. She assumed my parents were derelict.

That was one of several times in my life when I have done something really risky and survived, often because of an angel who appeared on the scene.

I am not sure you could call it courage. Can a small person, not yet two years old, have courage? Was it bravery or just a baby wandering mindlessly?

When I was three years old my mom gave birth to a son, and then one year later another son was born. My two brothers were very close; people thought they were twins. They did everything together. Michael, the older one, was chatty and outgoing but cautious. Kevin was quiet and introverted but fearless. From the time they were little dudes, when they'd go on an adventure outside, like sledding at the big hill, Michael would tell Kevin to go down the snow-covered slope first. If Kevin survived, then Michael would go. Sixty years later as adults, their lives have played out along the lines of the safety-seeking and risk-taking patterns of behavior established in their childhoods.

Some kids are naturally brave, and some kids need a gentle nudge to step out of their comfort zone to discover their inner source of strength. Because the truth is, courage is there, inside each of us.

There is a fun movie called *We Bought the Zoo* in which a father, trying to rebuild his family's life after the death of his wife, buys a new house—with a zoo. When his son becomes a teenager and expresses angst about a girl, the father gives his son a priceless piece of advice. He says, "You know, sometimes all you need is twenty seconds of insane courage—just literally twenty seconds of embarrassing bravery—and I promise you that something great will come of it."

I have often contemplated that advice: all you need is just twenty seconds of insane courage, twenty seconds of embarrassing bravery.

Courage underpins almost everything midwives do. Of all the skills that midwives learn, courage may be the hardest quality to impart to our students. It is beyond boldness, it is beyond valor, and it is beyond daring.

Courage is a hard quality to teach because it is not a skill; it is an internal compass. Courage is the willingness, no matter how afraid a person might be, to walk through life with an attitude of fearlessness.

There is no courage without fear, no courage without facing risks. Often, living a courageous life and living a comfortable life are not compatible.

Every midwife I know has breathed through the frightening process of freeing a baby stuck in its mother's birthing canal, or worse, stared death in the face. Some midwives have opened their office doors to police, been charged with criminal activity for practicing midwifery, and sat in courtrooms while judges determined their fate. Some midwives have kept their office doors open to any pregnant person that needed their support, even when the cash flow to continue was critically low. And other midwives have worked in faraway countries where death of women in childbirth–poor, undernourished, anemic—was common-place and supplies to provide healthcare were nearly nonexistent. And yet, each of these midwives had the courage to carry on.

Most midwives refuse to let fear paralyze them into inaction.

The willingness of midwives to cultivate courage is grounded in their passionate belief in what they are doing. Our work connects us to a larger, fiercer world. It connects us to a quintessential drama known to all people, through-out all time, and across all races, cultures, and creeds. We are awake, night after night, sometimes guided by the moon sometimes in complete darkness, but always engaged in events steeped in the cycles of life. One never knows what will happen; things can change on a dime.

I remember one moonless frosty night long ago when I strapped my six-month-old nursing baby onto my back and tromped through the snow down our long driveway to my car. When I got there, my car was stuck in a snowdrift. I shoveled for a long time until I finally got it free and could drive away.

It was a dark and solitary hour-long drive to my destination. This was in the days before cell phones and GPS. When I arrived at the lane leading to the log cabin where the birth was to occur, the driveway was snowed over. Once again I hoisted my baby onto my back, grabbed my birth bag, and hiked through deep snow to the house.

It was a profoundly hushed star-filled night in deep winter. It was gorgeous and I felt strong and brave. I felt like a midwife of the olden days. The trouble it took to get to the woman's side was a small act of courage (some might say lunacy) but it was all of a piece.

Poet David Whyte calls it "living on the cliff edge."[105] It is about the courage it takes to follow an individual and destined path that leads us off the prescribed path. Living on the cliff edge takes us in directions that terrify us even as they call on the best of us. Over time, fearlessness becomes a way of walking in the world. It becomes a guiding light.

Courage may not be a virtue that comes naturally to everyone, but it can be learned and cultivated and practiced in any setting.

To be a midwife is to be willing to confront fear, pain, adversity, and danger in the forms of professional challenges, political confrontations, oppressive attitudes, and medical dominance in order to live the kind of life you are destined to live. Because we have woven courage into the fabric of our beings, midwives are able to model it, able to inspire it in others.

What does courage have to do with risk-taking in childbirth?

In 2017, a midwife-researcher and professor, Missy Cheyney, and colleagues conducted a first-ever study to look at the relative risks of community birth (planned home birth and birth center births) using the largest available dataset on physiological birth in the US.[106]

The study was conducted after some of its authors participated in a debate undertaken in the *British Journal of Obstetrics and Gynaecology* around the prompt, "Homebirth is unsafe." The opposing viewpoint countered, "Safe for whom?" and argued that the literature certainly supported the safety and efficacy of homebirth, but safety was dependent on getting some things right. This included three key factors: a healthy client, a well-trained midwife, and a plan for transfer to a higher level of care should complications arise.[107] Community births were also safest, they argued, when they occurred within an integrated system so that transitions between levels of care were seamless and collaborative.[108]

The subsequent research by Cheyney and colleagues, called Perspectives on Risk, was designed to clarify how different risk factors impact outcomes for community birth and sought to answer the question, *for whom is community birth safe?* This study was born out of a commitment to maternal autonomy and informed, shared decision-making.

Among the salient features of this research was this. As part of prenatal care, midwives give pregnant people information about the relative risks of community birth—statistical, numerical, written, verbal and graphic information. And each woman filters that information through her own lens of perception—her system of values, beliefs, personal history, feelings about her own body and about childbirth, religious affiliation, and experiences with the medical establishment prior to her pregnancy. All of this shapes her reality and determines where she will draw the line for what constitutes 'acceptable risk.' And the perception of acceptable risk among low risk women varies widely person-to-person.

Many people who choose community birth do not see the hospital setting as risk free, but rather as a setting that carries another set of risks. And research bears out this fact. For example, a woman who had a cesarean section with a previous birth, in which she did not feel in control of making her own decisions, and for whom the postpartum recovery was dreadful, and thus she grappled with significant regret, may consider a one-in-three chance of having a repeat cesarean section in the hospital too risky. Especially if the hospital in her community has protocols that severely limit or fully ban access to vaginal birth after cesarean (VBAC). This woman would also have to weigh the risk of being out of the hospital for her birth, and if a complication or emergency were to arise, she would have to accept another kind of risk.

A friend who is also pregnant may say to this woman, *Wow, it takes courage to have your baby at home.* And the woman may be thinking, *Wow, it takes courage to go to the hospital.*

And the point is this: a risk-free option is an illusion. It does not exist. Birth is risky. Life is risky.

Consider this. A woman has a statistically greater risk of being injured or dying in a car crash while driving to the hospital to give birth than being injured or dying if she stays put and gives birth at home. And more to the point, although there is a very high success rate among people who attempt a VBAC in the community setting with trained midwives, the risk associated with a labor after cesarean in the community setting when there has been no previous vaginal birth is higher for neonatal injury or death.[109]

Yet large studies, like the one cited above, can never tell an individual woman what her specific risk will be, or what path she should take. Any woman can have mitigating circumstances that will make her a lower or higher risk. The results of this type of study are not prescriptive; they are tools for a conversation.

Maternity care providers would be wise to follow a counseling sequence with parents, such as this. Be up-to-date and provide all of the available evidence on each maternity choice, and without bias give clients a broad sense of the risk landscape. Then narrow the conversation to the client's individual profile, considering her values, needs, and beliefs. Identify specific practices that can improve outcomes. Help clients determine their psychosocial and clinical needs. Have conversations that explore all aspects of informed consent and informed refusal. Answer questions honestly. Engage in shared decision-making. And trust birthing people to make intelligent choices. Then support them in the decisions they feel are best for them, which fit their worldview and their value system. After all, clients will be living with the decisions they make their whole lives.

It takes courage to make decisions around childbirth in our culture.

Unlike other Western countries where it is an accepted norm that women will choose where and with whom they want to give birth and practitioners will follow the women's lead, in the USA we have what anthropologists call "the home-hospital divide." This gulf puts women in an either/or position: *Either I can birth at home or I can birth in the hospital, but I do not have the safety of an integrated system.* A smooth and respectful transfer of care among providers, who collaborate together for the benefit of mothers and their infants, does not exist in most places. And this kind of setup in the US actually increases risk, not only for mothers and babies, but also for maternity care providers and institutions.

We have to go beyond binary, limited, either/or thinking. We must create the circumstances for collaboration across the entirety of a woman's pregnancy, birth, and postpartum period. And the fact is, even without collaboration, outcomes for births are inevitably intertwined within a community.

Information is essential for parents, but it is not enough. While people are making informed decisions about childbirth risks based on the information they review, they are simultaneously dealing with something far more nebulous—fear of the unknown.

Fear is part of life, a constant companion, necessary for our survival, neither inherently good nor bad. Fear can be a wise guide or a warning signal, a protector or an inhibitor. We live in challenging times where most of us can no longer view the world as safe or predictable, some of us with less safety and predictability than others. Day-to-day living can be dangerous for some people. Because of our social and political climate, life can be risky business for almost everyone.

That brings us to birth—one of the most challenging, all-encompassing upheavals we will ever face in life. The reality of birth is that it is overwhelming, it shakes us right down to our roots, and it changes us. We never know if we will come out of it physically and emotional well—stronger, braver, empowered—or not well—weaker, disillusioned, disempowered. The stakes are high.

About 25% of all American women are affected by 'excessive fear' of childbirth, from moderate to intense feelings. Excessive fear has been associated with all of the following pregnancy complications: preterm labor, post-term pregnancy, small-for-gestational-age babies, precipitous labor, prolonged labor, increased pain in labor, increased incidence of fetal distress, increased use of medical interventions in labor, increased cesarean surgeries (both elective and nonelective), increased incidence of postpartum depression and other postpartum adjustment problems, and impaired maternal–infant bonding and attachment.[110]

These fears cannot be taken away. But midwives and other care providers are in a position to help lessen them and help women find the courage to give birth.

Because of the powerful mind-body connection, our beliefs and expectations will color all our thoughts and actions. Our beliefs about 'what reality is' will affect how we see our place within our reality, and how we perceive who we are. What we believe will ultimately affect how we behave. And how we behave will shape who we actually become.

Because midwives recognize what an important and influential player fear is in American childbirth, and how it can change a perfectly normal situation into a complex conundrum, we have learned to intentionally work with courage. It is a key characteristic in our bag of tricks, and it is something we aspire to teach or enhance in our clients.

Pregnant and birthing people need to have their fears noticed and to be listened to as they work through them. Yet most people's gut response is to want to 'fix' the suffering of others, take away their fears. Instead, midwives encourage their clients to make friends with fear, acknowledge it, face it, feel it, use it, and learn from it.

Each woman brings her own 'bag of stuff' with her into labor—beliefs, personality, resilience or lack thereof, fears, and life experiences—which positions her at a certain level, greater or lesser, for anxiety.

Of the countless fears women bring into labor—and some researchers have grouped them into ten key categories—**the number one fear is loss of control**. Some say all the other fears boil down to this one overarching fear. Especially for women who have had experiences over which they had no control and which put them in danger or harmed them, fear of loss of control is an even greater factor, and certainly justifiable.

I believe, as do many of my midwife colleagues, that what goes on in a person's womb—menstruation, fertility, pregnancy, birth, menopause—can be a source of fear, and it can also be our greatest source of courage.

Our womb, that round, blood-red, magnificently muscled organ in the very center of our being is the locus of our creativity, the seat of female power. It is from this power spot that we make babies, birth social justice movements, create works of art, feel pleasure, and imagine a world nurtured by mother love.

The female womb has the capacity to be both creative and destructive. We bleed, feel pain, and slough off a layer of our bodies each month in order to prepare the way for something new and mysterious to arise. The womb causes us to live within repeating cycles, in sync with the moon and the tides. There is no other organ, or energy center, in the human body quite like a womb.

Once, I read the lyrics of a song by an Indigenous musician named Nahkohe Parayno that began, *'courage is birthed from the womb.'*

I wondered what the author meant. Was the womb itself the place where courage originated? Or was it the time we spent in our mother's womb that suffused each of us with courage?

Either way, this is the place we midwives start with women in helping them reclaim their power. Womb power—physically and metaphysically—is not only the power to give birth. Ultimately it is the power to birth any creative endeavor a person desires to manifest. It is the power to take a courageous leap into daring, trusting, connecting, unfolding into the creative mystery of their lives.

The womb is a dark and mysterious chamber. In ancient times the womb was thought to be a woman's spiritual center, the source of intuition, emotional wellbeing, and physical vitality. It is not too dramatic to say that in modern times, helping women connect with their wombs and find the courage to give birth, especially in a culture that insists on instilling deep fear about the nature of childbirth, is a game changer for many women.

Sometimes we help women deal with vulnerabilities and needs, terror and grief, memories of abuse and neglect.

Sometimes in the process of finding one's courage, wild longings emerge, fierce and unpredictable, as women return to the feminine flow of energy that is their birthright. The process strips away the false sense of control and exposes real innate power.

The process of giving birth is a journey of reclamation for people with a womb. It will knock you off your feet, bring you to your knees, and toss you about. It will pull you under, breathless, like being caught in the clutches of big ocean waves. But the process will also carry you, caress you, transform you in ways you could never have imagined.

Succumbing to fear can destroy a person; summoning courage can remake them.

For women and birthing people, the processes of pregnancy and childbirth are like a yearlong Heroine's Journey,[111] larger than life, mythological, a major rite of passage. Every stage of the mythic Heroine's Journey is present. Separation from a comfortable and ordinary world. Travelling solo to an unknown place. Encountering unexpected challenges. Finding the skills, allies, and capacity to meet the challenges. Triumphing over adversity. Crossing a perilous threshold. And finally, returning home with a gift from the gods and a realization that you have been utterly transformed.

Yes, giving birth is all that.

Midwives help people to summon their own courage, find strength to intrepidly navigate though the wily and serpentine waters that pregnancy and birth can present, and make it safely and triumphantly to the far shore. And the satisfaction that comes from reaching the far shore, under your own stream, is exhilarating. It is worth every step of the long journey.

The winning formula that increases courage has four components—trust, honestly, confidence, and choice.

Trust, and the nugget of truth is this: the female body is exquisitely designed for the challenges of gestation, birth, and lactation; trust your body, trust yourself.

Honesty, and the nugget of truth is this: do not deny the difficulties; birth is hard work, no bullshit, but you are competent, capable, and fit for the challenge.

Confidence, and the nugget of truth is this: surround yourself only with people who unwaveringly believe in you and who help you believe in yourself, and confidence will become contagious.

Choice, and the nugget of truth is this: make your own decisions, take responsibility for guiding your personal Mothership, and know that however you choose to navigate the waters of childbirth is absolutely the right way.

It takes profound fearlessness to let our vulnerabilities and our raw humanness be seen, and to allow ourselves to become deeply connected with others who are willing to hold us at our most vulnerable times. Maybe just that—allowing ourselves to be vulnerable—is that twenty seconds of insane courage, the embarrassing bravery that is needed to conquer fear and accomplish something great.

And here is the beauty—allowing ourselves to be held in kindness, in confidence, and in tenderness is like returning to the womb.

lineage matters

Lineage is an immanent force that is present in the sensitivity in our hands,
the knowledge in our minds, and the trust in our hearts, and originates
from a pool of women-centered wisdom as old as time.

In the late 1980s I was part of a group of nine women who bought eighty acres of old-growth forest in the Upper Peninsula of Michigan. The land is in the Huron Mountain Range, a gorgeous, intriguing area of over 1,000 square miles devoid of towns and roads.

The Huron Mountains are filled with peaks and valleys. There are hundreds of pristine inland lakes and waterfalls, so numerous that many of them do not appear on maps. The headwaters of several classic wilderness rivers flow within this region, many with impenetrable swamps. The high ridges of the Huron Mountains have spectacular views of the vast, deep blue water gem that is Lake Superior. Unending white pine and hardwood forests form a spacious canopy that, seen from below, looks like a swirling ceiling of every shade of green. There is far more wildlife in the Huron Mountains than people. Even the locals—known for being tough and hardy—consider this region to be seriously rugged.

Southwest of Lake Independence, situated along the Yellow Dog River, is where we purchased our eighty acres. It was remote, undeveloped, and the pathways to get to our spot were primitive at best. The first time we went to the land we had to ski in following the old stagecoach path. The only use of the land by previous owners had been for hunting.

We bought the land for one reason: to save the trees and provide stewardship of natural resources. The nine of us had to pool our financial resources in order to purchase the land. We formed a nonprofit to house our collective inheritance and called it WWU—Wild Women Unlimited. Wild women in partnership with the wild forces of nature. The backstory will explain why we did it.

The Annishinaabeg Tribes—who formed a governed confederacy known as the Three Fires Council and inhabited the Great Lakes Region—were the first to fell trees in the area, but their approach to harvesting had little impact on the forests.

In the early 1800s the Territory of Michigan was formed, the Native peoples were systematically ousted from their homelands and confined to reservations, and the western expansion by Europeans to 'settle the land' began in earnest.

At this time the Michigan Territory was a densely forested wilderness. The virgin pines and towering hardwoods were a haven, and the lumber was believed to be inexhaustible. Harvesting was inevitable. The nineteenth century became the now legendary lumbering era. Very quickly Michigan became the leading lumber-producing state in the nation, producing as much lumber as its three contiguous states combined. It was an era filled with romance and tragedy, and a period when extraordinary wealth was produced. During the nineteenth century, Michigan's forests yielded more money and created more millionaires than did all the gold mined during California's Gold Rush. It heralded the great financial and industrial rise of the State of Michigan. But it was disastrous for the forests.

The mighty white pine was the most plentiful tree in the forest. It's a beautiful tree, sturdy with soft sea green needles. It was also the preferred tree to harvest as it was easy to work with because it grew tall and straight. Other abundant species were maple, elm, basswood, and yellow pine. Lumbering continued all century, and between 1889-1890 the peak of Michigan's great timber harvest was reached. Mills cut 5.5 billion board feet of lumber, mostly pine. By 1900 most of the pine trees in the Lower Peninsula were gone. The virgin stands in the Upper Peninsula lasted until 1920. Essentially all the merchandisable pine had been cut or destroyed by fire. By the boon's end, logging had stripped 19.5 million acres of Michigan forests.[112]

During the depression of the 1930s, one of the projects assigned to the Civilian Conservation Corps (CCC) was to repair the damage done to the nation's forests by clear-cutting. The CCC planted millions of seedlings and over time most of Michigan's barren areas were reforested. However, some areas known as stump prairies still exist, even though it has been over a century since they were stripped of trees.

Today, forests cover over half of Michigan's landmass. Logging, which never disappeared altogether, continues, especially in the state's northern counties. But the lumber companies say logging is being done selectively, to preserve and protect the remaining old-growth forests.

For unknown reasons, the eighty acres we bought in the Huron Mountains managed to dodge the lumberman's ax, and later, the industrialist's chainsaws. Maybe it was preserved because it is high on the mountain ridge and hard to reach. When we bought the land, timber companies were lumbering all of the large tracts of land around us. Our small eighty acres of old-growth forest is one of only several pockets in the state that were missed in "the big cut." They are the survivors, never-felled elder trees of the Michigan woods.

From a scientific perspective, old-growth forests—both the overstory and the understory—have a lot to teach us about the dynamics of a biosystem. When we first bought the land we invited a biologist from Michigan State University who specialized in old forests to visit and advise us on how to be good stewards. We took him to the area of deepest woods and pointed to the tall majestic trees. He looked upward only once, acknowledging their magnificence.

Then he got on his hands and knees and crawled around looking at the forest floor. He would stop and caress certain sections. It was as if he were connecting to each fiber in the matted weave of the forest floor, as if it were a covering of skin, a living pulsating body. He picked up a small clump of dark soil and smelled it. He twisted a mass of moss between his thumb and forefinger and tasted it. He took out a penknife and cut a wedge out of the thick, black humus, which looked as rich and sweet as a slice of blackberry pie. It smelled earthy and nutritious.

Sounds were escaping from the scientist, low murmurings that were tender, like the hushed conversation between lovers, or a parent's quiet singing to a beloved child. He was lost in some kind of revelry we did not understand. We thought he was acting strange. We looked at each other unsure whether we should be worried.

Then the biologist shook his head back and forth, touched his forehead to the ground, and unfurled a breathy elongated sigh. After a long while he gathered himself, stood up slowly, and announced that the trees were amazing, but the vegetation in the understory contained species he had never seen before.

He said, "There are things on the forest floor I have only seen illustrated in books."

He explained that garden soil is tilled, pulverized, homogenized and fortified, perhaps containing nutrients but not inherently fertile. But the soil in this undisturbed forest, he said, was a hundred times more nutritious. Layer upon layer, it was testimony to relationships that had developed naturally over time, woven together in a complex tapestry of living processes.

He said, "These relationships demonstrate the best of nature's interconnectedness and interdependency. We do not often see them undisturbed. And they cannot be replicated."

He said, "What you have here is the gene pool of the Huron Mountains. Very old, very rare, very precious." For a biologist to make this 'discovery' was a really big deal, and it had caught him off-guard. He was trying to hide the tears in his eyes.

The biologist helped us look at the old-growth forest in the context of a broader landscape. He explained that the age of the trees was not the only feature of the eighty acres that interested him. He said the real value of this piece of land was in the biodiversity it has been able to nurture and sustain over a long period of time. Our old-growth forest had a great capacity for retaining moisture, fixing nitrogen, preventing erosion, suppressing diseases, and creating a womb in which plants could grow. It was also proficient at providing food for animals and habitats for insects and birds, and in monitoring air pollution. These were tremendously important features.

But what the biologist was most excited about was that this particular old-growth forest was a refuge for seeds and spores that were old-growth dependent in order to disperse easily, grow, multiply and survive. The protection that the overstory afforded coupled with the richness of the understory helped the continued preservation and conservation of biodiversity, sustaining habitats in the entire region.

That is when it sunk in: *What you have here is the gene pool of the Huron Mountains.* We had just become guardians of a holy place.

Throughout human history sacred places have been distinguished and revered for their spiritual, ecological and cultural importance. I have been to places on the planet that, at once, felt sacred to me. Iona, an island in the Inner Hebrides of Scotland with its ancient crumbling sanctuaries and centuries-old labyrinths. Hagar Qim, the prehistoric megalithic temples of Malta with its statues of abundantly corpulent goddesses guarding the entryways. Dharamsala, a mountainside village surrounded by cedar forests on the edge of the Himalayas in Northern India, sanctuary of the Dalai Lama and the Tibetan government in exile. And many others.

The old-growth forest in the Huron Mountains came to be a different kind of sacred place for me. This rare place had a special presence. Eagle families made their nests in the towering trees. Black bears left gouges on the upright posts of our small hunting cabin from sharpening their claws. Endangered timber wolves built dens for their young cubs in the rocky caves hidden in the hillsides. The woods were alive with the music of songbirds singing, coyotes howling, insects buzzing, hawks and owls screeching, and, occasionally, black bears bellowing. It was an orchestra of diverse sound and vibration, a cacophony of life.

Ultimately, this place was sacred because of the cumulative presence, the synergy of beings that found this to be a place of refuge and renewal. And what made it even more special is that it almost got erased from the face of the earth.

By some good fortune, the line of ancestors for hundreds of species had been preserved and had flourished here.

Once I really understood the significance of both the *overstory* and the *understory*, I realized this old-growth forest represented an unbroken continuity that reached back in time to preserve something precious in a way few other places in my region, or the nation, ever could.

Lineage is like that. It reaches back in time and preserves memory and substance for future generations.

Midwives come from an unending lineage of ancestor midwives. They may be blood relatives or the family tree of midwives of the past. Our family tree of ancestors has many branches—Indigenous, African, Latina, Asian, European, and all manner of foreign-born people that feed and nurture our midwifery roots all across the land.

The midwifery family tree, like the old-growth forest, is old, rare, and precious. Midwifery has survived repeated efforts to clear-cut and supplant its ancient knowledge and practices with new, fast-growing, profit-driven systems of care.

Lineage is an immanent force that is present in the sensitivity in our hands, the knowledge in our minds, and the trust in our hearts, and originates from a pool of women-centered wisdom as old as time.

Scientists have recently conducted research on the remains of our earliest common human ancestor, dubbed 'Lucy,' particularly her pelvic bones, in order to discern what childbirth must have looked like for both mother and infant over three million years ago.

Researchers found that because our earliest ancestors had bigger brains than their chimpanzee cousins, human babies fit very snuggly in the birth canal, and had to make several internal rotations in order to be born. For primate relatives of humans, like bonobos and chimpanzees, this outward passage was much more straightforward. This tricky business of human childbirth, scientists conjectured, required the mother to give birth in the upright position, not on all fours, which most favorably facilitated the birth process. Researchers hypothesized that the mechanism for birth would benefit from having helpers. Human mothers generally required some kind of help during childbirth to assist with a relatively large infant head and broad rigid shoulders. Researchers stated that no time in the history of *homo sapiens* is it likely that mothers would have consistently given birth without help.

Thus, the scientists who studied the evolution of human childbirth concluded, "The origins of midwifery may very well extend back over three million years."[113]

Just as the biologist helped us look at the old-growth forest in the context of a broader landscape, we must look at midwifery in light of the bigger picture, too. Women have always been giving birth. Women have also always been midwives and healers. Healing is part of our heritage, our herstory, our birthright.

Modern midwives have evolved from predecessor midwives who existed in all corners of the planet. I have always felt it comforting to know we are direct descendents of such powerful and earthwise people. Those who came before us continue to inspire and impact us today, and their essence still reverberates inside us.

In the United States, before the existence of contemporary professional midwives there existed in every part of our country the iconic 'community midwife.' These practitioners, healers, *parteras, curanderas, sages femmes,* and medicine women preserved and practiced the knowledge and skills handed down woman-to-woman, generation after generation.

Midwives played an essential role in maintaining and sustaining health in their communities. Not only did they receive babies into their hands, they also ministered to the sick and injured and dying, and brought all manner of healing acumen to tribes, clans, and communities. They are the Wisdom Keepers on whose shoulders every present-day midwife stands.

Keeping the memory of that lineage alive, and safeguarding the seeds of wisdom we have inherited from our ancestors is important to me. But it has not always been easy.

The systematic elimination of community midwives from the US public health and maternity care systems is a long and fascinating story that unfolds the events of an 'official plan' to eliminate 'the midwife problem.'[114] The 'problem midwives' were primarily women of color, and the elimination plan focused on Black midwives in the South.[115] 'Man-midwives,' precursors to modern obstetricians, led the movement in the 1800-1900s, and the plan was to eliminate the competition posed to 'new medicine' by popular and beloved community midwives. What had customarily been considered 'women's work' was in the early 1900s refashioned to come under the jurisdiction of male doctors. The OBs believed that only surgically trained physicians with specialty training in obstetric physiology and pathology were competent to circumvent the many ills of childbirth.[116]

The plan to eliminate community midwives was calculated and reprehensible. The new midwifery that was reformulated and regulated under the auspices of the medical men became more like obstetrics, medical and interventionist in nature. The old midwifery, with its embedded patience and trust in nature's wisdom and its focus on the life circumstances and needs of individual parturient women, was squashed.

Just like the clear-cutting of old-growth forests that destroyed trees that were hundreds of years old and disrupted layer upon layer of heirloom seeds and spores embedded in the forest floor, something invaluable was lost with the eradication of community midwives whose traditions and practices were rooted in a time-honored lineage.

I am not overly romantic about the history of midwifery. To be clear, some midwives, like some doctors, were not competent to practice. And consequently, women and infants suffered. But history also tells us that for the most part the 'midwifery system' worked well for eons—still works well—in most human cultures.

Today in the USA there is a small but mighty cadre of community midwives, perhaps not more than several thousand in a country where only a century ago there were hundreds of thousands. Though fully trained and qualified, community midwives do not work inside large healthcare structures where their nurse-midwife colleagues work. Rather, they have small independent practices where prenatal, intrapartum, and postpartum care is provided, home visits are still the norm, and most clients give birth out-of-hospital in birth centers or private residences. Although their training, practices, and ethics of care are contemporary, their philosophy of care is classic.

In the USA community midwives are endangered like old-growth forests, the timber wolf, and the spotted owl.

I am the curator of a wooden sculpture given as a gift to the Midwives Alliance of North America by the illustrious and highly accomplished Trinidadian midwife, Venus Mark. It is an image of the Sankofa, handcrafted of ebony wood, from the Akan people of Ghana. Sankofa is a mythical bird that has its feet firmly planted forward with its head turned backward while it cradles an egg in its beak, symbolizing the future. It implies, "One must return to the past in order to move forward while keeping the precious egg of life alive." The Sankofa has been adopted as an important symbol in the African diaspora in the Americas and the Caribbean. The Sankofa teaches that whatever has been lost, forgotten, or taken can be reclaimed, preserved, and perpetuated.

When Ms. Mark entrusted us with the gift of the ebony Sankofa she also gave a powerful speech to a large assembled audience of hundreds of seasoned midwives, as well as those just beginning their midwifery paths. She said the Sankofa was a reminder to the midwifery profession of the need to pause and reflect on the past in order to build a successful future. She said reflecting on our ancestors is an important source of 'intuitive knowing.' Venus also reminded us that we are connected to a powerful lineage, past, present, and future. She cautioned that in the highly competitive world created by the modern healthcare industry, we need each other to survive and thrive.

In her final statement Venus made a call to action for midwives and mothers to be brave and bold. She told us: "Never forget the value of the good and the bad experiences from the past that have shaped you. Take back what was lost because it belongs to you. Connect the past with the present to impact your collective future. Protect your future by keeping the precious life within the egg alive and safe."

At the time Venus Mark gave her speech and presented us with the Sankofa sculpture I recognized her as a wise matriarch midwife. I was completely awestruck with her, and over the years she was a kind and patient mentor to me. In the intervening ten or fifteen years since then, time has been a swiftly flowing river of experiences. Now, I, too, have become an elder in our midwifery lineage and I, like my peers, have inherited the legacy. Venus stood on the shoulders of generations of midwives that came before her. I stood on Venus's shoulders. And younger midwives now stand on mine.

The lineage of midwifery in America has many branches that come from Indigenous peoples of North America, African peoples, Latin American peoples, Asian peoples, European peoples, and other countries from around the world.

Our lineage grows like a grapevine—connected to a single root but dependent on the intertwining of every branch to produce fruit. The harvest of each generation produces its own varietal whose taste and texture enriches the inheritance of the entire lineage.

Looking backward and looking forward I can see how preserving old-growth forests and preserving the lineage of midwifery have something in common.

Some say old trees are holding our whole world together. Old trees store more carbon emissions in proportion to their size than young trees. Some scientists say old trees are the frontline warriors in the battle against climate change.

Research has shown it is not just a matter of planting more trees to make up for deforestation because new managed forests take up a lot less carbon than old unmanaged forests. Humus in the ground of old-growth forests also sequesters more carbon, converting it to fertile topsoil. Humus provides resilience by storing moisture, like a reservoir, and acting as a barrier against flooding and an aid against drought. Today I read in the headlines that the Amazon Rainforest is disappearing at an alarming rate because the government is slashing environmental protections by exploiting biodiversity and opening up some of the most protected Indigenous reserves to mining. I felt despair.

Everywhere, our relationship to old-growth forests has shifted from reverence for living beings towards commodification of its material resources.

When I think of our old-growth forest in the Huron Mountains I have come to understand what scientists have found. *We cannot replace centuries-old trees in a biosphere and expect the same results that nature has evolved over time.*

That is why my small collective of Wild Women Unlimited is trying to save the venerable old trees and the precious ground on which they grow. Because they matter, not only for their inherent value as elder trees, but also for the survival of hundreds of species dependent on them, including humans.

Some say the lineage of midwifery is the reservoir and the sanctuary of our unique and successfully human way of giving birth. Some say midwives are the frontline warriors in the battle against the medicalization and dehumanization of female procreative processes.

When I stand on the logged landscape of childbirth in American, when I hear the chainsaws of industrial medicine that continually cut away at nature's plan for normal physiological birth, and when I watch women and infants continually trying to adapt to the commodification of the experience of giving birth and being born, I feel despair.

On the same continuum that holds my understanding of the value of old-growth forests, I have come to understand this truth. *We cannot replace centuries-old childbirth wisdom and expect the same results that nature has evolved over time.*

That is why the lineage of midwifery—all types of midwives in all settings—is trying to shelter a place for women and infants to do what they have known how to do, instinctually, all along. That is why the lineage of midwifery is trying to preserve the heart and soul, and the ancestral knowledge, of what it means to give birth and be born.

The good news is resistance to systems of exploitation is growing. While limitation is real, so is liberation. While development is inevitable, so too can we learn to reframe the way we 'develop' the earth and our systems. Sacred places and sacred rites of passage should matter, even to business folk.

Collectively and individually, we must remember whatever has been lost, forgotten, or taken can be reclaimed, preserved, and perpetuated. Collectively and individually, we have an opportunity to reshape our despair and mindfully hold the space for something new to be born.

It's about the big picture. It's about the long view. And that matters for our children and our grandchildren and all the generations to come.

Essence and Intention of The Midwife Matrix: 12 Qualities That Matter

In The Midwife Matrix each of the 12 Qualities That Matter is unique yet interconnected. Each quality is like a distinct color of thread in a tapestry, which is perpetually woven together with every other quality, blending essence with intention to create a unified and elegant whole.

1. **Context** is not a neutral aspect of maternity care and will, to a large degree, determine meaning, define who is in power, and have a profound effect on those giving birth, those being born, and birth workers.

2. The **content** of maternal and child healthcare is defined by the model of care, and is the substantive and fundamental features of *what* health services are delivered to women and babies, and *how* those services are delivered.

3. **Holism** recognizes that what affects one part affects all parts because everything is intimately connected—body, mind, and spirit.

4. **Nature** has masterfully designed the elegantly complex processes of pregnancy, birth, lactation, and mother-infant attachment, and in most cases, no amount of tampering can improve them.

5. There is a **sacred** and invisible domain through which women and infants must pass to give birth and be born. Birth is not just physiologic; it is a soul journey.

6. It is an essential longing of humans to be in **relationship** with one another.

7. **Compassion** is not a luxury, it is a biological imperative because our brains are hardwired to care about one another.

8. At the core of **self-determination** is a critical question: Are women in charge of their bodies, their births, their babies, their decisions, and their lives, or not?

9. Committing oneself to **service** contributes to actualizing the attainable vision of the Beloved Community, a society based on justice, equity, inclusiveness, and love of one's fellow human beings.

10. **Activism** is about ordinary citizens standing up to preserve human values and behaviors of integrity, standing firm for what will benefit humanity and all living beings, especially amidst disorder and degradation.

11. **Courage** is the willingness, no matter how afraid a person might be, to walk through life with an attitude of fearlessness.

12. **Lineage** is an immanent force that is present in the sensitivity in our hands, the knowledge in our minds, and the trust in our hearts, and originates from a pool of women-centered wisdom as old as time.

PART TWO

why midwives matter

just the facts

I love the rigor of scientific research.

I love the process of allowing my mind to be curious, becoming an intrepid explorer, digging deeply, and unearthing evidence. It is thrilling when insights and intersections begin to emerge and I am able to place puzzle pieces into a framework of a larger perspective and interpret what I see.

When I was first learning the scientific research process as part of my master's degree program at Case Western Reserve University, our instructor asked us to write a research question. She explained to my class how to go about it. We must specify our concern or issue, decide what we wanted to know about our concern or issue, and turn what we wanted to know into a question that was not too broad, not too narrow, and was answerable.

After a lot of contemplation I wrote what I believed was a brilliant question. When I presented it to my professor she frowned. She told me to try again. On my second attempt she gave me a mini-lecture on the difference between quantitative and qualitative research. She said try one more time. On my third try she threw her arms up in annoyance and said, "You keep coming up with *qualitative* questions. In this department we do *quantitative* research."

I said, "This is how my mind works. I'd like to do a qualitative study." She replied bluntly, "Then I cannot help you."

I was baffled. I asked if there was anyone in the department who could guide me in doing qualitative research. She thought for a moment and then turned up her nose. "Only one person does *that kind* of research," she said, and gave me the professor's name. "Her office is at the far end of campus. You'll recognize her. She has flaming red hair."

I smiled and thought, "My kind of woman," and off I went to seek my mentor.

My personality is more suited to doing qualitative research—exploring the stories of people's lived experiences (individuals and cultures) based on beliefs, opinions, and motivations, and inquiring about how people make meaning of their lives. The qualitative method of scientific inquiry makes me better understand what it might be like to walk in another person's shoes or culture. Quantitative research—gathering numerical data and performing statistical and mathematical computations related to phenomena—is more suited to personality types different than mine.

Yet there are times when I need a more analytical approach, and I crave the numerical analyses of data, which is valid, reliable, and generalizable to a large population. Sometimes I really want to see vast sources of information summarized, stripped of all the emotional details, with all the names removed and all the tears wiped away.

In analyzing our maternity care system, I need clean, precise data points to back up the stories I have gathered of people's lived experiences.

Stories without closed-ended analytical data can be limiting; analytical data without open-ended stories can be shallow, even heartless. Integrating these two scientific methodologies into a compatible marriage of comprehensive data provides a more complete story.

Unpacking the Evidence

In Part 1 of this book, which outlines the 12 qualities that matter to midwives, I used a combination of stories and statistics to make my point. In this section about Why Midwives Matter, I feel compelled to lead with numerous hard cold facts. Let's unpack the evidence that supports the primary assertions I have continually made throughout Part 1 of this book.

The first assertion is this... *Evidence shows that midwives save lives. When maternity care is provided by midwives who are trained, regulated, licensed, and integrated into healthcare systems—quality of care increases, maternal and newborn health improves, customers are more satisfied, and costs are reduced.*

And the second assertion is this... *In today's high-tech, low-touch, fast-paced healthcare system, what midwives offer is not only skilled, knowledgeable, and compassionate care; what midwives offer is also unique, ephemeral, artisanal, precious, and rare.*

Let's look at the evidence.

30 Facts That Change Everything

1. Globally, about 300,000 women die each year while pregnant, giving birth, or shortly thereafter—over 830 women die every day, more than 34 every hour—and most women die of *preventable* complications related to pregnancy and childbirth.[117]

2. Nationally, the USA ranks worse in maternal mortality of all developed countries, showing an increase in severe maternal complications that have more than doubled in the past twenty years, and an increase in maternal mortality from 2000-2014, while the international trend is an overall reduction in maternal deaths.[118] Black and Native American women are at highest risk for preventable maternal death.[119]

3. Beyond the women who tragically lose their lives in the USA, many thousands more are gravely harmed during pregnancy and childbirth, and each year more than 50,000 American women experience severe complications or have near-death experiences around childbirth,[120] and Black and Native American women are at highest risk.[121]

4. Globally, every year over 3 million babies are stillborn or die in the first month of their lives, and most die of *preventable* causes such as preterm birth and low birth weight.[122]

5. The USA has a higher infant mortality rate than peer countries (ranking 51st internationally), and infants of color and infants from lower socioeconomic status rank even worse.[123]

6. Women who have access to midwife-led care are less likely to experience preterm birth and fetal loss before 24 weeks gestation.[124]

7. Skilled midwives, with the equipment and support they need, can mean the difference between life and death for close to 300,000 women each year, and ten times that many infants, especially if gender-responsive, equity-driven, and rights-based approaches are used, with an emphasis on quality of care.[125]

8. Women and men have different healthcare needs, but have an equal right to live healthily. Yet of all the United Nations Millennium Development Goals (MDG) for 2000-2015,[126] the goal to improve maternal health made least progress, and was the most underfunded of all the MDGs.[127]

9. Midwives were identified as critical in achieving the 2000-2015 MDGs related to maternal and child health because they are the only health professional specifically educated to address the needs of women, babies, and their families across the continuum of care from pre-pregnancy through the postnatal period.[128]

10. Globally, we do not have enough midwives for the need that exists; the lack is estimated to be about 350,000 midwives.[129] Nationally, we do not have enough midwives for the need that exists; midwives attend only about 10% of all US births.[130]

11. The quality of maternal and infant health—ostensibly important to all—is poor nationally and globally due to discrimination against women, racism embedded in systems of care, and lack of political will and commitment to improving vital healthcare for women, including inadequate resourcing of midwifery services.[131]

12. A new study in the USA (2019) found a large percentage of pregnant and childbearing women experienced one or more types of mistreatment, such as verbal abuse, stigma, and discrimination. One in six women reported they were harassed, had their requests ignored, or were mistreated during childbirth, and the number is higher for women of color.[132]

13. A recent large-scale study (2017) found the US medical system performed worst on measures of access, equity, quality, efficiency, and healthy lives among eleven similar countries, all while spending more money on healthcare than any other country.[133]

14. Research shows that a subset of the US healthcare system—the maternity care system—is in crisis due to large expenditures and troubling performance.[134]

15. Numerous studies on US maternity care have called attention to the fact that despite the availability of evidence-based guidelines that could produce optimal outcomes in maternal and child health, there remains widespread and continuing underuse of beneficial practices, overuse of harmful or ineffective practices, and uncertainty about effects of inadequately assessed practices.[135]

16. While there are numerous ways to care for women and babies in the birth year, evidence-based maternal-infant care models focus on practices that are *effective while being least invasive.*[136]

17. The countries that consistently show the very best outcomes for women and newborns are those with midwifery services integrated into their healthcare structures, and where midwifery care is accepted, respected, and valued as a cultural norm.[137]

18. A recent study in the USA (2018) found that in states where midwives are a part of maternity care systems there were significantly higher rates of spontaneous vaginal birth, significantly higher rates of vaginal birth after cesarean (VBAC), lower preterm birth rates, lower rates of low birth weight, fewer obstetric interventions, fewer adverse neonatal outcomes, and significantly higher rates of breastfeeding at birth and at six months.[138]

19. In the largest global study of midwifery personnel ever conducted (2470 midwives from 93 countries) midwives stated they faced barriers to practice. These included: complex hierarchies of power; hindrance for creating change through a lack of voice for delivering solutions; discrimination and harassment in the workplace due to gender dynamics and inequality; low salaries or lack of proper financial compensation; disrespect at work particularly by senior medical staff; devaluing of midwifery care in the workplace; and inadequate resourcing of midwifery services, among other factors.[139]

20. Across all countries, races, and ethnicities, women who received midwife-led continuity models of care reaped substantial benefits for themselves and their infants with no adverse effects compared to other models of care.[140]

21. In a reversal of decades-long trends, more women in the USA, about 86%, are choosing to have children; that's over 4 million births each year.[141]

22. Women in the USA who were cared for by Certified Nurse-Midwives (CNMs), mostly in the hospital settings, compared to women of the same risk status cared for by physicians had fewer technological and invasive interventions including: lower rates of cesarean section (9.9%) compared with the national average (32%); lower rates of labor augmentation and induction; lower than the national average rate for episiotomy; significant reduction in third and fourth degree perineal tears; and lower use of regional anesthesia.[142]

23. Women cared for by CNMs in the USA also had a higher readiness for labor and birth; increased sense of control during the labor and birth; higher chance for normal vaginal birth; higher rates of satisfaction with care; and their infants had higher rates of breastfeeding.[143]

24. Women in the USA who were cared for by Certified Professional Midwives (CPMs) in out-of-hospital settings, mostly planned home births, had high rates of normal physiologic birth and low rates of interventions without an increase in adverse outcomes for mothers and babies. Outcomes included: a remarkably low rate of cesarean section (5.2%) compared with the national average (32%); high rate of vaginal birth (94%); high rate of vaginal birth after cesarean (87%); low rates of prematurity and low birth weight—97% of babies were carried to full term and weighed an average of eight pounds; 98% of infants were exclusively breastfed at six weeks; and only 1% of infants required transfer to the hospital, most for non-urgent conditions.[144]

25. Babies born in the USA to low-risk mothers having planned home births with CPMs had no higher risk of death in labor or the first few weeks of life

than those in comparable studies of babies born in hospitals to mothers of similar low-risk pregnancies.[145]

26. Within the US healthcare system, childbirth is the leading reason for hospitalization, and 23% of all individuals discharged from hospitals are mothers or newborns.[146]

27. Childbirth in the USA is uniquely expensive, and maternity and newborn care constitutes the single biggest category of hospital payouts for most commercial insurers and state Medicaid programs. The cumulative cost of approximately 4 million annual births is well over $50 billion.[147]

28. The American way of birth—centered in hospitals with obstetric and neonatal specialists—is the costliest in the world, and in the last decade costs rose 49% for vaginal births and 41% for cesarean sections, with average out-of-pocket cost for consumers rising fourfold.[148]

29. Giving birth in a US hospital with an obstetrician is more expensive than anywhere else in the world, but a full package of prenatal, labor, delivery, and postnatal care with a midwife in a hospital is a fraction of the cost compared to similar care with an obstetrician. Full-scope midwifery care in the community setting (freestanding birth center or home birth) is even less costly. Research confirmed that pricing is not synonymous with quality. A higher pricetag does not necessarily reflect superior medical care.[149]

30. Evidence is clear that there is no better return on investment anywhere in the healthcare realm than investing in midwifery care for all women and newborns in all settings.[150]

drop dead serious

Big picture evidence is shocking but compelling. To many of us, the modern maternity care landscape reads like a postmodern dystopian novel: intrigue, greed, ignorance, trauma, widespread failures, death of innocents.

After her near-miss childbirth experience, Serena Williams expressed thankfulness and said the medical staff had saved her life, which is a fact. But they also almost let her die of a pulmonary embolism, and that's a fact, too.

When Serena opened up about her story it was a watershed moment. Women's stories from all over the country, and around the world, started flooding media sites. Among them, superstar Beyonce shared her traumatic birth story. She had preeclampsia, emergency cesarean surgery, and her twins spent many weeks in the NICU.

Researchers are finding that near-miss incidents related to pregnancy and childbirth are becoming so common worldwide that they have identified a new name for it: **maternal near-miss syndrome**.[151]

What happens to over 50,000 women per year in the USA who survive near-miss childbirth ordeals in which a grave obstetrical complication nearly kills them?

Women's own stories are supported by research studies that confirm that traumatic childbirth can cause post-traumatic stress disorder (PTSD).[152] Severe maternal morbidity that results in unexpected outcomes of labor and delivery can result in significant short- or long-term consequences to a woman's health.

There are definable ways in which post-traumatic stress plays out for a survivor of childbirth trauma.[153] Women can have a constant preoccupation with the near-tragic event, imagining what might have happened. They can become detached from loved ones, including their newborns, avoiding intimacy, and becoming irritable, withdrawn and depressed. They may experience loss of interest in their daily activities or social life, or may experience a sense of 'not belonging' with family, friends or colleagues. Women can suffer difficulties with sleep, appetite, relationships, sex, or career. Women can suffer loss of meaning in their lives, 'waiting for it to be over,' develop a preoccupation with death, suffering, tragedy, or a pessimistic feeling of 'what's the point?' Women can feel that surviving was a mistake, thinking 'I shouldn't be here,' resulting in feelings of guilt or unworthiness. Some women are unable to have more children because of injury; some choose not to have more children as a result of their traumatic experiences.

The effects of maternal near-miss syndrome can be temporary. Or trauma can have lifelong implications for mental health for women, and quality of life for women and their families.

For every 70 women who experience a near-miss ordeal in the USA, one more woman dies. Over 700 women per year in the US perish of complications related to pregnancy and childbirth. Google 'maternal mortality' and you will get more than 25 million results.

What does maternal death look like for newborns and families?

A father or partner will be in profound shock as they carry a perfect newborn baby out of the hospital, alone, and returns home without the baby's mother. Stunned disbelief, an internal sense of injustice, outrage, unfathomable sadness, and overwhelming confusion will infuse the home and every conversation among those who knew this young woman who was alive only the day before. Statistics about the other 699 women who died this year will mean nothing, because this one woman was *their woman, their beloved, their mother*. And the baby's birthday will always be the day their mother died. Imagine carrying that burden?

And that is just the tip of the iceberg. It will take months, years, maybe decades to get over this loss. In the meantime, a newborn infant will suffer, the surviving parent will suffer, grandparents, sisters, brothers, aunts, uncles, and friends will suffer. And that suffering will manifest in untold ways, from mild physical, behavioral, emotional, and psychological consequences to severe ones. Even communities will suffer the loss of mothers.

Between 2017 and 2018, the trend in maternal mortality caught the attention of several news media including ProPublica, National Public Radio and *USA Today*. Curious journalists could not understand why maternal mortality was increasing in the USA but decreasing in every other developed nation. These journalists conducted in-depth investigations. They asked the questions, *What is happening? Why are our mothers dying?*

They concluded that causes for maternal death were linked to a cluster of reasons in four general categories.

First, there is a widespread misconception that mothers rarely die in childbirth in the USA, and thus hospitals do not have effective protocols in place to protect mothers from complications related to childbirth. This mistaken belief accounts for why practitioners are trained, by and large, to respond to complications and emergencies in the newborn and not the mother. Delayed response to complications is cited as one of the most deadly mistakes made by healthcare teams.[154]

Second, the rise in cesarean surgery has been associated with obstetrical complications like hemorrhage, blood clots, and uterine rupture, and is considered a primary factor in the dramatic increase in maternal deaths.

Hemorrhage is a primary cause of maternal death and is often associated with a condition caused by cesarean surgery called placenta accreta. This occurs when the placenta is attached to the scar from a previous cesarean, the placenta grows too deeply into the uterus, and all or part of it will not separate after birth. Consequently, the woman hemorrhages. A woman with a prior c-section is also at greater risk of uterine rupture, a rare but serious childbirth complication. A woman's risk of uterine rupture increases with every cesarean section. In addition, blood clots from a c-section that occur postpartum can cause hemorrhage, which might occur in the hospital, or worse, once the woman is at home. Also, a pulmonary embolism can occur when blood clots break away from the uterine site and travel to the lungs, which can be deadly.

Third, maternal conditions or diseases, such as obesity, diabetes, or late-life pregnancy can lead to complications such as high blood pressure and preeclampsia. The journalists found, however, these conditions typically could have been managed better with proper prenatal care and oversight. But too often, a woman's blood pressure rose, went untreated or was caught too late, she had a stroke, and died. Women are also dying of untreated, life-threatening infections.

And fourth, limited access to healthcare causes a set of conditions that can lead to complications or death, especially if a woman does not have enough insurance to cover the care. The journalists confirmed what other studies like the Institute of Medicine's seminal report found: **access to healthcare is unequal in the USA.** Women of color, women who are poor, immigrant, disabled, and otherwise vulnerable or marginalized people experience unequal and discriminatory treatment and face greater barriers to high quality maternity care.

As an overarching umbrella to the entire investigation, the journalists affirmed what other research studies have confirmed: women of color, particularly Black, American Indian, and Alaska Natives are three times more likely to die of pregnancy or childbirth-related causes than white women.

But the bottom line of this report was shocking.

There was consensus by all journalists—Nina Martin of ProPublica,[155] Renée Montagne of NPR,[156] and Alison Young of *USA Today*[157]—about the most devastating conclusion of their independent and comprehensive investigative research: **Most of the maternal deaths could have been prevented.**

Do the Facts Change Anything?

Learning these facts prompted the National Conference of State Legislatures to publish a sobering report in January 2019. Bipartisan policy makers—who cannot seem to agree on much of anything in the US legislature these days—agreed on this topic: US maternity care is in crisis.[158] The headline on their website homepage quotes the *USA Today* report, affirming, "America's regretful status as the most dangerous place in the developed world for a woman to have a baby."

As a result, a limited but bipartisan coalition of US policy makers are in consensus that the steady and unremitting rise in maternal mortality and morbidity demands action. And they are finally calling for change.

Not a Trick Question

Yet, calling for change and actively making change happen in ways that immediately make the lives of people better are two different things.

Here's the rub. If the well-established facts are these—the American way of giving birth is unfavorable and even dangerous; midwifery is a favorable model of maternity care; community birth settings are as safe as hospital birth; and more midwives should be added to the US workforce and integrated into our system of care—**why aren't things changing in the USA at the speed of light?**

a new way of thinking

In order to answer the question, *why aren't things changing in the USA at the speed of light?* we must first ask another question: *"What time is it on the clock of the world?"*

As you remember, in Part 1 of this book, I introduced the latter question. It was the signature probe used by activist and mentor Grace Lee Boggs to get people to scrutinize the context in which they were trying to affect social or political change. She said the question was the foundation for informing whatever actions people would take.

Today, our US maternity care system is just one of many systems plagued with seemingly untenable problems. Currently in the postmodern world, we are witnessing the simultaneous collapse of social, political, religious, moral, economic, and environmental systems. It is a runaway train, which some scholars and scientists believe cannot be stopped. The levels of disorder, disruption, and degradation all around us provoke many of us to feel overwhelmed, even despair.

In the midst of unending national and global chaos, one brilliant scholar and system analyst, Margaret Wheatley, asks us to consider yet another question: *"Who do we choose to be?"* This question also begs contemplation.

We are confronted with so many provocative questions.

When I was in my late twenties I was the midwife for a Native American family. Not only was I invited to the powerful homebirths of their two sons, but my entire family also attended. After that, their children called me 'auntie' and our family was brought into their family circle and that of the local Native community.

Over the years we were privileged to sit at the feet of a Native American Elder named Poonse. He was generous in sharing the teachings of his people and culture. I remember long weekends in late winter when we would collect sap from dozens of trees and make maple syrup in the wood-fired sugar shack outdoors. Then in the evening we would share a potluck dinner, sit by the blazing hearth fire, and listen to Poonse tell stories. He was an old, small, wizened-looking guy, sort of like Yoda with that same twinkle in his eyes. Poonse spoke slowly and deliberately as he imparted his wisdom with ornamental detail. His stories were enchanting as well as inspiring.

One of the most important lessons I learned from this beloved elder has stayed with me my whole life. Poonse said, "The truth is never found seeking answers. Always ponder the questions, always seek the right questions, and your answers will naturally follow."

Now I am in my late sixties. Now my peers and I are the elders in our midwifery tribe. In the intervening forty years between my late twenties and late sixties I have learned there is real power in honing the fine art of asking the right question. The wrong question is almost guaranteed to generate the wrong answer.

The right questions will always coax us to think in a new way about the issues.

So here are the three questions on the table. Each question naturally leads to the next question, and they are all interrelated. *Why aren't things changing in the USA at the speed of light? What time is it on the clock of the world? Who do we choose to be?*

At the same time, let us reflect on the overarching question in Part 2 of this book: *Why do midwives matter?*

What We Can and Cannot Influence

In the early 2000s, when I first became a member of the board of directors of the Midwives Alliance of North America, and later its president, I studied Margaret Wheatley's theories and writings on leadership. She was one of my favorite systems analysts. She was an acclaimed trainer and persuasive guide on how to apply the new science to influence organizations and business management, and make significant changes in large systems.

Wheatley's work was based on science—biology, systems theory, chaos theory, and quantum physics—fields of study she claimed were remodeling our understanding of how the world worked. She acknowledged that we lived in a time of chaos, but that it was rich in potential and possibilities because "life seeks order." She saw evidence everywhere of "webs of cooperation that connect us."[159] Wheatley became a leading voice in how to affect changes in large political, social, governmental, and environmental systems. She mentored leaders all over the world—from officers in the US Army, to CEOs of Fortune 500 companies, to environmental organizations and nonprofits. (For more information go to: https://margaretwheatley.com/)

Now more than twenty years later, Margaret has changed her way of thinking about what we can and cannot change. She has studied the very destructive forces at work that are "destroying the future, destroying people, and destroying personal motivation." She has concluded that due to the overwhelming complexity of systems, the mega-power that most large corporations wield, coupled with the degree of degradation that has already been perpetrated, we have reached the tipping point where we can no longer affect global mass destruction. The window of opportunity when we might have made significant global changes has now closed. She believes we can no longer "save the world."

Islands of Sanity[160]

Wheatley asserts that what is left for us to do is: face reality, claim leadership, and restore sanity. She beseeches those who are "warriors for the human spirit" to create resilient and inspirational "islands of sanity."

She asks us to ponder the question, *Who do we choose to be?* as we seek answers for the reality in which we find ourselves.

Wheatley, and other futurists, scientists, philosophers, activists, and everyday people suggest that what we *can do* is choose to preserve and protect local systems and local networks, and choose to be the kind of people we want to be. Each one of us has that power.

According to Wheatley, islands of sanity are places where interested citizens cooperate together and learn how to use their influence and power, their insights and compassion, for the good of all.

Islands of sanity, Wheatley tells us, "lead people back to an understanding of who we are as human beings by creating the conditions for our basic human qualities of generosity, contribution, community, and love to be evoked no matter what." Islands of sanity "make it possible to experience grace and joy in the midst of tragedy and loss, in the midst of wildly disruptive seas." Islands of sanity are places within local communities where everyday people work together "to preserve what is sane, good, just, and equitable."[161]

Asking the Right Questions

What time is it on the clock of the world? is a question that demands clear thinking about what we can and cannot do. This vital question guides our dreams and our actions about what is possible to achieve in these troubled times. This question also invites us to embrace a deeper acceptance of things as they are, of the world as it is, and in so doing, see the everyday beauty, compassion, intelligence, bravery, and kindness available to us, and to all human beings.

Who do we choose to be? is a question that invites reflection on what we stand for, how we choose to spend our time, and how we'd like to be remembered. It also awakens a call to action, beckoning us to discern what is needed now in our own backyards, and offering us an opportunity to contribute in whatever way we can with whatever resources we have.

We can apply this contemplative approach to seeking answers to any area of human need.

For example, my oldest daughter, Maya, is a public health warrior in the arena of harm reduction policies, programs and practices. She does research in the field as well as works on the ground in communities all across the country, and in several places in the larger world. She and her colleagues have proposed a different set of questions, and arrived at a different set of answers, than state and federal agencies have used in their approach to the 'war on drugs.'

Research suggests that the USA's law-and-order approach to drug selling and drug use has been ineffective and counterproductive, and consequently the economic and human costs are staggering. US policies have impeded the implementation of a more humane and effective public health model, namely harm reduction. Harm reduction is a set of ideas and interventions that seeks to reduce the harms associated with both drug use and ineffective, racialized drug policies. Principles and practices of harm reduction seek to promote public health and protect human rights and stand in stark contrast to the punitive approach to drug use adopted by government and law enforcement agencies. Harm reduction is based on acknowledging the humanity of people who use drugs and bringing them into a community of care, in order to minimize negative consequences and promote optimal health and social inclusion.[162]

Maya, and public health activists like her, works tirelessly to preserve people's rights, justice and dignity in a world where substance use and substance users have a changing profile. Consequently, they understand that harm reduction efforts must continually adapt to the reality of 'what is,' and meet the needs of real-life people in real-life situations.

Acknowledging each person's essential humanity—no matter what—and bringing them into the circle of inclusive community is soulful, necessary work.

Why do midwives matter? They matter because like other public health warriors, they aspire to acknowledge and attend to each person's essential humanity and individual needs within the context of the lives they are living.

The truth is, every person, and every contribution, matters. No part is too small to play. No contribution is too insignificant to count.

There is no doubt—we must bring a new way of thinking to the challenges we face. As the ancient Tao Te Ching advises: *When you change the way you look at things, the things you look at change.*

standing at a threshold

A threshold is a significant frontier, an opening or a gateway to a new realm. It is a place of confluence and transformation that divides worlds: life in the womb and birth; childhood and adolescence; adulthood and middle age; old age and death.

As a civilization we are standing at a threshold of inevitable change that will inexorably transform our world.

Many of the greatest thinkers and philosophers of our times are talking about a concept coined by author, activist and Harvard professor David Korten. They say we are in the midst of The Great Turning, a time of revolution in which people are rejecting corporate globalization and envisioning an 'Earth Community,' which will be a life-centered, egalitarian, sustainable way of ordering human society based on democratic principles of partnership.

Joanna Macy, an American environmental activist and scholar of systems thinking and deep ecology, talks about The Great Turning in this way: "a shift from the **Industrial Growth Society** to a **Life-Sustaining Civilization.**"[163] In her writings, films and workshops, Macy teaches, "our planet is a living system, and we belong to it, like cells in a living body everything is hitched to everything else. We cannot find anywhere on Earth where we are not connected."[164]

Macy and other prophets of our time, and also poets, philosophers, scientists, futurists, and everyday people know this: *everything is shifting.*

We are standing at the threshold of a major revolution, a metamorphic moment in human history, which is similar in scope and magnitude to two other major human revolutions in which everything changed.

To understand The Great Turning we must look to the past for the context of the two most recent major shifts: the Agricultural Revolution and the Industrial Revolution.

A brief history will create the context for our present moment, and provide further background for answering the question, *What time is it on the clock of the world?*

When Everything Shifts

In relatively modern times, the first big shift in everything was the Agricultural Revolution, which occurred between 10,000 BCE and 2,000 BCE. It was the transformation of human societies from hunting and gathering to farming. The Agricultural Revolution brought about experimentation with new crops, new methods of crop rotation, better food output, and advancements in irrigation and drainage that further increased productivity. This revolution took thousands of years to fully manifest across the planet. In the mid-seventeenth to late-nineteenth centuries, the Agricultural Revolution took a quantum leap with an unprecedented increase in agricultural production in Europe that impacted the spread of modern global agricultural practices.

The Agricultural Revolution triggered a profound change in society and the way in which people lived. Impermanent and migratory dwellings and traditional hunter-gatherer lifestyles, practiced by humans since earliest times, were swept aside in favor of permanent settlements, stationary farming, and a reliable food supply. Out of agriculture, cities and civilizations grew. Because crops and animals could be farmed to meet demand, the global population skyrocketed—from about five million people 10,000 years ago, to more than seven billion today.

The major effects of the rise in agriculture (very briefly) were these. Decreased migration and increased permanent structures, villages, and eventually cities. Increased food supply due to better crop yields, new crops, and improved livestock breeding. Better nourished and healthier societies. Increased population growth. Rise of plantations and decrease in smaller farms. Increased need of laborers. Rise of slavery for planting, harvesting and tending land. Genocide of Indigenous peoples due to disease, conflict and warfare to acquire their lands. Decreased civil rights for certain groups of people. Enclosure laws that limited the common land available to small farmers. Negative impact on forestlands. And water stress due to crop irrigation, among others.

The second big shift in everything was caused by the Industrial Revolution that occurred between the mid-eighteenth and twentieth centuries when agricultural societies became more industrialized. Most eighteenth-century Americans lived in self-sustaining rural communities, but the Industrial Revolution witnessed the evolution of large urban centers, such as Boston, New York City, and Detroit, and spurred a massive internal migration of workers. People moved en masse from farms and tribal reservations to cities. Manufacturing of goods moved from small shops and homes to large factories. These industrial and economic developments brought significant social and cultural changes.

There are three significant aspects of the Industrial Revolution that transformed our modern society. They were: the rise of steam power, including engines, trains, and cross-nation railways; the assembly line, which afforded mass production of goods, increased efficiency, reduced costs, and enabled more to be produced; and the rise of digital technologies. With each of these three advancements the world around us fundamentally changed.

The major effects of industrialization (very briefly) were these. Urbanization. The factory system. Rise in capitalism, socialism, Marxism, and communism. Exploitation of the working class, particularly women and children. Increase in population. Opportunities to improve the standard of living. Rise in materialism and consumerism. Technological advancement. Transfer of wealth and power to the West. Globalization. And pollution and destruction of the environment, among others.

The most recent effects of the Industrial Revolution are with regards to digital technologies, which were initiated to combat challenges in the manufacturing sector and have grown to include every conceivable aspect of business and society. Some consider digital advancement to be its own separate revolution. The major effects of digital technology were: mass communication democratically available; robotics; Internet of things (IOT); artificial intelligence (AI); and big data.

Unlike the Agricultural Revolution that took millennia to unfold and proliferate in human cultures, the Industrial Revolution took only a couple hundred years to spread across the planet like wildfire.

Gateway to the Next Revolution

Now we are standing at the threshold of The Great Turning, the third revolution of comparable scope and magnitude as the Agricultural and Industrial Revolutions. Some refer to it as the ecological revolution, the environmental revolution, or the sustainability revolution, while others simply call it The Great Turning. Those who are studying the phenomenon say this revolution will be equally as comprehensive as the first two revolutions. They also say it must happen much faster than the other two revolutions because the stakes are high and time is running out.

Joanna Macy says, "The living systems of earth are coming apart under the onslaught of the Industrial Growth Society, scrambling for the last dollar."[165]

In order to disrupt the patterns of organization in the Industrial Growth Society and shift to the Life-Sustaining Society, we have to change the whole mindset of who we are and what we are in relation to the living planet of which we are a part. And that task is huge, complex, overwhelming, and perhaps, not solvable.

Some leading thinkers claim global change is possible. Others, like Margaret Wheatley say we cannot solve global problems globally, but we must work at the local level to manifest change.

Others, like eminent historian Howard Zinn assert, "We don't have to wait for some grand utopian future. The future is an infinite succession of presents, and to live now as we think human beings should live, in defiance of all that is bad around us, is itself a marvelous victory."

Top-down, Bottom-up, All-around Change

Every movement has its pioneers. Every revolution has its visionaries. Every transformational change process has its tipping point where established systems break and new systems emerge.

In the USA, and in our world, we are at an unprecedented twenty-first century moment of dramatic and inevitable change. And change is happening simultaneously from top-down institutions and bottom-up actions by grassroots citizenry. People are making change on four critical and interrelated levels simultaneously: changing hearts, changing minds, changing structures, and changing policies.

While a full exploration of the topic of transformational change is beyond the scope of this book, it is heartening to see the plethora of examples that demonstrate the number of people and corporations that are agents of change. (Please consult the wealth of information that is available on the topic.)

The Great Turning is a possibility not a prophecy. We do not know what is going to happen, but we do know a revolution has begun. It is gaining momentum through the actions of countless individuals and groups around the world. It is abundantly clear: we are standing at a threshold that holds infinite possibilities.

Microcosms Within Macrocosms

Let's bring our attention back to the main focus of this book—The Midwife Matrix and its impact on the bodies, minds, spirits, and lives of people who give birth, people who are born, and people who care for them. Regardless of your perspective on whether we can save the world, most of us can at least agree we stand at the threshold of the next big shift in everything.

The story I am telling in this book is about a microcosm of one system (the maternity care system), nested inside a macrocosm of global systems. I am also making a case for why midwives matter in this complex puzzle. The state of affairs around our current maternity care system, and its impact on the health and wellbeing of women and infants, and thus on our society as a whole, is a small slice of a big picture. However, this book was born from my desire to place the needs of women and children at the heart of our conversations about transformational change.

The great challenge of our times is to create sustainable systems and sustainable communities that support, not destroy, the web of life, the planet on which we live, and the bodies, minds, and spirits of the Earth's living beings.

Sustainability Is at the Heart

The ancient lineage of midwifery in its postmodern manifestation as a healthcare profession is a sustainable model of maternity care trapped in the grips of an unsustainable healthcare system.

What is *sustained* in sustainable systems and communities is not economic growth, development, market share, profits, or competitive edge.

What is sustained is the entire web of life—living networks, food and water systems, and other life-supporting systems that make our lives better without compromising the ability of future generations to meet their needs.

How Will You Know?

Among the ways in which you know you are shifting consciousness towards a Life-Sustaining Society are these. You feel you are not who you once were. You feel motivated to change. You crave a more meaningful life. You are consuming less and connecting more. You feel less like sticking your head in the sand and more like contributing in some way. You are becoming more creative. You understand that what affects others also affects you, and what affects you also affects others. You feel increasingly mindful that every choice you make, every action of doing or undoing, has a consequence that matters, because it's all connected. You are finding, more and more, you want to give yourself to love.

Each person, in their own community and realm of influence, and in their own unique and invaluable way, is needed to take part in this emerging and potent revolution.

The Voices of Midwives

A crucial piece in shifting paradigms and insuring transformational change is to make sure all of the stakeholders are brought to the table, and all of the voices are heard and given equal weight in analyzing existing structures and creating alternative structures. For maternal and child health that includes parents, providers, policymakers, insurers, business leaders, legislators, everyone.

It is a fact that the voices of midwives—as important as they are—are often missing from policy conversations about maternal and child health. Often their input is missing at local, national, and international policy-making tables.[166]

When we include the **voices of midwives** in the dialog about maternal-infant health, here's what happens. We gain an understanding about how vital it is to facilitate a maternal and child healthcare system that is built on love, respect, compassion, justice, and autonomy.

When we include the **skills of midwives** in maternity care, here's what happens. We gain a model that promotes an indispensable combination of meeting the physical, psychosocial, and cultural needs of women and people who give birth, ensuring better pregnancy and birth outcomes, and promoting better health across the lifespan of people and families.

When we include the **essential assertion midwives make** that women and people with wombs are powerful, proficient, and intelligent enough to take control of their bodies and their lives, here's what happens. We reinforce the fundamental human right each person has to self-determination. And we uphold the human rights people have to make their own choices about their bodies, their lives, and what matters most to them.

And when we include the **philosophical viewpoint midwives hold** that birth is a precious miracle that must be treated like a sacred rite of passage, here's what happens. We shift from 'controlling' to 'empowering.' We begin to dispel the myths that keep people disconnected from their bodies and deeply afraid of giving birth. And we return the soul-nourishing aspects of mystery, ecstasy, and joy to the experiences of giving birth and being born.

These are the contributions midwives can make in the process of transformational change.

The midwifery perspective—both theory and practice—is a shift from an economic-based healthcare system focused on commodities, profits, and unlimited growth, to one that is ecologically sustainable, life-affirming, and socially just.

midwives are changing the world

Sometimes I laugh at myself when I make such sweeping statements as 'midwives are changing the world.' I chuckle even as I write because I know that every person who does work that ignites their passion, enriches their spirit, and makes a difference in the lives of others thinks their little piece of the pie is the juiciest and tastiest of all. I am no exception.

But I have also seen, firsthand, the evidence of this bold statement. I know midwives all over the country and around the world. I have heard their stories and in many cases visited their homes and their workplaces. And I have observed them in action.

The cultural narratives midwives offer are often different from those espoused by the purveyors of the US healthcare system. When you change the defining stories of the mainstream culture, you change the ways in which we understand the world around us, and you change reality.

I will tell you a few stories of midwives who are changemakers. Midwives who see the patterns around them and figure out ways to solve problems. Midwives who act on the possibilities they have imagined for the world. Midwives who are nudging, unleashing and causing social cascades.

And then you decide for yourself: *are midwives changing the world?*

In Guatemala

Several years ago in the early 2000s, in the highlands of Guatemala near Quetzaltenango, my friend Judy Luce and I were staying with our friends, Indigenous midwives Antonina Sanchez and Berta Juarez. Our relationship with the Mayan *comadronas* began small. We brought midwifery supplies to them, swapped stories and tricks of the trade, and sponsored them to attend midwifery and herbal conferences in the USA.

One morning as we were enjoying coffee and tortillas made from corn harvested on their land and cooked on an open fire, we talked. Antonina and Berta described how midwives attended the majority of births in the area, which still occurred at home, but lacked the most basic equipment or opportunities to increase their knowledge and skills. The government was unsupportive and in fact was trying to eliminate community midwives, even though they were the primary birth attendants for the majority of women all across Guatemala. Doctors and hospital staff tended to disrespect them. When midwives brought patients to the hospital for care, they were often blamed for problems their clients developed that the midwives had no way of treating because they stemmed from severe malnutrition, too many pregnancies, limited access to medicines and preventive care measures, and the devastating aftermath of recent civil war. In addition, Indigenous midwives had substantial responsibilities in their own domestic lives, were often illiterate, and received little compensation for their midwifery work.

One day we went for a walk to the small town of Concepción Chiquirichapa. On the way I took a photograph of Antonina and Berta standing in a very large field of ripe cabbages. I can still see it: two women dressed in colorful handwoven clothing, standing amongst plump green cabbages, smiling, with a bright blue sky overhead. They told Judy and I about their vision of building a midwifery center and clinic at this site. They asked if we would help, and we agreed.

For the next several years, Judy was instrumental in planning, raising funds, organizing support from midwives in North America, and assisting with on-site work. I helped with fundraising to bring Guatemalan midwives to conferences in the USA in order to demonstrate their case and ask for financial support. The Guatemalan midwives organized their community and did the heavy lifting.

The next time I visited Concepción the cabbage field had been transformed into a much-needed birth and community center. In June 2004 there was a grand opening celebration to dedicate their vision-made-reality. *Casa Maternal de Nacimiento y la Comienza de Esperanza* (Maternity Home and the Beginnings of Hope) featured a birth center, educational and community space, health clinic, and guest quarters. And that was just the beginning.

Twenty years after their vision was conceived, Antonina and other seasoned midwives provide training for community midwives, young and old, to ensure sustainable, long-term, community-based care that is culturally grounded and accessible to all. The training preserves their traditional medicine and sacred

Maya childbirth practices while blending modern clinical midwifery skills and equipment. They provide full-scope midwifery care to community members, including preventive healthcare like screening for cervical cancer, a leading cause of death in Guatemala, which the midwives are determined to eradicate. They host monthly community health days for screenings and education.

The midwives received a grant from an international humanitarian organization, Every Mother Counts, for a mobile clinic—a 4-wheel-drive vehicle equipped with everything the midwives needed for a prenatal clinic, including lab capabilities and a portable ultrasound machine, which the midwives were trained to use. For a long time, Guatemala has had the region's highest maternal mortality rate, and due to lack of services and respect, the rate among rural Indigenous women has been double that of the national rate. Every month the midwives visit four remote areas with their mobile clinic, one village is four hours away, to provide maternity care to women and infants in areas where there are no other healthcare providers. The midwives hired a female, very progressive, and respectful obstetrician from Quetzaltenango, a town known as Xela, to accompany them and provide consultation on complicated situations.

Even before they conceived and built the birth and community center, the Guatemalan midwives created a midwifery association called *Asociación de Comadronas de Area Mam* (ACAM), Association of Midwives of the Mam-speaking Region. Because of what they have accomplished in their region, the ACAM midwives have become the official representatives with the Guatemala Ministry of Health in drafting and implementing standards for training community midwives and replicating the ACAM model nationally. Last month they celebrated the fifteenth year of opening *Casa Maternal de Nacimiento y la Comienza de Esperanza*, and 25 years as ACAM.

The midwives have been successful in their work because they are trusted members of their communities, and because they have found ways to successfully create bridges between community midwives, hospitals, and other maternity care providers for the benefit of the women and families they serve.

After several decades of civil war and devastating losses on every level possible, the Mayan midwives have woven the fabric of their communities back together with golden threads of loving kindness and hard work.

The midwives have realized the vision they held while standing in a cabbage patch. And with the allyship from midwives and supporters in the USA—emotional, financial, technical, collegial—the Guatemalan midwives have been able to manifest their dream in ways even more vast than they originally imagined. Now, the silver threads of heartfelt advocacy from American midwives have also been woven into the story of how transformational change took shape and blossomed in Guatemala.

In Haiti

Ninotte Lubin is from Jacmel Haiti. In 2013 she was in the United States to complete her midwifery training in Michigan and she attended my wedding. She was in the process of earning a Certified Professional Midwife certificate. Her training took five grueling years.

But Ninotte was a young woman with a vision. She knew that the neonatal, infant, child, and maternal mortality rates in her home country of Haiti were the highest in the Western world, with rates similar to those found in Afghanistan and several African countries. She worked in two nonprofit birth centers following the 2010 earthquake in Haiti that killed over 200,000 people. She spent a lot of time studying the health indicators in her native country, including the fact that 80% of Haitians live under the poverty line and 54% live in abject poverty. She also learned that due to both violence and AIDS, Haiti had the highest percentage of orphans of any country in the Western Hemisphere. She came to believe that the development of any society, and the future of Haiti, depended on how the children were birthed, cared for and raised.

Ninotte envisioned a community-based birth center that was owned and operated by Haitians where "women and babies are served respectfully in a loving and compassionate way for a better future." She conceived the idea for Grace Community Birth Center (GCBC). It took years of planning and fundraising. It took many conversations with community members to get buy-in, particularly from the men, and specifically around the concept of birth control.

Sometimes the most transformational change comes when we change our minds, imagine a different way, and live into that new way of thinking and acting.

This one-woman powerhouse has been working tirelessly and her dream is becoming manifested, step-by-step. Today, the first phase of GCBC is located on three acres of property in Grand Bassin, in northern Haiti. While Ninotte's vision includes a brick and mortar health center, currently GCBC is an open air education center in which Ninotte holds prenatal and postpartum sessions for local women, teaches monthly sex education classes for teens and young adults, and runs monthly men's and women's groups. The property supports gardens and beehives and is abuzz with new life and new energy. The mission of Grace is "to provide affordable, accessible, respectful maternity care and family planning education for the women, children, and families of Haiti."

Last week Ninotte was in Michigan to meet with friends and supporters, and to continue her fundraising campaign. To date, she and her allies have raised $50,000, one-third of the goal for their capital campaign to build the birth center. Michigan midwife, Kathi Mulder and her husband Craig have been Ninotte's continual companions on this long journey. Not only have they been to Haiti several times to offer on-site support, but stateside they provide technical, business, managerial, and fundraising support, too. At the recent gala event that the Mulders organized and that was attended by a large portion of the homebirth community and other supporters, funds were raised, a meal was shared, and updates on the project were given. Craig described the architectural renderings for Grace Community Birth Center displayed on the wall. He outlined how the center will be integral to the community and ecologically sustainable, both structurally and functionally. Ninotte presented a PowerPoint and shared statistics and stories about the amazing progress that has been made since we saw her the previous year at the Grace fundraising event.

It was inspiring to see what has been accomplished. Among my favorite stories were the ones about the men's group. To me, it's a no-brainer for women to easily have buy-in to a birth center concept. But it is typically more challenging to 'bring the men along.' Ninotte is doing it, slowly but surely, because she is committed to making Grace a valuable addition to the whole community. She has taken care to provide special group activities for each sector of the community—women, men, teens, and elders. She has even added a special group for kids, because they came to her and said, "We want to be included too."

This little oasis in a poverty-stricken and trauma-torn country exists because of one midwife's vision, hard work, and determination to make things better. Ongoing support from local people in Haiti and North American allies make it possible for Ninotte's vision to be manifested. There is a circle of support, but it is decidedly a Haitian-led project. Ninotte and her community are making transformational change on their own terms and in their own way.

Ninotte said she chose the name 'Grace' because of its implication of God's love and kindness offered to the entire human family. Life is difficult for Haitian women, and she wanted to create a place of compassion, support, and individualized care when women needed it most.

Ninotte said, "In giving grace through the form of professional, compassionate care to the women and babies, I hope to see this generation regenerated through love, respect, and education." Grace, indeed.

In Nigeria

Beginning in the mid-2000s I had the pleasure and privilege of being a delegate on the Governing Council of the International Confederation of Midwives (ICM) as a representative of the Midwives Alliance of North America. The ICM's mission is to strengthen midwifery globally and it has midwifery member-associations from over 100 countries. I served on the ICM Governing Council during three triennial conferences, held in Scotland, South Africa, and the Czech Republic. For years I had been gathering stories of the transformational work midwives were doing in the Americas. But it was at these international meetings that I came to understand the profound impact midwives were making in countries all over the world, particularly under the most extreme circumstances, and in the lives of individual women and their families.

I met midwives from Nigeria who said, frankly, their country was a risky place to give birth and be born. Even though Nigeria is the wealthiest nation on the African continent, maternal and infant mortality rates are desperately high. Nigeria is also a war torn country. As the insurgents started gaining ground in particular regions, many of the doctors and health workers fled, leaving only a handful of obstetricians to care for a vast number of pregnant women and girls.

In northeast Nigeria where conflict is the greatest, about 250,000 people give birth every year. Midwives rose to the challenge of serving this population. They worked in small, whitewashed, barebones clinics for thousands of internally displaced people, with no electricity or running water, where the nearest hospital was eighty miles away. But they saved women from pregnancy and childbirth complications, and death, which frequently occurred during unattended home births.

Other midwives were part of a squad of 'flying midwives,' a cadre initiated by UNICEF that flies into war-torn areas and Nigerian refugee camps. The midwives said they do this hard and dangerous work because they believe "no mother, no matter where she is, should experience the tragedy of losing her child or her life while giving birth."

If securing the basics of survival—food, water, shelter, and clothing—is a constant challenge in war-torn regions, imagine also being pregnant, and equally as important, searching for practitioners to distribute reliable birth control methods.

The role of midwives in conflict zones around the world has become even more critical than in peaceful regions. These midwives are recognized for their tireless, skillful, lifesaving, and immeasurably important contributions in making the world a better, safer place.

In the Caribbean

I met midwives from the Caribbean islands of Trinidad and Tobago and became friends with Debrah Lewis, a Trinidadian nurse-midwife and vice president of the ICM. She told me that in the Caribbean region, pregnancy is often the first time women encounter the medical system and too frequently that system does not respect their choices. Childbirth is often very dehumanized and the staff is completely in charge of making decisions for the woman and her family.

For years Debrah had been fighting hospital policies that kept fathers out of the delivery room. In most hospitals in Trinidad, as in many other Caribbean territories, fathers were not allowed to be with their partners, or witness the birth of their children. In most hospitals there were too many hoops to jump through, too many conditions to meet, and even if a father satisfied all the requirements, including attending childbirth classes, there was no guarantee he would be allowed to attend the birth of his own child. The final decision was up to the whim of the staff that often came up with reasons to keep fathers out, such as "we are too busy," or "we do not have time to deal with that," or "it is our decision."

Debrah and her colleagues argued that it was not up to the staff; it was up to the parents because it was their right to choose.

In the early 2000s, Debrah and other midwives began meeting informally to share concerns about the challenges their clients were facing within the healthcare system. They began to dream about a place where women and their families could meet, get information and support, receive maternity care, and have a natural childbirth experience. Their dream was a place for "safe, accessible, equitable, nonjudgmental, woman-centered healthcare."

With meager financial resources and little support from the medical community, in 2004 Debrah and three other independent midwives co-founded a nonprofit, community-based, nongovernmental haven—Mamatoto Resource and Birth Centre—to help address the demand for family-centered, individualized, culturally appropriate care.

Mamatoto was committed to three key values for childbearing women and their families: respect, empowerment, and self-determination through informed choices. The midwives knew the philosophy and maternity care practices at Mamatoto were replicable and could be easily adopted throughout the Caribbean Islands. But they insisted it required each woman be empowered to make informed choices, determine who she considered to be family members, and decide whom she wanted with her as she labored and gave birth. Mamatoto's philosophy stated that those things were basic human rights.

They also asserted that men have to be educated and prepared to be equally involved in raising their children. Therefore, Mamatoto—a Swahili word that means 'mother and baby'—provided access to a free, multimedia library with materials on reproductive health and breastfeeding. The Resource Center offered sessions for prenatal yoga and childbirth education, and free support groups for teens, fathers, and families who experienced a miscarriage, stillbirth, or infant loss. The freestanding, midwife-led Mamatoto Birth Centre offered family-centered care that was individualized to meet each family's needs and choices. Debrah and her colleagues encouraged their clients to ask for what they needed in order to get what was rightfully theirs, whether they gave birth at the birth center or in the hospital.

Almost two decades after their dream took shape out of a desire to create transformational change in maternity care practices in the Caribbean Islands, Debrah Lewis is now the Executive Director of Mamatoto Resource and Birth Centre, which is going strong and has a large degree of community support. Slowly but surely Debrah, her colleagues, and their community members see that social change is possible because of the transformational change they have manifested at Mamatoto. Debrah said, "Our vision for the future is to have a greater impact on national policy to ensure that the care we provide is seen as the model for all healthcare in Trinidad and Tobago."

In Indonesia

Robin Lim is a Filipino-American who has lived in Indonesia much of her adult life. She is a midwife, mother of eight, wife, grandmother, mentor, and community organizer. She and her family moved to Indonesia twenty-eight years ago after her sister and her sister's baby died of childbirth complications. The same year Robin's best friend, who was a midwife and delivered one of Robin's children, was killed in a car crash. In that same year another best friend also died. Robin needed a change.

Robin told me, "I had to look deep to find my own answers to the question, 'Why am I alive?' I found my only reason for living was *love*, which drove me to become a BirthKeeper."

I do not think Robin could have foreseen that in her 'grief walk' she would come to be the epitome of transformational change and a beacon of light for so many others.

Shortly after Robin moved to the Ubud area, to the tiny village of Nyuh Kuning in Gianyar on the Indonesian island of Bali, people learned she was a midwife. They came knocking at her door asking her to assist them in childbirth.

Because Robin's style was both skillful and loving, the demand for her midwifery services grew so steadily that she, along with the help of other midwives and local people, opened Bumi Sehat Clinic to provide maternity care and childbirth classes. Services were provided to everyone free of charge. The clinic depended on donations from those who could afford to pay and the generosity of donors from around the world. Her patrons began to mount, and today they include everyday people and famous people such as Christy Turlington, an American model, human rights activist, and founder of Every Mother Counts. The people of Bali call her Ibu Robin (Mother Robin).

Robin also cofounded Bumi Sehat Foundation. One of its key activities is to go to disaster areas to provide humanitarian aid where people are injured, homeless, displaced, and starving. Robin and her team focus their efforts on pregnant, birthing, and postpartum women, babies, children and families. Robin knew that when disaster struck babies would still be born, even if the mother was homeless, unhealthy, thirsty and hungry. Robin and her team arrive promptly to disaster sites, set up a no-frills clinic, a birthing tent, and provide expert mother-baby-family care.

In 2004, Lim along with Bumi Sehat's team of midwives and medics responded in the aftermath of the earthquake in Ache on the island of Sumatra. It was a devastating megathrust earthquake that registered a 9.3 magnitude. After earthquakes struck Yogjakerta in 2006, Padang in 2008, Haiti in 2010, and Nepal in 2015, Lim and her colleagues traveled to these sites. In 2013, they were called to set up birthing units in the Philippines after the super typhoon. More recently in 2017 and 2018, Bumi Sehat and Ibu Robin were called upon to respond to the eruptions of Bali's volcano. Also in 2018, when Lombok Island suffered devastating earthquakes, and Sumatra had earthquakes and a terrible tsunami, once again, Lim and her team responded with timely, loving, and professional humanitarian healthcare and human services.

In the aftermath of disasters, mothers suffer from malnutrition and post-traumatic stress disorder, which can cause stress-related symptoms like hypertension and premature birth. With the expert care of Ibu Robin and Bumi Sehat's midwives, women who may not have survived do survive. Against all odds, twins, breeches, and premature babies have also survived.

The Bumi Sehat birth data show that even in the lowest-resource and highest-risk settings such as disaster zones, the loving, respectful Midwife-to-Mother Model of Care is so effective that the Bumi Sehat outcomes are better than the national statistics for childbirth in the countries in which Bumi Sehat provides care.

Currently in Indonesia, Bumi Sehat has community health and childbirth clinics in Bali, Aceh, Lombok and Papua. In coastal areas of the Philippines hardest hit by recent typhoons, a partnership between Bumi Sehat and Wadah Foundation created birthing-related maternal and infant health services with Bumi-Wadah Clinics located in Leyte and Palawan.

In 2017 Bumi Sehat provided 83,218 people with care. In 2018 Bumi Sehat delivered health, education and human services for 146,671 people. As early responders to disasters, which are fueled by the increased temperature of the Earth's crust, in the shadow of the climate crisis, Ibu Robin and the Bumi Sehat team are always prepared and increasingly busy.

At an international gala in 2011 televised worldwide, Robin was awarded CNN's prestigious Hero Award, which every year highlights the extraordinary commitment of everyday heroes that give selfless service to others. I watched the coverage on TV. I listened as Robin accepted her award and told an international audience of millions of viewers, "every baby's first breath on Earth could be one of peace and love. Every mother should be healthy and strong. Every birth could be safe and loving. But our world is not there yet." Sadly, that is true.

In June 2017 I met up with Robin in Toronto at the ICM Triennial Congress. It happened to be my birthday, and she gave me a hand-beaded bracelet of my favorite colors—turquoise, purple, coral. In the center is a small, delicately carved bone face surrounded by a circle of beading. It looks like a moon face, and it also looks like a newborn baby just as it is emerging from its mother's body. Every time I wear this beautiful moon face, baby face bracelet I think of Robin's work and mission. She fiercely asserts, "We can change the world one gentle birth at a time, addressing one mother at a time." And so it is.

Around the World

It was my good fortune to become friends with midwife, mother, educator, and visionary, Bridget Lynch, from Toronto, Canada. After a long and successful career in the professionalization of midwifery in Canada, Bridget became passionately involved in the politics of midwifery at the global level and worked her way to the world's top midwifery post—president of the International Confederation of Midwives. She became a pivotal voice in the struggle to identify midwives as the key to reduce the tragically high death rates of mothers and infants in developing countries. She told me that of the nearly half million women who die every year, 90% are from low-resource countries, and their deaths could be prevented with proper midwifery care within functioning healthcare systems.

Bridget became convinced that midwives were the solution to reducing the dismal mortality rates because midwives are the experts in birth and care for women and their newborns in the community. More than half of all mothers in the world give birth out of hospital and midwives are often the first care worker to which women reach out. The problem Bridget witnessed was that midwifery training and the way midwives practiced was different from one country to the next. In many low-resource countries midwives were controlled by nursing standards and physicians, and most importantly, they lacked the autonomy needed to provide exemplary midwifery care.

When Bridget became President of the ICM, her vision was to create global standards for an autonomous global midwifery profession. With the support of the ICM Council, board, and staff, and generous financial support from the Swedish government, the ICM recruited midwifery leaders in education, regulation and association development and established three task forces to develop global standards in each area. During the triennium between 2008-2011 the task forces consulted 100 ICM national associations along with global partners, and developed basic standards in what has become known as the **'Three Pillars' of midwifery: education, regulation and association (ERA).** The Three Pillars are interdependent, and they embody ICM's vision to strengthen midwifery worldwide in order to provide high-quality, evidence-based care for women, newborns, and childbearing families.

In 2011, I attended the ICM Triennial Congress in Durban, South Africa, where over 4,000 midwives had gathered for the first Triennial Congress ever held in Africa. I walked 5 kilometers with hundreds of midwives singing, dancing, and celebrating this historic event. During the three-day ICM Governing Council, which took place before the Congress, I represented MANA and joined midwifery leaders from across the planet to endorse the new ICM global standards. During her final speech to the Durban Congress, Bridget announced that the WHO, UNFPA, and the international societies for obstetricians and pediatricians all not only endorsed these standards, but committed to supporting their use in all countries globally. In Durban, in 2011, **midwifery became the first healthcare profession in the world to have achieved global standards for the education and regulation of a healthcare workforce.**

Another first that took place during the Durban Congress was the release of the State of the World's Midwifery: Delivering Health, Saving Lives (2011) report. This report produced by the ICM, UN agencies and over 30 global partners is a comprehensive analysis of midwifery services and issues in countries where the needs were greatest. It grew out of the first global Midwifery Symposium, which Bridget chaired at the Women Deliver Conference in Washington, DC in 2010, convened to highlight to global agencies the essential role of midwives in reducing maternal and newborn mortality. The report confirmed that the world lacked some 350,000 skilled midwives—112,000 in the neediest 38 countries surveyed—to fully meet the needs of women around the world, and called for a unified effort to develop the profession of midwifery globally.

The new global standards, alongside the information provided by the State of the World's Midwifery report, were total game changers. Low-resource countries had the data and the guidelines needed to work with UN Agencies and donor countries and agencies to begin to develop a sustainable midwifery workforce. Today, the standards continue to provide the foundation of the midwifery profession in all countries globally and the State of the World's Midwifery report is in its 4th edition (2020).

Throughout our friendship, I came to understand that Bridget's vision, and her deep commitment to mothers and their newborns came out of her personal commitment to motherhood. Bridget told me that being the mother of five children, being able to love them and watch them grow surrounded by opportunity, is what made her strive so passionately for the mothers of all the world's children. She said, "Every child deserves what my kids have had. It all starts at birth."

In Indian Country, Straddling the USA and Canada

Imagine how it would shape your view of reality, and your own sense of self, if your origin story began, "I was born in my grandmother's big iron bed, sliding out of my mother's warm body into my grandmother's waiting hands. I was surrounded by generations of my women. There was my mother, who was born in this same bed, my grandmother, who caught all the babies in the region, and my aunties and cousins who were waiting nearby to welcome me."

That is how the story begins for my friend and colleague, Tekatsi' tsiah:khwa 'Katsi' Cook, who is a descendant of the Original People of North America.

Imagine if you knew exactly where your original homeland was and you could trace an unbroken alliance with the land, as the Mohawk Nation can, from the northeastern region of what became New York State, extending into southern Ontario and Quebec. If you knew where your people lied buried, and you could hear their voices on the wind, would that make your connection to your land, and your desire to preserve and protect it fiercer and stronger?

This confluence of personal and cultural histories is the energy that inner-vates and motivates Katsi Cook's work. Her work is informed and nourished by the worldview of her Indigenous peoples, rooted in the geography of a specific place on Mother Earth.

Katsi was born on the St. Regis Mohawk Reservation and is a member of the Wolf Clan of the Mohawk Nation. Because she belongs to a matrilineal society, the story of where she comes from begins with her mother who was from the Mohawks of Kahnawà:ke, where she was born. Katsi's name in Kahnawà:ke Mohawk, *Tekatsi' tsiah:khwa*, means, *she is picking up flowers*.

Katsi is a mother, grandmother, elder, women's health advocate, educator, researcher, and activist. She grew up under the guidance of her grandmother, Kanatires, "knowing the medicines, the plants, and their relationship to the Mohawk people of the Great Lakes Basin and St. Lawrence River."[167] She watched her grandmother carefully, who was the community healer, as she ministered to people from cradleboard to coffin. Katsi grew up steeped in the historical narratives of her ancestors, knowing her kinship structure, retaining cultural memory and knowledge of traditional ceremonies, and immersed in political action to preserve the rights and lifeways of her people. She was born into a family of people who used their service and their lives to make a difference.

Transformational change, the kind of lasting change that influences entire sectors and ecosystems, is sometimes a matter of preserving, protecting, or restoring what we already have. Many Indigenous people are that kind of change agent.

When Katsi was in her mid-twenties, she attended the Loon Lake Conference of 1977; an important internal meeting of activists of the Haudenosaunee (Six Nations of the Iroquois Confederacy—Mohawk, Oneida, Onondaga, Cayuga, Seneca, and Tuscarora). At this pivotal meeting attendees decisively articulated 'five areas of sovereignty'. These included: "control over our land base; control over the jurisdiction of that land base; control over our education; self-determination of our psycho-spiritual life; and self-determination and control over our bodies and reproductive health."[168] The Loon Lake meeting was the catalyst for Katsi to actively pursue midwifery, a calling she knew she wanted to follow from a very young age at her grandmother's side.

For over five decades, Katsi has led her people in a wide array of initiatives at the potent intersection of reproductive justice and environmental justice.

A key motivator for Katsi's midwifery work was recognizing how much self-knowledge and cultural knowledge around reproduction had been lost by Indigenous peoples, due to colonization. "This awareness, coupled with community concern about the sterilization of Native women, led Katsi to reclaim childbirth as key to community healing and survival, and a process of empowerment through which women revive Indigenous culture and restore Native peoples' connections to ancestral land."[169]

Reviewing Katsi's lifework, it is almost as if her activism has followed the pathway of the Medicine Wheel. She has initiated projects in each of the Four Directions, in the four stages of human development—child, youth, adult, and elder.

In 1981 Katsi conducted her first award-winning research by initiating the Akwesasne Mother's Milk Project to monitor and document industrial pollutants in breast milk of Mohawk mothers. Although Mohawk ancestral lands were once a vibrant sanctuary of rich woodlands and clear lakes and rivers that sustained the Native peoples for centuries, polychlorinated biphenyls (PCBs) were found in the groundwater under General Motors' property, and later in private wells near and on tribal lands. The St. Lawrence River ran through reservation land and was in close proximity to GM's auto plants and waste dumps. The surrounding communities experienced high numbers of miscarriages and birth defects, and concern mounted among women on the reservation about the safety of breast-feeding. The Akwesasne Mother's Milk Project evaluated PCB levels in breast milk. It also addressed the environmental impact of industrial development of the St. Lawrence Seaway, which began in the 1950s. The Mother's Milk Project provided services and advocacy for residents of Akwesasne, the most severely polluted of 63 Native American communities. The Mother's Milk Project was later cited as emerging 'reproductive rights activism'. It challenged the feminist movement's focus on 'pro choice', pushing it to go beyond abortion rights by adopting a broad social justice agenda related to a full spectrum of women's health and human rights.

In the mid-1980s Katsi served as program director for First Environment Collaborative at Running Strong for American Indian Youth. Running Strong's mission was to help American Indian people meet their immediate survival needs—food, water, shelter—while implementing and supporting programs designed to create opportunities for self-sufficiency and self-esteem. 'Women as the First Environment Collaborative' supported community-based health projects that sought to empower Native women of all ages and increase knowledge concerning reproductive health.

Katsi beautifully sums up this concept by saying, "Women are the first environment. In pregnancy, our bodies sustain life. At the breast of women, the generations are nourished. In this way, women are an embodiment of Mother Earth."

Around the same time as the Women as the First Environment Collaborative was gaining momentum, Katsi became a founding aboriginal midwife of the

Six Nations Birthing Centre in Canada where she assisted with student training, curriculum development, and community education. Several years later she participated in cocreating the National Aboriginal Council of Midwives and was instrumental in drafting midwifery legislation in Ontario that protected the rights of Indigenous midwives and women. Her midwifery has always been informed by ancestral knowledge and energized by returning birthing to Native peoples so that childbirth traditions can take place in Native communities and within the wisdom of their own cultures.

In 2009 Katsi was a cofounder of the Konon:kwe ('women') Council, a women-led, community-based council in Akwesasne which sought to empower women in the community and advance woman-centered policies to stunt cycles of violence in the community. Katsi explains, "Taking Kahnistensera, or 'Mother Law', as its foundational principle, members of the council work as daughters of Sky Woman, weaving 'webs of women's wisdom' with prayer, healing ceremonies, and grassroots activism to empower and transform their traumatized communities."[170] Katsi teaches about how midwifery can be an antidote to traumatic processes Indigenous communities have endured, because midwifery returns birth to the community and provides culturally appropriate primary care close to home.

And most recently, Katsi has initiated Spirit Aligned Leadership Program, which elevates the lives, voices, and dreams of Indigenous Elder women who are working to heal, strengthen, and restore the balance of Indigenous communities. They address these issues: violence against girls, women and the Earth; leadership of Indigenous girls and women; healing from historic trauma and oppression; and Indigenous education.[171]

Katsi said, "We feel that the life knowledge of traditional Native women, particularly those who have stepped out courageously to create healthy paths for their generations, deserve to be celebrated. As the Spirit Aligned Leadership Program now begins to unfold through the eyes of a circle of women brought together to think and act on how to heal, we strengthen and restore the balance of Indigenous communities."[172]

Across the spectrum of life—child, youth, adult and elder—Katsi has led transformational initiatives that have changed, enriched and empowered the lives of Indigenous peoples. She has been celebrated as a mentor and leader by a whole generation of women who became mothers and social activists under her guidance, and who honor her extensive body of work.

As an aboriginal midwife and an Elder, Katsi "pulls the threads of her ancient matrilineal knowledge from the teachings of Sky Woman and weaves them together with threads of Western science and political discourse and activism." In this way she contributes to the legacy of embodied Indigenous knowledge that is helping to recreate healthy pathways for current and future generations.

Katsi believes it all begins at birth.

"An empowered community is made up of empowered individuals and empowered families, and to me empowerment is feeling at home with who you are, and that begins with the moment of birth," Katsi said. "So my own birth story is a great source of strength to me."

"When you ask the question about our children," Katsi says, "I have to go the long way around and say it all begins with the way they get born."[173]

In Mexico

"*Todo tiene vida y merece un gran respeto*," says midwife-healer Doña Enriqueta Contreras Contreras…"everything has life and deserves great respect."

Doña Enriqueta is a Zapotec of the Sierra Juárez in the southern Mexican state of Oaxaca. Like Katsi Cook, Doña Enriqueta is also a descendant of the Original People of North America. One woman is from the north and one is from the south.

Doña Enriqueta grew up in a region of rugged mountains, dense forests, and immense biodiversity. The Zapotec call themselves *las gentes de las nubes* (people of the clouds) because for many months each year everything is cloudy and they live inside those clouds. The Zapotecos say behind the clouds there is clarity of life.[174] The 'clarity gem,' bequeathed by the ancestors to their descendants, is this teaching: center one's life on the important value of respect. And respect, Zapotec folkways teach, extends to all living beings and especially to Mother Nature.

Doña Enriqueta is a revered elder as well as a *partera tradicional, curandera,* and *herbalista* (traditional midwife, medicine woman, and herbalist.) She is also the author of an herbal *materia medica*—an encyclopedic body of knowledge that describes how her people have used plants therapeutically throughout the ages.

I first met Doña Enriqueta, fondly called Doña Queta, in the early 2000s at conferences where she sold herbal remedies and offered hands-on workshops. But in the late 2000s, I got to know her personally at a conference hosted by the Midwives Alliance of North America in Chiapas Mexico. Doña Queta was facilitating the opening circle of the gathering. She was dressed majestically in traditional Zapotecan clothing and she wielded several ceremonial accouterments. She and others had created a spacious ritual circle that was circumscribed with flowers and herbs, nuts and seeds, ribbons and feathers. In the center of the circle was an altar with a fire in a large cast iron pot, statues, candles, a pitcher of water, a bottle of mescal, baskets of herbs and flowers, a bowl of eggs, semi-precious gemstones, and other sacred objects.

My friend and younger colleague, Cristina Alonso—a potent agent of change in her own right—was the founder and chief operator of a birth center in San Cristobal de las Casas in Chiapas and the local coordinator of the MANA-Mexico conference. As the lead conference organizer Cris was the co-facilitator of the opening ceremony along with several Indigenous elders. Because I was MANA's president, I was invited into the center of the circle to help with the ritual.

When all the preparations were in order Doña Queta led the procession of ritual makers around the periphery of the large circle that contained over 200 people from several Latin American countries, the USA, Canada, and over a hundred traditional Mexican midwives, who had taken buses out of their mountain villages to be at this meeting. It was an auspicious gathering. We were privileged to be in ceremony and enacting rituals together that were thousands of years old, which began by respectfully acknowledging each person's presence, and value, in the circle.

Doña Queta's resoundingly sonorous voice, and her very presence, spoke of dignity, power, and wisdom. I knew I wanted to sit at her feet and learn from her. For several years thereafter I saw her at conferences and attended her workshops, both stateside and in Mexico, and eventually I visited her home in Oaxaca.

In her home Doña Queta's has a large room that is her clinic and apothecary. The first time I saw it I was blown away. The brightly painted indigo walls had colorful shelves, floor to ceiling, and were filled with herbal remedies of all kinds, organized by type. There were salves, soaps, extracts, oils, capsules, leaves, roots, and tinctures. Each medicine had been grown or wild-harvested, prepared, bottled, cataloged, and curated by Doña Queta. During one visit to her home I was privileged to experience a *temascal*, a 2500-year-old ritual sweat bath housed in a small adobe structure with a wood fire, which functions similarly to the sacred Native American sweat lodge ceremony.

During other visits we simply talked. I learned that Doña Queta was the granddaughter of a Zapotec midwife-healer and that she watched her grandmother as she delivered babies and ministered to the people who lived in the isolated ranches and villages. As a child, Enriqueta was interested in what her grandmother did and wanted to learn more, and her mind recorded every detail she observed.

Growing up, Enriqueta was one of the youngest of seven children, and her family was very poor. Resources were scarce on every level and they often did not have enough to eat. Her father died when she was three years old. Her mother worked and did her best to care for seven children, but when Enriqueta was six years old she was "given away" to another family. This family required her to be a goat shepherdess. She was a hungry working child who tended her flock on foot. When she could hardly bear her hunger pains, she began to eat tender leaves, fruits and herbs of the plants that grew on the mountainside. She found that if she would just listen, the plants would speak to her. In this way she began to learn about medicinal and edible plants. Within a few years she became very knowledgeable and people began to seek advice from her about plant remedies that could treat their ailments.

Doña Queta says, "I was born with the gift of healing."[175]

During the time she was a shepherdess, Enriqueta saw her very first birth when one of her goats went into labor and was having difficulty. Enriqueta lovingly attended to the goat mama until the baby was successfully born. When Enriqueta was a teenager she attended her second birth. She was midwife to her sister, also a teenager, who lived on a remote ranch. Word traveled about the remarkable teen that knew the plant medicines and could deliver babies. Before long people were seeking Enriqueta's services. This is how Doña Queta's lifetime work as a midwife-healer began.

Over the years she delivered babies for several generations of women in rural and remote mountain villages. She also became the medicine woman for people who would otherwise have no access to healthcare of any kind. She said, "I knew all those villages like the back of my hand." There were no vehicles. In order to reach a woman in labor or a person ailing with an illness or injury, Doña Queta had to walk on foot carrying her supplies, often walking six to ten hours a day over gnarly and steep mountain terrain.

In 1974 Doña Queta attended formal classes and was trained as a first aid emergency worker for the Mexican Red Cross. In 1990 she was trained as a rural community health worker on behalf of the National Indigenous Institute (NII), which gave her the knowledge, tools, and clientele to conduct public health services. Over her long career she had many other continuing education opportunities.

The story of Doña Queta's career as a community midwife and healer spans six decades. There were numerous twists and turns, some of which were very challenging requiring enormous sacrifices. For many years she worked for the National Indigenous Institute, covering all the villages in the Sierra Juárez, but it was not always easy. Not only was the work physically demanding—and she had her own family of five children to care for—but she also encountered staff physicians who did not respect her work. One doctor maliciously dug up her herbal plants and destroyed her medicines. But Doña Queta persevered. She planted more herbs, made more medicines, and she also spoke to her supervisor. She told him that she extended respect to her colleagues for their work, and because her work was also valuable, she expected respect in return. She told him, "Either my work is respected or I am going to leave the National Indigenous Institute."

Doña Queta then called the regional manager of the NII programs for health and traditional medicine to inform him of the conflict. Because her work was important to the mission of the NII, arrangements were made for her to be transferred to the state headquarters in the capital city of Oaxaca de Juárez. She continued to do fieldwork and her responsibilities expanded. Her reputation as a *cuandera* (medicine woman) grew. First, she became respected and well known in her region, then in the state of Oaxaca, then all over southern Mexico, and finally her reputation transcended national borders. Eventually, she became a sought-after teacher and mentor in her own right, known for her ability to master the energies that heal body, mind, and soul.

Doña Queta advised and guided the creation of the Ethnobotanical Gardens of Oaxaca, Mexico, a unique gem that features the biodiversity of the region and explores the relationship between plants and people by highlighting more than 140 botanical families. University professors from the USA brought students to Oaxaca to study ethnobotany with her in order to discover the medicinal and spiritual uses of plants. Anthropologists came to her to learn Zapotecan cultural norms and perceptions about health and wellness including protective dimensions, and to learn about traditional birthing customs. Student and seasoned midwives took classes from her to learn practical midwifery skills and herbal remedies for pregnancy, childbirth, infancy and childhood ailments.

Doña Queta became a living legend, a multifaceted treasure.

Doña Queta is not only a master healer and herbalist with over sixty years of experience; not only a midwife who delivered over 2000 babies never losing a mother or child; not only the repository of centuries-old Indigenous knowledge; not only an internationally renowned and beloved teacher; she is also a master shape shifter.

All her life Doña Queta walked a fine line. She continued to use traditional Zapotec medicine while at the same time learned and mastered modern public health therapies. In Mexico, as in other countries, there is a clash between the worldviews of Aboriginal and Eurocentric peoples. Doña Queta is a Wisdom

Keeper and Protectoress of cultural traditions and Indigenous medicines that have survived since the sixteenth century despite devastating and unremitting impact of European invaders. Nonetheless, she demonstrates what true 'collaborative practice' in healthcare can look like, when practitioners work in partnership to offer differing models of care, from differing worldviews, for the benefit of their diverse pool of clients and patients.

In our multicultural world, it takes someone who is astute and stealthy to straddle two distinctly different worlds and emerge as a leader who embodies the fine art of creating cultural harmony and nurturing respectful relationships.

Doña Queta is such a person. She has transcended her time and is a living example of what it is like to walk in the world as an emissary of peace, and as one who teaches reverence for all of life. She models respectful behavior and teaches her students the skills of living in harmony with nature and with other human beings.

She says the blood of her ancestors runs in her veins and the compass they gave the Zapotec people guides her through all the seasons. She remembers their teaching…*everything has life and deserves great respect.*

Doña Queta teaches, "*Es imperativo que haya un cambio de conciencia mundial en el cual se dé énfasis al cuidado de los demás, de nuestro medio ambiente, de las plantas, del agua y de todo nuestro universo.*" [176]

"It is imperative that there be a change of world consciousness in which we emphasize the care of others, our environment, the plants, the water, and everything that is our universe."

Doña Queta says we must carry respect with us everywhere we go. Respect for the space that offers us something to eat, the space where we have a conversation, the space where we work, and the space where we live.

She says, "People must raise their consciousness to find their own path, their light, and their hope to live."[177]

At this moment in history, a time of increasing fear, turmoil and acrimony in a world that seems to be self-destructing, it matters that people use their power, passion, influence, and intelligence in service of "a change in world consciousness."

It matters that people evoke respect, reverence and love as they mend and reconnect the web of life.

It matters that there are people who are living archives, and that the knowledge and wisdom they embody is given generously, and abundantly, in order to make the world a better place.

Doña Queta is an inspiring exemplar. When you see her walking through the market, when you watch her conducting a ceremony, when you listen to her speak, you know she acts with the clear understanding of the change of consciousness and the change of heart that is required of each of us.

In Miami, Florida

Sometimes the most valuable thing you can do to change the world is to offer sanctuary to people who need a refuge—a safe place where they feel welcome to talk, and share, and just be.

A sanctuary might look like this: a two-story art deco house in an urban setting converted into a comfy gathering place. One large and luscious mango tree. Two white rockers on the front porch. And a dozen ways to get community support from peers, and then in turn, give that support back to the community.

My friend Tamara Taitt, whom I call Younger Sister because she is the age of my oldest daughter, and her partner Michelle Fonte had a vision. Tamara told me, "Long before we opened, we had an idea for creating a space—just a place to gather—for families, women in particular, because so many people were looking for guidance and friendship on their journey of birthing and parenting children."

After much work, in 2011 they manifested their vision. The Gathering Place in Miami became a community resource center offering professionally led classes, workshops and peer support groups. The Gathering Place was open to all comers, about half were people of color, and each person that crossed the threshold was looking for something. They were people who had been baffled or battered by the system looking for answers; people who did not yet even know what to expect from maternity care and were looking for inspiration. The Gathering Place provided tools that empowered families by giving them information, confidence and camaraderie.

"There is a sense of warmth when people come through our doors," Tamara says, "like you've arrived somewhere you didn't know you were trying to find."

Tamara was born in Barbados, an eastern Caribbean island. Like many children of Caribbean immigrants, her mother came to the US to make a better life for her children by working and sending resources back home to the family. Tamara's grandmother was her primary caretaker from age five to ten. One summer when Tamara was visiting her mother in the US and her grandmother was visiting a friend in New York, Tamara took a trip to Disneyland. During that trip her beloved grandmother unexpectedly died in a massive house fire in Brooklyn. From then on Tamara lived with her mother in the US. For the past 30 years she has gone to school, worked a variety of jobs, and become an entrepreneur. And last year she became a citizen of the USA.

Michelle is Tamara's partner in life and in business. They paint a beautiful picture in contrasts: one is very dark with long black dreadlocks; one is very light with long red hair. One is bold and assertive; one is gentle and soft spoken. But both women are fierce and dedicated to the work they do. Together they have been able to unfold the miraculous flames of creative transformation in Miami because their personal stories led their vision.

Michelle's story is that she is the mother of six children. Her first birth was in the hospital and although she felt confident that she could direct the course it took, she couldn't. She wanted a natural birth but ended up with an epidural, which numbed her from the waist down. She had vaginal cutting for which she was not consulted and did not give her consent. Her recovery from the birth might have been customary except for the intense pain and dysfunction she felt from the episiotomy, which took over a year to heal. Michelle says, "When women's bodies are cut during childbirth, whether it is an episiotomy or a cesarean, the scars are both physical and emotional, and they can take a long time to heal."

Michelle had five more births, some in the hospital and some at home. She became a doula and taught childbirth classes so that other women would be more knowledgeable, feel more confident, and "would not fall under the control of the system as I had done." She has been working for twenty-five years as a childbirth and postpartum doula and educator, yoga instructor, breastfeeding advocate, community organizer, and advocate for childbirth reform.

Tamara's story as an immigrant and a Black woman has led her to understand implicitly the dynamics of those who feel vulnerable. In order to best use her talents in serving humanity, Tamara earned a degree in psychology at Princeton, became a licensed midwife in Florida, earned a master's degree in marriage and family therapy, and pursued a PhD. Tamara has married her two professional sets of expertise, midwifery and family therapy. She zeros in on the vulnerable and marginalized, those who are abused, ignored or neglected, those who need to find their voices, and those who want to feel more powerful. She brings her therapist's mind and her midwife's heart to every encounter.

Tamara has described the experience of 'living Black', a phenomenon in which the cumulative effect of stress results in such things as prematurity, low birth weight, and infant mortality for Black babies, and poor health, increased morbidity, and a higher death rate for Black women. Her concern about perinatal health disparities that disproportionately impact Black women and their families fuels her passion to make a difference. "Even when a Black woman and a white woman have similar socioeconomic protective advantages, such as marriage, health insurance, higher income, and education," Tamara said, "the Black woman still has a much greater chance of a poor pregnancy or birth outcome."

Tamara insists, "Addressing health disparities in infant and maternal mortality is the battleground on which midwifery will be proven to be the gold standard of maternity care."

Tamara and Michelle—who met in 2008 to resurrect the consumer group Florida Friends of Midwives—found fertile ground in Florida for their collaborative work. Their strategy for transformative change was to change cultural norms that are commonly accepted as 'the way it is'.

The city of Miami had one of the highest cesarean section rates in the country. Tamara and Michelle were concerned, actually hopping mad, about this. Cesarean is the most commonly performed surgery in the US, but performed even more commonly in Miami. And once a woman had a primary c-section, there was no place for her to have a vaginal birth after cesarean (VBAC). For about ten years in Miami-Dade County, the number of surgical births and vaginal births for low-risk women were nearly equal.[178] In 2015, Consumer Reports found that Baptist South Miami had a c-section rate of 59 percent, and a smaller facility called Hialeah Hospital had the astounding rate of 64.6 percent.[179]

Consumer Reports found the hospital in which a woman chose to give birth—not her medical risks or her personal preferences—was the most likely indicator of whether she would end up having a surgical birth.[180]

Hospitals with similar populations had very different cesarean section rates (from 7 percent to 64 percent) depending on "the culture of the obstetrical unit and the attitudes of providers."[181] They also found hospitals with a culture that valued and promoted spontaneous physiological labor and birth, vaginal birth, and encouraged vaginal birth after cesarean had lower c-section rates. And hospitals in which midwives were an integrated part of the maternity care culture also had lower c-section rates.

Tamara and Michelle wanted to challenge the medical norms that supported and encouraged the 'standard' way of doing business. But more than that, they wanted to save women's lives and preserve their reproductive rights.

Picture this: You are young, healthy, and pregnant for the first time. Your infant is growing normally and your excitement about being a parent is growing exponentially with each tiny baby kick. You have done everything right—eaten well, exercised regularly, taken your vitamins, gotten prenatal care. You are considered 'low-risk', which comforts you. You go to the hospital nearest your home in Miami to give birth. At this hospital you have a 50% chance of having a surgical birth. High odds. If you do have a cesarean section, you have a greater chance of hemorrhaging or having complications during or after surgery than with a vaginal birth. Your baby has a higher chance of suffering complications, particularly respiratory problems, and being sent to the NICU immediately after the birth. With cesarean surgery, you are also at greater risk of dying of complications. If you are Black, Brown, or Native your chances of complications or death skyrocket. If you do survive, your chances are greater of having a longer and harder postpartum recovery because of having surgery. You feel you have no choice but to roll the dice and take your chances. The sobering odds: one in every two laboring women will have major abdominal surgery at your local hospital. Even if your dice roll is very lucky and you escape surgery, in this environment chances are high you will consent to, or be subjected to, numerous other medical interventions, and so will your baby.

This is a realistic picture, *and it's not personal*. They are not gunning for you, but you may have to dodge a bullet. It's simply the way the system works and how cultural norms and institutional policies are played out within the system. Besides, you have walked into a maternity unit with five high tech operating rooms and a neonatal intensive care unit with thirty beds and expensive equipment. You are surrounded by skilled surgeons and pediatric specialists who were not trained, and do not get paid, to sit on their hands.

However, The Gathering Place, Tamara says, *is personal*. For some women it is a haven where they can go to escape 'business as usual' and learn about alternatives to standard obstetric practices. For some it is a safe harbor where they can process traumatic birth experiences, confusion, disappointment, sorrow, physical and emotional scars, and receive both friendly comfort and professional counseling. Online testimonials virtually shout the indescribable happiness people feel to have discovered The Gathering Place. The online photo gallery leaves no doubt: it is a haven, a safe harbor, a community home.

The Gathering Place is not like a typical maternity care environment in which care is provided in tidy spaces with predictable assembly line procedures. The Gathering Place is like a village, colorful, busy, noisy, peopled. There are couches with bright pillows and throws; birth art is on the wall. There is free coffee, tea and healthy snacks available, toys for kids and baby-changing tables, three-ring binders of community resources, and an active parent network. There is lots of hugging, chatting, crying, laughing, and cuddling.

"Women swap stories, they talk about the maternity care scene in Miami, they nurse babies, they give and receive advice, they learn from one another about parenting, and they make friends," Tamara says.

The Gathering Place is where people can go to become knowledgeable about birth options, take childbirth preparation classes, find midwives and doulas, learn which doctors to choose or avoid, and receive breastfeeding support. It's also a place for nurturing the more nebulous but powerful task of building women's confidence and empowering them to make well-considered choices for their reproductive lives. At The Gathering Place families find the kind of comfort that has been lost in our fast paced, fragmented lives, disconnected from our extended families, but that is desperately needed during major life transitions like pregnancy, childbirth, and early parenting.

Free community workshops and support services are not the only things Tamara and Michelle envisioned. They also conceptualized a birth center, which was intended to be the moneymaking aspect of their business plan. But for several years they battled the City of Miami over regulations and zoning requirements that would keep them from adding a birth center to the building. In the process they depleted their financial resources on rent and expenditures. Yet they were relentless in making their dream a reality. In May 2015 they found a new building, and in February 2016 they opened the doors of Magnolia Birth House, and relocated The Gathering Place within the same building. They finally had everything they envisioned under one roof.

Tamara and Michelle feel strongly that taking birth out of a hospital dominated by medical technology designed to treat sick and injured people, and putting it back into a social environment within the community that is designed for healthy people engaged in a normal function, is a pivotal game changer in transforming cultural norms.

They believe there are four reasons birth centers like Magnolia are so popular. It is an environment that is peaceful, relaxed, and individualized to each person's needs. Midwives and doulas are primary care providers. They have better birth outcomes (for example, 10 percent cesarean rate for US birth centers versus 32 percent nationally for customary hospital care).[182] And cost of care is significantly lower.

Community birth centers are an increasingly popular location for birth. The number of US births in freestanding birth centers grew by more than 75.8% from 2004 to 2014.[183] Birth centers are associated with lower rates of medical intervention, positive outcomes for women and newborns, and higher rates of satisfaction.

The online reviews of Magnolia Birth House are gushing with gratitude, written in superlatives with lots of exclamation points. Some descriptors are: changed my life; amazing service; felt 100% protected; great team of professionals; loving people; gentle care; sincerity; sense of calm; loads of education; peaceful atmosphere; never felt rushed; most beautiful experience ever; dream birth place; cannot praise enough; inspiring; magical; grateful; happy; perfect place to welcome our daughter into the world. And one final comment: "I don't even know where to begin there's so much to say about this jewel of Miami."

There are many more comments but you get the idea; the comments leave no doubt. People are hungry for a childbirth experience that is loving, peaceful, joyful, satisfying, and personal. They are thirsting to be in a place where they feel safe, protected and respected. It matters to people, matters deeply. But our modern 'healthcare culture' does its best to obscure the deep longing for a good experience.

Michelle says, "It confuses people at the level of their gut instincts by making them afraid and convincing them that their only concern should be 'safety,' and the only place they will be safe is in the hospital with medical specialists."

Yet for all its outstanding qualities, a birth center is undisputedly difficult to keep open in any city or small town in the USA. This is because Medicaid, which is the payer of over 40 percent of all US births, is not consistently cooperative in reimbursing birth centers.[184] Neither are other insurers. Nationally, midwives collect only about 40 percent of all birth center reimbursements, which means they give away a lot of care.[185] Legislation and oversight of birth centers varies state-by-state, and regulations can be restrictive for these small owner-operated businesses. As the administrator of Magnolia Birth House, Tamara spends untold hours trying to collect reimbursement for services they have provided and dealing with overly burdensome regulations and paperwork.

And still, Tamara and Michelle, like others who own birth centers across the country, continue to provide care to those who want it.

The key difference between community birth settings and hospital birth settings is the emphasis on woman-directed childbirth.

At the Magnolia Birth House, as in other birth centers, women are in charge. They are encouraged to have support people with them, whomever they choose. They go into labor without any pharmacological augmentation. They are free to move, walk, eat, drink, and find comfort on their own terms. The Magnolia Birth House staff accommodates birth in any position the woman chooses—standing, squatting, hands and knees, on a birth stool, using birth slings, or in a birthing pool. All of these practices are fundamentally different than the standard practices in almost every US hospital, small or large, urban or rural, where hospital policies and medical staff are in charge, not the women.

The Gathering Place and Magnolia Birth House offer services to people who are planning to give birth in any setting—home, birth center or hospital. Tamara and Michelle claim the most critical service they and the other professionals (doulas, childbirth educators, midwives, counselors) offer is *access to information*. They say all women, across the board, lack information on how the complex maternity system really works, and how to get what they want and deserve from the system.

"Women across every spectrum of class, race, ethnicity, and educational level," Michelle says, "are equally underinformed, and equally disempowered."

At Magnolia they teach women how to put themselves—not anybody or anything else—smack-dab in the center of their own experiences. They do this by providing evidence-based information, building confidence, respecting choices, and encouraging women to surround themselves with people who will unfailingly advocate for them to create and achieve a joyful birth on their own terms.

"There is nothing more powerful," Tamara says, "than the overwhelming tidal wave of labor and birth. It tries to lay you low and pull you under. We attempt to paint a realistic picture of childbirth, no sugarcoating. With a few good tools and innate instincts, women can succeed."

"Women are still caring for women," Tamara says, "in the same way we have done for ages. There is something soul-deep and honest about that. And I came to understand that carrying the past into the present, and maintaining those traditions, and roots, and truths, is priceless."

Tamara also notes that our world has long suffered from the toxic dominance of male rule. Everyone suffers, she contends, but particularly women and children. In a recently published book she is quoted as saying, "The whole way that we birth is the biggest misogynist sexist plot ever."[186]

"Males and females alike," says feminist writer, scholar, and cultural critic, bell hooks, "share accountability for our sustained investment in patriarchal domination. It is our destiny as males and females to work together to restore our original state of connection, rooted in inescapable bonds of mutuality and devotion to cultivating human wellbeing."[187]

What does it take to bring a community together? What does it take to empower people? What does it take to change the status quo?

Sometimes all it takes is *a place to gather*. A place with a roomy porch, where we can sit in an old white rocking chair under a mango tree, and do the life-changing work of creating the kind of future we can imagine, together.

In Detroit, Michigan

Other times, what it takes to make the world a better place is to work from the inside out. Transforming existing systems is some of the hardest work of all.

Cathy Collins-Fulea is a nurse-midwife who received her basic nursing and midwifery training in England in the early 1980s. She returned to the USA and opened an in-hospital birth center in Detroit at a time when there were only five certified nurse-midwives (CNMs) practicing in the whole State of Michigan. Ten year later she joined the Henry Ford Health System, a comprehensive, nonprofit, managed-care healthcare organization in Metro Detroit.

Henry Ford, as you remember, was the internationally acclaimed industrialist who changed the world when he popularized assembly line techniques for mass production of automobiles, and also incorporated his techniques in implementing the first assembly-line style maternity care unit in the country. In 1915 Henry Ford founded the Henry Ford Hospital, and in 1992 Henry Ford's descendants and others established the Henry Ford Health System. Today the system boasts twenty hospitals, sixteen emergency departments, forty general medical centers, and seven specialized medical centers. It is one of the largest corporate healthcare systems in the country, run by a board of directors and advisory trustees. Depending on the year revenues range between 3 and 4 billion dollars annually. And the Henry Ford Medical Group is one of the largest group practices of physicians and advanced practice providers in the nation.

It is into this seemingly impenetrable and complex system that Cathy Collins-Fulea strode. Actually, she may have ridden in on her motorcycle. Either way, knowing Cathy, I am sure she made an impressive entrance.

In the 1990s, Cathy and six other CNMs started a new midwifery practice in the Henry Ford Health System. The practice grew into one of the most respected midwifery practices in the state, with twenty-two midwives providing care at two hospitals, and practicing in twelve outpatient centers in Metro Detroit.

The trajectory of Cathy's long career, and her pioneering work in systematically bringing nurse-midwifery into a very physician-dominated health system in an urban area of great need is awe-inspiring. It was a long hard journey to achieve the profound inroads that Cathy and colleagues were able to manifest.

Particularly noteworthy, Cathy authored research on "models of organizational structure of midwifery practices located in institutions with residency programs,"[188] which provided both theory and structure for collaborative care practices among members of maternity care staff in hospitals.

The literature suggests that an interdisciplinary team model that includes midwives, obstetricians, family practice physicians, nurses, nurse practitioners, and anesthesiologists confer benefits to all involved. Collaborative care can improve access to care for women and their infants, improve efficiency, provide greater patient choice, and improve safety and clinical outcomes.[189] For healthcare providers, collaborative care can improve communication and teamwork, inspire mutual respect, improve job satisfaction, and decrease job-related stress.[190]

Cathy and her colleagues had another aspiration—to instill this type of collaborative model into the training of student nurse-midwives and resident physicians. Henry Ford Health System is an academic medical center that offers training for professionals. Cathy and peers found that when resident physicians and student nurse-midwives were trained using an interdisciplinary team model of collaborative care, not only was there an opportunity for interprofessional education, but also a **culture of collaboration** became the accepted standard of care. Cathy and her colleagues were able to observe, document and experience this phenomenon: when midwives and physicians are trained together—which is becoming more popular in Canada, France, the USA, and other places—they learn to work better together. Plain and simple.

Cathy told me, "The resident physicians leave with a clear appreciation that care is best provided in this collaborative model, setting them up to spread the model once they graduate from residency."

Cathy and colleagues were change-makers who pioneered the birth of a collaborative model of maternity care in the USA. They demonstrated how collaborative care offered their patients an expanded set of choices from care providers who possess a diverse set of skills. They demonstrated the high quality value of integrating nurse-midwives into hospital maternity care teams. Collaborative care practice became a success story in Detroit in the Henry Ford Health System—one of the largest corporate healthcare mega-businesses in the country.

The collaborative care model became a win-win situation for everyone—women, infants, families, midwives, physicians, administrators, and those in the process of learning the art and craft of high quality maternity care.

Regardless of the outstanding strides made on collaborative care at the Henry Ford Health System, more work has yet to be done. While Metro Detroit boasts medical systems with highly rated obstetric and neonatal units, infant and maternal mortality among African Americans remain high. The fact that the USA has the highest maternal and infant mortality rates among comparable developed countries is bad enough, but the survival rates of African-American mothers and their infants are even more dismal.[191]

In Detroit, African-American women across the income spectrum and from all walks of life are dying from preventable pregnancy-related complications at three to four times the rate of non-Hispanic white women, while the death rate for Black infants is three times that of infants born to non-Hispanic white mothers.[192]

With a population that is 83 percent African-American, Detroit has a greater proportion of Black people than any big city in America. Hence, the tragic racial and ethnic disparities in maternal and infant mortality that impact Detroit's families and neighborhoods are devastating.

Another band of brave midwives in Metro Detroit—a new generation of midwives—is addressing the issue of Black women and infants dying of preventable causes. They are tackling the problem head on, and they are doing it neighborhood-by-neighborhood. Heather Robinson is one of them.

In 1997, after finishing a tour with the Peace Corps in Honduras, Heather gave birth to her own daughter at home, fell in love with midwifery, and wanted to bring this model of care to her hometown of Detroit. She became a childbirth educator, a doula, a licensed paramedic, and in 2015 she became a Certified Professional Midwife (CPM). Soon thereafter she cofounded Mosaic Midwifery Collective. It is a Detroit-based collaborative by three homebirth midwives (Heather Robinson, Jahmanna Selassie and Cynthia Jackson) committed to training midwives of color.

Heather told me, "We wanted to make culturally congruent midwifery services available to Detroit women, who are primarily people of color."

The midwife collective has provided prenatal care and counseling, homebirth midwifery services, postpartum care, free community-based informational sessions, and hospital doula support for hundreds of women and families in Metro Detroit.

Their social media site says, "We love serving our community as midwives and we are committed to the legacy of Black midwives in our community."[193]

Recently, Heather was part of another awesome innovation: Detroit Pop-up Midwifery Clinic.

The pop-up clinic was cofounded by Heather and two other midwives, Nicole Marie White and Jahmanna Selassie. The midwives were keenly aware that birthing parents and babies did not have the best odds in Detroit, and health disparities disproportionately impacted Black families. They live in the city, work in Detroit communities, and the majority of them are members of the impacted population, which makes their mission incredibly personal.

Their collective vision was to bring education and resources, free of charge, right into Detroit neighborhoods. Their goal was to assist parents and parents-to-be in learning about options for maternity care, becoming proficient in using healthy and protective behaviors during pregnancy, building resiliency for giving birth and caring for newborns, and feeling empowered about decision-making.

The group chose locations for their first pop-up clinics by identifying neighborhoods with the highest infant mortality rates, some with heartbreakingly high rates of up to 24 infant deaths per 1,000 live births. To put that number in perspective, the most recent overall rate for infant mortality in the USA was 5.8 deaths per 1,000 live births.[194]

Detroit Pop-up Midwifery Clinic is not a 'clinic' per se. It does not provide hands-on clinical or diagnostic care. Although the founders of the clinics are midwives who do provide maternity care through established midwifery practices, and some founders offer doula services and childbirth education, the mission of the traveling cohort of midwives is to provide information and suggest resources based on people's identified needs. They share information about a whole host of resources that are available in Detroit about which people may not be aware.

The pop-up clinic midwives believe **knowledge is power**, and when people have knowledge they can make the choices that are best for them.

But the key feature of the Detroit Pop-up Midwifery Clinic is that the midwives are committed to *listening before acting*. They want to know what is missing from people's experiences of pregnancy, birth, and postpartum care that contribute to disparities. They want the community to drive the discussions and suggest the content of programs that the midwives present in each neighborhood.

The midwives believe that when members of the community identify gaps in healthcare services and resources, and define the barriers they have had in accessing high-quality healthcare, including discriminatory treatment and racism, members of the midwife collective can be more effective in providing the support and assistance people need to achieve the healthcare experiences they desire and deserve.

Some people will choose community birth and some people will choose hospital birth. Some people will choose to seek care from midwives and some will choose to seek care from obstetricians. The point is to help people feel more confident and prepared regardless of where, with whom, and in what manner they choose to give birth.

"We talk about choices and knowing your rights," says midwife Nicole White. Her goal is to inform and empower. When people go into the hospital, she wants them to know they have a right to make informed decisions and ask for help when they need it. And they have a right to ask for more time in the processes of laboring and giving birth, rather than being forced to conform to routine obstetrical practices that might not suit their individual needs or circumstances.

Pop-up clinics are becoming 'a thing' in major cities across the country. They are trying to fill the gap in a country where access to healthcare is unequal, where over 33 million people still do not have healthcare insurance, and where due to physician shortages, among other things, many pregnant people cannot get an appointment with a physician until their second trimester of pregnancy.

Detroit Pop-up Midwifery Clinic pops up in different neighborhoods every month.

The work of this innovative, grassroots, community-based approach has drawn the attention of other service-oriented organizations in Metro Detroit. As a result, Detroit Pop-up Midwifery Clinic has expanded its network, increased its invitations to pop-up in neighborhoods and at civic centers, and has received grant monies to continue its work.

The midwives also have plans for creating a freestanding wellness and birth center (not affiliated with a hospital), which would be the first in Metro Detroit.

"It will be a place," says Nicole, "where families can come, be respected, loved, and nurtured with the kind of care that is the spirit of midwives."[195]

When it comes to the ongoing work of the Detroit Pop-up Midwifery Clinic, midwife Jahmanna Selassie says, "We believe the connectivity between community-based midwifery and people in our communities, is what will uplift our communities."[196]

That's what transformational change looks like: building networks of support so that pregnant people and birthing families are uplifted. It is possible—and not that difficult to manifest—when we are committed to treating people with dignity, supporting the choices they make for themselves and their families, and fighting hard so that they not only survive, but also thrive.

As demonstrated in Detroit—when we seek to transform existing systems, sometimes change comes from the inside, sometimes it comes from the outside, but when it works well it always comes from the heart.

In My Own Backyard

Sometimes transformational change can only be grasped in retrospect.

In 1977 I had my first child at home. From a midwife point of view it was a normal pregnancy and an enviably quick first labor and birth. I was attended in this process by a handful of young women who were self-taught midwives. My former husband and I were do-it-yourselfers, so 'do it yourself birth' fit the ethic of our lifestyle. I joined with other self-sufficient women in my community, each of us helping the other to give birth, learning the craft of catching babies empirically.

After a year or so, we found there were pockets of women in several parts of the state who were also acting as birth attendants in their respective urban and rural communities. In 1978 we organized the first meeting of what would become the Michigan Midwives Association (MMA). In 1982 we incorporated as a 501(c)(3) nonprofit organization. A meeting was held in Detroit hosted by Marta Hoetger and Diane Foss, operators of Motor City Midwives, and I was elected to be the first president of the MMA.

From the beginning, we were dedicated to accountability and integrity in our practice of midwifery. Without any mentoring, but with a lot of background in grassroots community organizing around women's health and social justice issues, we designed an apprentice-style, competency-based midwifery training program. We created a midwifery certification process and credential that we called the 'Certified Midwife.' This credential preceded the current national certification called the Certified Professional Midwife or CPM. We implemented a peer review process and a means of gathering statistics on our pregnancy and birth outcomes.

In 1982 I became the first MMA Certified Midwife, or CM, in Michigan, and as such, I was one of the first certified direct-entry midwives in the country. Later we learned that there were other midwifery organizations in various states in the USA that had simultaneously created a similar direct-entry midwifery credential just as we had in Michigan. Curiously enough, most of them were called 'Certified Midwife.' Several years later the national Certified Professional Midwife credential was created and patterned upon those early regional models.

We were, however, keenly aware that we operated 'outside the system.' Most of the time our births were well within the range of normal. But occasionally, when we had to transport a client to the hospital, all hell broke loose. For so many reasons that system of non-collaboration did not work well for anyone—hospital staff, midwives, and most specifically, for mothers and infants who were often treated poorly in the transfer. We knew that being integrated into the healthcare system in a way that would assure our client's safety and emergency care was a preferred model.

Let's skip the long story about the dozens of intervening years—the struggles, the heartaches, the conflicts to get midwifery regulated—and jump into the recent past. The MMA and a citizens' nonprofit called Friends of Michigan Midwives banded together to get a law passed that would license and regulate direct-entry midwives in Michigan. We hired a savvy, scrappy, small-but-mighty lobbyist and we found a legislator to champion our cause. We became very familiar with ICM's Global Standards for Midwifery Education, Regulation, and Association. The process was grueling and took nearly a decade to complete.

But miraculously, on January 3, 2017—after years of hard fought advocacy by midwives, parents and other stakeholder partners—the governor signed into law a bill to license Certified Professional Midwives in the State of Michigan.

In what felt like a dream, or most certainly an act of coming full circle, I was appointed by the governor to the first Michigan Board of Licensed Midwifery. By this time I was already a licensed Certified Nurse-Midwife, and I had practiced in hospitals, birth centers, and homes. It was the responsibility of our twelve-member midwifery board (two consumers, seven CPMs, one CNM, one OB/GYN, one pediatrician) to promulgate rules for the practice of community midwifery (out-of-hospital) in the State of Michigan.

And very recently, on August 1, 2019, on my grandbaby Margaret's second birthday, I got the best gift besides her. The state issued the very first midwifery licenses to CPMs in Michigan.

In retrospect, it took nearly forty years from conception to fruition—nearly my entire midwifery career—for women in my state to have access to a full range of choices in childbirth by trained, skillful, licensed midwives in every setting.

It took developing business and negotiation skills to overcome regulatory barriers and advocate for legislative solutions. It took strategic planning and implementation to get legalization and professional recognition for midwives who work in community settings.

It took holding an unwaveringly vision for equity, informed choice, safety, and seamless access to high quality midwifery care as the right of every birthing family.

But sometimes that is the way change happens … slowly, steadily, over time, but inevitably.

10,000 More Stories

Midwives are engaged human beings. Some strive to preserve our ancient lifeways and ethics, some create the conditions for new and imaginative solutions to emerge. In hard times, they choose not to flee, but rather, to step up. Midwives hold the space, generate the energy, and exert heroic effort to make amazing things happen. I know midwives all over the country, all around the world, and the stories of midwives-as-changemakers are endless.

Sometimes change happens slowly. Sometimes change comes from the inside out and sometimes from the outside in. Sometimes change affects an entire community. Sometimes change is seeded in worse-case scenarios. Sometimes change grows exponentially until it reaches critical mass. Sometimes change goes global.

My journals are filled with stories upon stories. Over the past forty-four years I have gathered thousands of tales that describe how midwives are changing the world.

Empowerment and equity—these are the radical energies that are at the center of the revolution. These are the themes that rise to the surface, over and over. This is the song we hear sung repeatedly by the people who are changing the world, like midwives and the birthing people they serve.

And *community*—this is ground zero, the axis of heart and soul by which people are inspired to change the world. Community is at the center of the universal drumbeat, sonorous and unending, affirming that we are not alone, we need one another, and we are all in this together.

Community is the eternal rhythm that pounds in our ears, forever reminding us: *Me in you, you in me. What happens to you happens to me. None of us is free until all of us are free. Me in you, you in me.*

Tipping Point

The tipping point is that magic moment when an idea, vision, or social behavior crosses a threshold, tips, and spreads like a wildfire.

In so many ways, we are almost tipping. The world—individuals, corporations, governments, international agencies—are beginning to grasp why midwives matter, and why the 12 essential qualities embedded in The Midwife Matrix matter.

We are at the threshold of reclaiming our bodies, our births and our lives.

Then You Win

As someone who has lived a life of advocacy for social justice, I have always loved a particular saying by Mahatma Gandhi. He led a successful nonviolent campaign for India's independence from British Rule. And in turn his campaign inspired movements for civil rights and freedom across the world.

Gandhi's predicted trajectory was this. "First they ignore you, then they laugh at you, then they fight you, then you win."

PART THREE

wild wisdom

wild is something you cannot tame

I had the great good fortune, in 2011, to take a journey to the Motherland.
I traveled to the furthest tip, to South Africa, for an international midwifery summit and remained in the country for a month. Before I left my place on the planet in Maple City, Michigan, my writing mentor Max Regan advised me, "When you journey to a new place don't think too much about what you are writing. Just write. You can sort it all out when you return home."

Six months after returning I finally had time to reread my journal, sort out my thoughts, review hundreds of photos, and create a booklet of visual images and written narratives. Almost ten years later, however, I am still contemplating what I experienced and learned on that journey.

The gathering of the midwife clans from all parts of the world for the triennial meeting of the International Confederation of Midwives (ICM) is a sight to behold. They stream in, midwives from north, south, east and west, with all the clamorous clatter of sailing vessels arriving at a swarming central seaport. In a wild frenzy they disembark from seven continents—Africa, Antarctica, Asia, Australia, Europe, North America, and South America.

Everywhere there are flashes of colorful native attire—kimonos, caftans, saris, dirndls, temple dresses, kiras, skirts, huipils, embroidered bodices, and sarongs. For the opening ceremony, people adorn themselves with unique headdresses, turbans, hats, belts, beadwork, jewelry, scarves, shawls, feathers, footwear, and carry all manner of accoutrements. Hair appears in unending variations, chic or casual, coiffed or windblown. Black hair braided and beaded. Blonde hair twisted and pinned. Red hair curly and flowing. Gray hair short and spiky. Pink and purple hair, bristly and balding hair, twisted and tangled hair.

And there is an unceasing buzz of hundreds of languages; a bedlam of sound, and shrieks, and laughter.

There is excitement in the air, and anticipation, and intention. We are drawn to an international gathering of like-minded people, as instinctively as honeybees to the queen's hive. We have traveled long distances, some of us at great sacrifice, for a unified reason: we devote our lives to the caretaking of mothers and infants, and to the health and wellbeing of families and communities across the globe. There are as many unique expressions of this caretaking as there are people present. But we all have one thing in common: in this lifetime we walk in the shoes of a midwife. That knowledge inspires us to greet each person we meet as a relative: sister, brother, auntie, grandmother, cousin.

We are drawn into the huge auditorium by the beat of a drum and the rise of a song so joyful we cannot resist moving our hips and swaying our bodies. The singing explodes into the vast open space of the auditorium, wraps its arms around us, seeps into our bodies, and lifts our travel-weary spirits. And then the pageant begins. South African children process up the long aisle from the back of an enormous auditorium and onto the stage. They each carry a flag from one of the countries whose midwives are present at the gathering.

We hear a booming disembodied voice over the sound system, as each flag bearer is individually welcomed to the stage. The voice proclaims, "Please welcome the midwives from Argentina… Australia… Austria." Loud applause and cheering accompanies the announcement of each country, and midwives jump out of their seats and cheer even louder when their own country is named.

"We are pleased to welcome the midwives from Ecuador… Estonia… Ethiopia." More cheering erupts accompanied by frenzied waving of flags and banners and scarves. We feel a deep down stirring in our souls when someone knows our name, calls it out loud, and formally welcomes us and our kin into the circle. It is electric.

"Let's hear it for the midwives from Iceland… India… Indonesia… Iran… Ireland… Israel… Italy." On and on it goes, the energy keeps building, from A to Z the names of more than one hundred countries are called out, from Afghanistan to Zimbabwe. And we are all welcomed.

As the flag-bearing and flag-waving assemblage of children converge onstage, we study their faces, beautiful, proud and jubilant. We take in the visual tapestry of colors, as the flags swirl and blend together creating a rainbow sea. There are waves of energy in the entire cavernous room, they are rolling and swelling, and I know I am not the only one moved to tears. This thing that make us cry is the feeling that lets us know who we are at our core. In this moment—a rare and blessed moment—we are diverse nations, diverse peoples united; one mind, one heart, one humanity.

The memory of that moment still lives in my bones—children laughing, adults clapping and shouting, praising and weeping, drums beating, heartbeats pounding, colors undulating, voices ululating. And when the South African choir broke into song, and danced with pounding feet that created an unending rhythm that resonated viscerally, the cacophony nearly blew the roof off. The room literally pulsed with a boisterous, exuberant, chaotic, sensual, thunderous, celebratory, uninhibited, multisensory ode to joy!

Wild is something you cannot tame.

Four thousand midwives were in that auditorium, one-third were African midwives, along with many others—scholars, heads of state, public health experts, healthcare practitioners, global policy makers, leaders of international agencies, and maternal and child advocates from all corners of the world. We had gathered in Durban, formerly called Port Natal, a major seaport in eastern South Africa, located on the coast of the Indian Ocean.

Some say that Durban Bay is shaped like a womb and the neck of it points to the open sea. It seemed more than coincidence that here at the bottom of the Mother Continent we would be nestled in the womb, rocked by the ebb and flow of the sea tide, advocating for women and children.

Necessity drew us together; intention united us. We made history in Durban.

We were the first audience to hear findings from The State of the World's Midwifery Report: Delivering Health, Saving Lives. This seminal report by the United Nations, ICM, and other global partners was a year in the making, and provided vital information on the evidence of need, evidence of what works, and the tools needed to tackle maternal mortality. It was the first comprehensive blueprint for governments and policymakers committed to addressing key deficiencies in healthcare provision to childbearing women and babies. It placed the strategy of midwifery at the top of the list. We were also present at the unveiling of the new, first-ever global standards for the education and regulation of skilled midwives and updated competencies for midwifery practice, which provided a practical framework for actualizing midwifery services in every country and region of the world.

There were hundreds of scientific workshops, networking meetings, and coalition-building activities. Durban was the first place I presented my theory of the 12 essential midwifery qualities—not yet called The Midwife Matrix—to an international audience, on the summer solstice (winter solstice in Africa), my birthday, with my very own mother in attendance.

The scope of the meetings is impossible to describe, all the collaborations impossible to track, but the impact of what got rolled out in Durban still reverberates all across the planet. The stakes were high. Africa was home to 18 of the top 20 countries with the highest rates of maternal mortality in the world. We were there to affect a change.

Let's just say it was multidimensional, like birth is, indescribably multisensory and mysterious. When a woman is in labor her whole body is on fire, soaked in life-giving waters, subsumed in the ethers, consumed by the mystery. But she is not merely her bodily functions, her blood pressure, her temperature, her contractions, and the data that our tools register about her. She is also humming with the stories or her life, her history, her dreams, her fears, her unique way of perceiving the world, what is happening in her family, what is happening in her life, comingled with what is happening the moment her baby enters the world.

Likewise, Africa was more than its devastating mother-baby statistics, more than its stunning geography and cultural diversity, more than its fierce cadre of midwife warriors. Africa was the true Motherland, the seat of creation of the human race, rich with stories and history that connected the races of the Four Directions together—black, yellow, red, and white. Africa was the place where every single one of our ancestors began, the place from which the entirety of the human family tree could be traced. The invisible silver thread of common DNA, both physical and psychic, wrapped itself around and within each of us, infusing us with the knowledge that whatever affected one part of the fabric of human life affected every other part. It could not be otherwise.

What happened in Durban is a story whose complexity and magnitude is hard to convey. It was the emergence of something new, and significant, and unique. There was a consensus of people from every continent on Earth that the toxic effects of patriarchal rule, to which we have been subjected for thousands of years all across the planet, had generated untold suffering for women and infants, and for men and other living beings, too.

There was a consensus that we must shift our consciousness from the fear and greed that patriarchal systems perpetuate to a matriarchal worldview. This shift would be inclusive, relational, nurturing, and built on shared power and shared resources. It would be cocreated from the best of feminine and masculine energies working in partnership to cocreate systems that are beneficial for all of humanity.

It was in South Africa that many of us came to understand *ubuntu*, a concept of the Nguni Bantu. Translated from the Zulu language *ubuntu* means, *I am, because we are*. It is a concept that speaks to our common humanity and oneness. Learning about *ubuntu*, and seeing it in action, helped us grasp more deeply the sentiment I had learned many years earlier, *you in me, and me in you*. It encouraged us to genuinely feel the interconnected web of life more profoundly.

In South Africa we demonstrated what cellular biologists and evolutionary scientists have been asserting for a long time: humans did not evolve through survival of the fittest modalities. Humanity's best survival strategies have been, and will continue to be, unity and mutuality.

There was wildness in the air, fueled by continual singing and dancing, but also by boundless imagination. Palpable untamed passion to make the world better and more humane infused every place we met. A thousand ideas were rolled out for how to manifest new maternal and child structures and innovations, new ways of engaging healthcare workers, new frameworks for designing MCH policies.

The atmosphere crackled with fertile energy. In a sense it was a creation story—a story about something that was born on the same continent that is the birthplace of *homo sapiens*.

In my journal, June 23, 2011, I wrote: "To be addressing the health of women everywhere while meeting in the Motherland, and to be seeking solutions to some of the most devastating problems facing women and their children using the global community of midwives as anchors, and our professional partners as helpmates, is an opportunity of extraordinary potency and vitality."

The meetings in Durban caused an evolutionary momentum urging us to rise to the next level of human potential. And the beauty was, we were not asked to do this alone. All around us were people willing to collaborate in transformational change. Each understood they had whatever was theirs to do, in whatever manner their body, mind and heart was able to do it. And we understood that we needed every single creative expression of intelligence and compassion to get the work done.

For those ten days—in ICM Governing Council meeting, ICM Congress scientific sessions, and all the other collaborative meetings—we moved as one force, a collective field of energy and strength. For ten days it was a synergy way bigger than the sum of its parts. It changed our lives, and in the future, it would change the lives of those we influenced.

Transformational change was unleashed…flaming, breathing, pulsating, roaring…simultaneously reaching inward and unfolding outward, a flow of energy seeping into every corner of the world.

Wild is something you cannot tame.

Those ten days were both exhilarating and exhausting. Afterward, my friend and midwife colleague Diane Holzer and I traveled to a place in KwaZulu-Natal, to a bushcamp operated as a tourism business that was environmentally friendly, designed for long term preservation of wildlife ecosystems. It was low-key and basic. In my journal I wrote, "It is very rural here in the Bushlands, very quiet, and very much removed from the hubbub of the last ten days in Durban. The room is sparse, the lighting is poor, the furnishings are bare, and the space is draughty, yet I am totally satisfied."

When you travel halfway across the world you must explore the region. As Fate would have it, three Dutch midwives were at the same camp. We lived and traveled together for a week, and Diane and I have had post-trip communication with two of the midwives, Suze Jans and Mieke Beentjes.

We had the opportunity to hear firsthand accounts from aboriginal people as well as Afrikaners about the experience of apartheid. Earlier, we had visited the prison in which Nelson Mandela had been kept captive for over twenty-five years before he was freed and elected South Africa's first Black president. The stories were sobering, appalling, humbling and inspiring, and provided a deeper understanding of South Africa's recent history.

The bushcamp provided us with an amazing safari guide, a young Zulu woman named Noxolo (*note-zo-lo*) whose nickname was Pinky. At 6 A.M. on our first morning, Noxolo had her jeep loaded and ready to go, complete with two coolers of food and blankets for us because it was miserably cold.

The thing about Africa is the immensity of it—its size, its history, its place in human evolution, its rich cultures, its cultural wars, its social and political problems and solutions, its beauty, and its diversity. It is huge. Africa, in all her aspects, is huge.

I wrote, "We drove in an open-air jeep across the African savannah and bushlands in search of wild animals. The uninterrupted landscape extended as far as the eye could see. It was open land with no encumbrances: no houses, buildings, lights, telephone wires, signage, electrical poles, satellite towers, or billboards. It was wide-open vast tracks of earth, and the experience of being in this immense undomesticated and untamed space was exhilarating. It touched a very primal place inside of me. It felt intoxicating."

Noxolo expertly led us through the game reserves along dirt roads that wound over 100,000 hectares of rolling land. The landscape was a kaleidoscope of patterns and colors. We saw the most gorgeous and intriguing assortment of wild animals.

Being 'in the company of wild things' is indescribably spectacular. We saw several antelope species, kudu, nyala, and impala. We saw thousands of wildebeests who are really impressive animals and whose tails are used as a sacred talisman by some medicine men and women of South Africa. We saw lots of warthogs, which were pretty funny looking.

We saw several family groups of giraffes, females and children, and some solitary males. We saw lots of vultures, their wingspans seemed 8-10 feet long, rather scary. Diane said they were as big as me. We saw scores of lovely smaller birds including zebra birds, bee eaters, crest-headed guinea hens, and numerous beautifully colored ones we could not name. The zebras were probably my favorite, so gorgeously striped, each pattern unique. I took a photo of an elegant pregnant zebra, which when I got home, I turned into a greeting card.

Many different times we saw the majestic Cape buffalo, and one time they covered an entire hillside. The way their horns curl is so gorgeous, their heads are massive, and they have beautiful regal faces. We saw one mongoose, a few monkeys, and a family of baboons. We saw one elephant, and though we were hoping to see a herd (there are about 500 elephants in the reserve), we were really grateful we saw this one. He was the last big animal we were searching to see.

I wrote in my journal, "The biggest gift of the day—amidst all the bounty and visual splendor—was when we rounded a turn and were surprised to see two cheetahs crossing the road right in front of us. Pinky said, 'Quick, quick, quick,' (meaning, get your photos), 'because they will be gone in a minute.' Not only are cheetahs shy and notoriously difficult to spot, but also there are only 40 of them in the entire Game Reserve of thousands and thousands of miles, less than 1,000 in the entire continent of Africa. And we saw two! The pair of young males was so exquisitely handsome, and within about ten seconds they crossed in front us, looked at us once, and disappeared into the bush. It was a rare and fortunate gift that moved several of us to tears."

There is no way to adequately describe what it is like to drive among herds of wild animals, many of them very large, some of them very dangerous and scary, and all of them breathtakingly beautiful. The entire experience was splendid beyond belief, a once in a lifetime affair.

In reality, it was much more than splendid. It was an experience that not many of us will have because there are so few places in the world where this mixture of wildness exists on the scale in which it exists in Africa. The variety and diversity of species that thrives in Africa is unique.

There is something about being in nature and among wild animals that makes you contemplate the natural order of things and the diversity that exists within it. For example, consider the family structure of various animals. While crocodiles are solitary and seem not to like the company of other crocodiles, hippos live in extended family pods and sleep all squished up next to one another for warmth. They put the smallest and youngest in the center of the sleeping pile. Many of the various kinds of antelope live in herds of females, children, and one male who spends much of his time breeding with the females and keeping other robust males away from 'his' herd. This is the same for the Cape buffalos, wildebeests, zebras, and rhinos. But two types of small antelope, the bushbuck and deerbuck, mate one-on-one with a single partner, often for life.

And one more thing. On the continent of Africa is a phenomenon that exists nowhere else on earth. Each year close to two million wildebeest, zebra, and antelope such as impala, eland, and gazelle gather up their young and start the long trek north from Tanzania's Serengeti to the Massai Mara in southwestern Kenya, following the rains, in pursuit of food and water. In terms of scale and size, it is the largest migration of wildlife on Earth.

The final entry in my journal said, "There is something that happens to your mind when your eyes become unhinged from looking at things closely, say, a computer screen or your dinner plate. When you look across vast expanses of land, day after day as we have been doing, there is a magical opening in the world. You can see the intersections and union of life more clearly. These past days of being on safari have been the best. Days of deep and rich meditation, a soulful journey into the heart of life, a discovery of one's place in the family of things."

Life on our planet is so precious, and the wild places so breathtakingly wondrous, my body aches to know that species and habitat are being annihilated at an alarming rate. The preservation movement is heartening, but the effort to tame and destroy is relentless. When that occurs, everyone, everything, loses.

Wild is something you cannot tame.

Places that are wild do not only exist outside of us; they also exist inside us.

Every night, in our dreams, we experience wild adventures. It never ceases to amaze me that every morning my husband Fred, who dreams prolifically, always prefaces his waking comments with, "I had the wildest dreams." And I always respond, "Are there any other kind?"

Our imaginations take us to wild places. Our bodies take us to wild places. Our loving one another takes us to wild places.

And birth is one of the last wild frontiers.

Birth: in its infinitely diverse expressions of individuality and creativity; in its unpredictably mysterious ways of opening and exposing us to something much bigger than ourselves; in its powerful insistence that we ride the waves of natural rhythms until we are utterly transformed and left breathless and speechless; birth has a wild power unlike anything else we ever experience.

Why, then, would we want to tame it?

It is a harsh story. Birth was taken from women, by men, for four reasons. *We did it too loud. We did it too wild. We did it together. We did it without them.*

Code words: Loud = *passionate.* Wild = *unpredictable.* Together = *woman-centered.* Without them = *on our own terms.*

Yet true as it is, it is only one side of the story. If women's reproductive lives were the dramas that drew us together each revolution of the moon, pulled us into the Red Tent, why did women *give up ownership* of their bodies, their births, and their initiatory and ritual spaces?

The reasons are numerous; we have explored them in this book. We made some regrettable mistakes, but ultimately, we were overpowered by intersecting socioeconomic constructs more powerful than our ability to resist.

As feminists, we said it before and we'll say it again: *the personal is political.* There is a connection between our personal experiences and the larger social and political power structures in which we live. Our personal lives cannot be addressed separately from the social and political constructs that exert power and control over us.

And the fact is, powerful forces of ordained social and political structures have been trying to tame the wildness in women for more than two thousand years.

colonizing women's bodies

The act of colonization is strategic. Whether it's colonizing cultures or colonizing women's bodies, the key to success is in time-proven formulas.

*Catch them unaware. Take them by force. Strong-arm them into submission.
Strip them of all that is familiar. Sedate them with substances. Punish, humiliate,
and disempower them. Threaten and use violence. Keep them in fear. Ban freedom
of choice. Make them dependent. Instill belief in inferiority. And ultimately, take
possession of and exert control over resources, knowledge, and systems.*

Essentially, that's how it works. Historical accounts and contemporary
cultural narratives all highlight some iteration of 'the colonization formula.'

The colonization of women's bodies in the USA has been historically successful, primarily because of the success of four interrelated, mutually supporting
social constructs: patriarchy, capitalism, racism, and white supremacy.

Patriarchy is social, political and economic power in the hands of men. *Capitalism*
is the pursuit of profits for private individuals or corporations, through selling goods
and services, often with little or poor regulation. *Racism* is the race-based belief
and practice of grouping humans into distinct groups, ranking them as inferior or
superior, producing prejudice, stereotyping, discrimination, and other injustices.
And *white supremacy*, in this context, has determined the laws and moral apparatus
to enforce "which women possessed wombs that represented profit for whites and
which women had the right to be mothers of the children they bore."[197]

Of course, there are other factors, but these four are at the forefront of
colonizing women's bodies. The antidote is reproductive justice.

Reproductive justice is a model to address "multiple, simultaneous vectors
of oppression,"[198] particularly for the most marginalized and vulnerable people,

and it marries human rights and reproductive rights. Reproductive justice aims to transform inequities so that "all people have the social, political, and economic power and resources to make healthy decisions" about their "gender, bodies, sexuality, and families."[199] This includes the right to have children, to not have children, to parent one's children, and to control one's birthing options.[200]

Another definition, articulated by Forward Together (Asian Communities for Reproductive Justice) states, "Reproductive justice is the complete physical, mental, spiritual, political, economic, and social wellbeing of women and girls, and will be achieved when women and girls have the economic, social and political power and resources to make healthy decisions about our bodies, sexuality, and reproduction for ourselves, our families, and our communities in all areas of our lives."

Multiple frameworks for reproductive justice have emerged to describe interlocking oppressions and ways in which women and girls have been dominated (colonized) and historically oppressed through unjust systems of power. In addition, Forward Together and others state that a queer analysis, which thinks beyond the womb and includes trans and intersex people, is also central to the principles and practices of reproductive justice for the liberation of all people.

A new generation of reproductive and birth activists—midwives, doulas, parents, and partners—is engaged in extending the conversation beyond the limits of most reproductive justice discourse. They challenge each of us to think in new ways about justice, autonomy and the act of colonization.

These activists are examining the intersections of race, class, sovereignty, and gender related to reproductive health. They are examining ways in which Black, Brown, Indigenous, and LGBTQI peoples, substance-using mothers, immigrants, people facing linguistic or cultural barriers, people with disabilities, and individuals and communities that experience the most threats are subjected to mistreatment and abuse within healthcare systems.

They are examining and documenting experiences of violence and discrimination in medical encounters during preconception, pregnancy, labor, childbirth, postpartum, and parenting. They are conducting collaborative inquiry and research, and teaching about civic and political engagement related to reproductive justice. They are articulating theories, practices, and principles around sexual and reproductive rights and gender politics.

In essence, they are disrupting the status quo in brave, bold and decisive ways.

Decolonize Birth Conference was created by Chanel L. Porchia-Albert of Ancient Song Doula Services, a health organization focused on birth and reproductive justice in New York. Chanel organized the first Decolonize Birth

Conference after attending various conferences within the birth and reproductive health arena. She realized that the voices of many marginalized groups were being left out of the conversation, or their views and opinions were overlooked regarding the work they did within their respective communities.

Numerous other reproductive justice organizations and individuals—mostly Black, Brown, Indigenous and queer—have joined forces to provide ongoing support for a Decolonize Birth Collaborative, and to draw more attention to birth justice for people of color.

Decolonize Birth website states, "We are facing racial and gender injustices, communities being pitted against one another, and an attack on the sheer autonomy over our bodies."[201] As of 2019, the Decolonize Birth Conference was in its fourth year, and at their 2019 conference they made action plans to address these issues.

I recommend that readers visit the websites of Ancient Song Doula Services[202] and Decolonize Birth Conference[203] where you will find stories about priority areas in education and advocacy, learn who their partners and allies are, and see reports about the amazing work being done by community-based doulas, midwives and educators to end racial disparities. I was particularly impressed with the report, Advancing Birth Justice: Community-Based Doula Models as a Standard of Care for Ending Racial Disparities.[204]

I also recommend the book *Reproductive Justice* (2017) as an excellent and comprehensive primer that elucidates an intersectional analysis of race, class, and gender politics.

Midwives and doulas are always named as key strategies in efforts to 'decolonize birth.'

This is because a foundational piece of midwifery training and practice is respecting choices people make and supporting people to realize the goals they have for their pregnancies and births. Likewise, doulas have been documented to be especially beneficial for women of color and for low-income and underserved communities. Their continual presence can reduce disparities by ensuring that pregnant people who face the greatest risks have the added support they need during and after pregnancy and birth.[205]

But it goes well beyond birth. Decolonization is the process by which an individual or group rejects the definition of itself as marginal in relationship to a conceptual norm that has been forced upon them from the outside.

Audre Lorde, writer and civil rights activist, described the mythical norm in the Western world as "white, thin, male, young, heterosexual, Christian, and financially secure." Lorde asserted that it is within this mythical norm that "the trappings of power for this society reside."[206] And finally Lorde cautions, "The master's tools will never dismantle the master's house."

Therefore, we must reframe maternal and child health in ways that are conducive to reproductive justice principles and practices.

And in this reframing, strategies have to shift from what is currently the status quo. The voices of the most impacted people must be privileged. They must be at every table where decisions that impact them are being made. They must be considered the experts in determining what their needs are. And they must be honored as the leaders and innovators in this movement. Those who identify as white or who have privileged status and influence within societies must learn to be respectful and effective allies and advocates for impacted people and communities, and be willing to follow their lead.

Birth decolonizers are leading the charge in reframing conversations, disrupting norms, taking power back, and inspiring people to reclaim control of their bodies, their births, and their lives.

These activists are challenging each of us to see things through a different lens, and adopt a new worldview that is diametrically opposed to the status quo. It involves taking risks. It involves taking direct action. And it involves standing up to those that abuse power. Fortunately, we have partners and allies all across the globe doing just that.

We have discussed two movements that seek to marry health equity with reproductive justice. Both the 'humanization of birth movement' in Latin America and the 'decolonize birth movement' in North America share common goals. Each movement seeks to: dismantle old forms of unjust, disrespectful, and inequitable systems; restructure new ways of providing and receiving healthcare so that the common resources of societies are shared equitably; and advocate for those who are suffering most from abuses of power and reproductive injustices.

In addition, professional health organizations and advocacy groups from around the world have joined forces to develop global initiatives to provide guidance and support for safe and respectful maternity and newborn care.

One global collective is the International Childbirth Initiative (ICI). The ICI provides a clear and unifying template for optimal care around which all relevant organizations can rally to promote quality maternity care in a comprehensive manner. Based on the most recent evidence and insights into what constitutes optimal maternal and newborn health, the ICI's 12 Steps to Safe and Respectful MotherBaby-Family Care provides a blueprint for implementing evidence-based maternity care worldwide.[207] At its core, the International Childbirth Initiative promotes compassion and dignity in care provision; access to affordable care; and adoption of midwifery and family centered maternity care guidelines.[208]

The fact that international guidelines exist attests to the magnitude of reproductive injustices that are currently being documented. Worldwide and in our own country, the rights of women, girls, and people with wombs are compromised and violated during pregnancy, childbirth, and the postpartum period. It's factual. It's documented. It's a problem.

It is not happening to just a few of us; it is happening to thousands and thousands of us, particularly our most marginalized and vulnerable people.

Not only do we have an urgent need to fix what is not working, but we also have a consensus on at least one outstanding solution to do it.

wild wisdom

And that brings us full circle, back to the beginning.

Midwifery is not simply 'an alternative way to approach childbirth.' **The midwifery model of care is *the radical pathway* we must take to achieve a better, more humane way of taking care of our mothers, babies and families.**

The Midwife Matrix is a vision of untarnished hope married with elegantly simple, evidence-based, and compassionately charged practices.

The Midwife Matrix is a simple, cost-effective model that can be applied to maternity and other healthcare systems, but also to other areas of human need.

The Midwife Matrix is a call to action to bring our finest human qualities and our best selves to the task of transcending and triumphing over the profound challenges we humans have created. It's a doable, sustainable code of behavior for actually making change and making a difference.

Whether you are a healthcare worker, chair of a coalition, businessperson, hospital administrator, volunteer, social reformer, philanthropist, parent, or person who cares about childbirth in America or simply in your own town, you can use the practices and principles of The Midwife Matrix to advance your cause.

The Road Back to Ourselves

A story is silent until the word is spoken. But when stories come alive, we can see, sense, live, learn, connect. With stories we can make sense of our world and our place within it. When it comes time for me to rest from my lifelong work, to finally step aside from midwifery and return to my life as an artist, a writer, a gardener, a sailor, and a grandmother, I hope that my story, and the small part I have played as a midwife, has paved a pathway that others can continue walking.

Because the truth is, the long road back to ourselves will take all the dedication we can muster.

Just as restoration ecologists are working to restore old-growth forests one chestnut, cedar, and hemlock at a time…

Just as Indigenous peoples are working to restore old-growth cultures one ceremony, language, and teaching at a time…

Just as midwives are working to restore old-growth midwifery one birth, one birth center, and one midwifery licensing law at a time…

…We the people will restore old-growth childbirth practices one woman, one baby, one family at a time. We will remember, and we will reclaim the birthright that is ours.

Of the unending possibilities of what it will look like, here is one image.

The night is dark and the wind is howling. The moon is hidden behind snow clouds, but the lights are on in the small neighborhood house that has become the community birth center.

In the birth room six candles are burning with a golden light, one for each of the birthing woman's grandmothers and great-grandmothers who she says "will guide me." She is deep in labor. She flails and howls with the wind, trying to get comfortable. Her own parents stand anxiously at the edge of the room, waiting and watching. They have never seen a natural birth. Two of the laboring woman's girlfriends kneel at the foot of the bed holding hands, softly murmuring reassurances to her.

The young woman does not notice them now. She is rocking her body rhythmically with each contraction, moaning her birth song, falling into a sleepy trance in between contractions. She is in transition. Her partner sits very close, whispering quiet words to her, holding their three-year-old daughter who is clutching her teddy bear.

My midwife partner and I are preparing for the birth, moving silently in tandem, gracefully and efficiently. When all is in order I sit down near the bed, reach into my handwoven basket, pull out the softspun green and lavender yarn, and continue knitting a baby hat.

The room is charged with the energy of life and anticipation. Abruptly the young woman snaps out of her trance, calls for me, and I go to her. She grabs my hand and says, "Here comes another one."

She squeezes my hand so hard that my rings cut into my fingers. When our eyes meet, she gives me the frightened look of a wild animal caught in a trap. But I simply stroke her and say, "You can do this," and I breathe with her and then she begins to find her own rhythm again. As the surge of energy dwindles, she closes her eyes, bows her head, and retreats into her own private world of sensation, and journeying, and mystery.

When the next contraction pulls her out of her deep trance, she struggles to ride the wave. She sways her hips from side to side, she moans, she bellows, she squirms. When the contraction subsides, she rests her whole body against her partner. She relaxes for a moment.

Then suddenly her eyes fly wide open, she is very still, and with a tremulous voice she says, "I have to push." I say, "Wonderful . . . push your baby out."

She no longer needs my eyes to reassure her. She no longer needs to hold anyone's hand. Instinctively, she squats at the side of her bed and pushes, gently at first, then more rhythmically, and finally with a burst of energy like an athlete in the last few strides of a marathon.

The baby descends quickly and then crowns, its head emerges and rotates into my waiting hands, that exquisite moment of half in and half out. Time stops for everyone in the room. Perhaps time stops in the entire universe to make room for one more soul.

We wait for the final contraction. Everyone is crowded around now, breathless, completely enraptured by being in the presence of this ordinary miracle. The three-year-old takes her thumb out of her mouth and says, "Is that my baby sister coming out?" Everybody laughs.

I say to the mother, "Reach down and touch your baby." When she touches the top of the wet slippery head an extraordinary calmness washes over her. She smiles, at peace. She knows the long dark night is nearly gliding into dawn.

I say, "With the next contraction your baby will be born. Push gently." And she does. She pushes confidently and with the power of a rushing river in springtime.

As the baby eases out, so does the rest of the amniotic fluid that always feels like a baptism to me. I whisper to the baby, "Welcome, little one." And in that holy moment the mother reaches down and lifts her baby to rest against her naked chest, heart to heart.

Then she throws her head back and in an ecstatic litany she cries, "Oh my God, oh my baby, oh my God!" And then, "It's a girl!"

The new big sister is clamoring for a better view. The new grandparents are sobbing. The girlfriends are kissing the new mama's feet and burbling congratulations. The baby's other parent is elated, weeping for joy. The room is abuzz with the sounds of an ancient chorus of gratitude and relief. My midwife partner puts her arm around my shoulder and we just watch this sweet nativity scene, feeling blessed to be a part of it.

Several hours later, after the baby and the mother have been examined carefully, after everyone is cleaned up, after the herb bath, after the family has been served breakfast, and after the champagne toast, we tuck the new family into the bed, pull the comforter up, hug them, and invite them to take a nap.

The new mother grabs our hands, pulls us to her chest, whispers sweet words of thanksgiving—like a prayer—into our ears, and kisses each of our cheeks. Then she lets go of our hands and we leave her gazing into the primordial pool of her newborn baby's eyes.

We tiptoe out of the room, go to the front door, open it, and step onto the porch. The light of a new day dawning rushes in. We hang out the big banner that says, "It's a girl."

Before long the honking starts from the neighbors in their cars who are passing by the birth center on their way to work. Whether young or old, strangers or friends, people in our community are eager to share in the celebration of life. They give us the thumbs up sign, and we wave to them.

Surges of joy course through our veins, overflow, and are carried away on the wisps of crisp morning air. The golden light of dawn lights up our neighborhood and we all understand…the way back to ourselves was through our hearts.

And all is well.

closing

There is a remarkable spirit of self-transcendence that is intrinsic to humankind.

Human beings can accomplish anything to which we set our minds. We have proven, time and time again, that we can expand beyond what appears to be a fixed boundary. If our minds can think it, we can accomplish it.

Consider the boundaries humans have pushed. Mastering fire, creating languages, developing agriculture, inventing automobiles, navigating ocean voyages, mastering flight, walking on the moon, climbing Mt. Everest, building the Great Pyramids, running the four-minute mile, creating art and music, developing the printing press, designing the World Wide Web, inventing microsurgery, extinguishing dangerous diseases, extending life expectancy, harnessing wind and solar power, and mapping the human genome.

And then there are the things humans have done—and then undone—to benefit humankind. Things like dismantling the Berlin Wall, outlawing slavery and Jim Crow laws that enforced segregation and disenfranchisement, saving endangered species, reversing deforestation by planting trees, ending wars, coordinating humanitarian efforts across countries, enshrining human rights in national and international laws, outlawing systems of institutional apartheid, ousting dictatorships and installing democratic governments, and guaranteeing all people the right to vote.

Human beings are paradoxical. We are easily the most creative and the most destructive of all creatures on earth.

But surely, if we can build international stations in space, we can build functional and equitable healthcare systems on earth.

Surely, if we can eradicate smallpox—a task in which partners all across the planet collaborated—we can eradicate preventable childbirth-related deaths of the world's women and newborns.

Surely, if we can harness atomic energy capable of wiping out the entire human race and the lives of all sentient beings, we can harness the powerful energies of ingenuity, compassion, and political will to protect and enhance those same lives.

It is all a matter of what we make up our minds to do.

The Only Home We've Ever Known[209]

Thirty years ago, on February 14, 1990, the Voyager 1 space probe drifted about four billion miles away from Earth. Before the spacecraft left our planetary neighborhood for the fringes of the solar system, Carl Sagan, the famed astrophysicist and astrobiologist, asked engineers to capture one final photo of our world, Planet Earth. The image was a tiny pinprick of light just over a tenth of a pixel in size. Caught in the center of massive scattered light rays, it almost looked like a mistake it was so minuscule. They named the photo "Pale Blue Dot" and later Sagan penned a book of the same title.[210]

Sagan famously wrote, "Look again at that dot. That's here. That's home. That's us. On it, everyone you love, everyone you know, everyone you ever heard of, every human being who ever was, lived out their lives. The aggregate of our joy and suffering…every hunter and forager, every hero and coward, every king and peasant, every young couple in love, every mother and father and hopeful child, every saint and sinner…on a mote of dust suspended in a sunbeam."[211]

Sagan further opined, "Our posturings, our imagined self-importance, the delusions that we have some privileged position in the Universe, are challenged by this point of pale light. Our planet is a lonely speck in the great enveloping cosmic dark. In our obscurity, in all this vastness, there is no hint that help will come from elsewhere to save us from ourselves."

Sagan concluded, "To me, it underscores our responsibility to deal more kindly with one another, and to preserve and cherish the pale blue dot, the only home we've ever known."[212]

This long view, one that gives us an opportunity to discern our lives not in terms of years or even generations, but in terms of geological epochs and cosmic infinitude, urges us to ask the vital questions. *What really matters? What do we choose to care about in a world that is both achingly precious and compellingly lonely?*

What Matters to Me

We will each find our own way. Moment by moment we will make choices. The trick, says my favorite Buddhist teacher, Pema Chödrön, is to "realize the importance of how we choose to orient our minds."[213]

As my 70th birthday approaches, I contemplate all the years I have walked in the shoes of a midwife, and the myriad places those shoes have taken me. I have distilled all that I have learned into a dozen truths that orient my mind. The nectar of these truths is sweet and savory, an ambrosia to nourish and sustain my life, and to help me live respectfully amongst all living beings.

Breathe life in through my senses.
Lead with my heart and not my head.
Become aware of what draws my attention.
Lean into my fears.
Trust my body.
Be curious and stay open to possibilities.
Extend loving-kindness to all beings.
Cultivate awareness that everything is connected.
Take time for wise discernment.
Do only what is mine to do and do it with intention.
Practice gratitude moment by moment.
Live by the mantra 'you in me, and me in you.'
Awaken to the wisdom of the wild within and follow her anywhere she leads.

The endlessly overflowing spirit vessel of being a midwife to birth, woven together with being a mother, an activist, and a soulful woman, taught me all this. No small lessons, distilled to their essences. And perhaps these lessons are just the kind that, when practiced faithfully, have the power to change the world.

I offer blessings for the survival, health, and wellbeing of all of our mothers and birthing people, fathers and partners, children and families in whatever way we define them. May we thrive—as the Hopi and other Indigenous peoples say— *for seven generations to come.*

May we live lightly, and with profound gratitude, upon our Earth Mother and in peace with all living things. So be it.

acknowledgements

I am grateful to my parents, Margaret and Earl Simkins for giving me life and providing a stable and stimulating home environment where diversity on all levels was welcomed and celebrated. My father's strong mind and fierce dedication to his family, and my mother's *joie de vivre* and unquenchable thirst for social justice are traits I have sought to emulate. My mother Margaret, now in her ninth decade, is my bright star of inspiration for living a life full of meaning and zest.

I am grateful to my friend and colleague Judy Luce for providing the spark for this project. Without her nudging and encouragement *The Midwife Matrix* would never have come to fruition. I am also grateful for her thoughtful reading of and suggestions for revisions to my manuscript.

I am grateful to the original twenty-five matriarch midwives who generously shared their life stories with me for my anthology, *Into These Hands: Wisdom From Midwives* (https://wisdomfrommidwives.com). I have learned so much from them. They are Marina Alzugaray, Rondi Anderson, Alice Bailes, Maggie Bennett, Patrice Bobier, Kate Bowland, Katsi Cook, Ida Darragh, Ina May Gaskin, Diane Holzer, Marsha Jackson, Jennie Joseph, Makeda Kamara, Abby J. Kinne, Kip Kozlowski, Casey Makela, Linda McHale, Shafia M. Monroe, Sr. Angela Murdaugh, Carol Nelson, Yeshi Neumann, Debbie Pulley, Arisika Razak and Saraswathi Vedam. They have demonstrated how the 12 Qualities That Matter are manifested in the real world, in real time, across a lifetime, and across the world. My gratitude runs deep and my respect for each of them is immense.

I am grateful to the midwives featured in the section Midwives Are Changing the World who allowed me to share the stories of the work they are doing to make a difference in the world. And I am grateful to all the midwives and other birth workers who serve pregnant and birthing people daily, all across the planet, who embody the 12 Qualities That Matter, and who understand exactly why they matter. I have tried to call out the names of as many midwives as I could. But it was only a fraction of the hundreds I know, and none of the thousands I have yet to meet.

I am grateful to the people brave enough to grow human beings in their bodies and courageously give birth to future generations. Bless each of you for nurturing the children with all of your hearts and for protecting them in an uncertain world. Bless all those who truly realize that every child deserves as much love and protection as their own children, and who take action to make the world a friendlier more equitable place for all to live.

I am grateful for Rita Lawrence (https://www.bitsybaby.com), the awesome photographer and motherhood advocate who allowed me to use her spectacular photos for the front cover and interior pages of *The Midwife Matrix*. The story behind the front cover photo is that this baby was the firstborn son of a woman whose husband was a quadriplegic. The couple doubted they would ever have children. This beautiful and hopeful image is perfect—it embodies the truth that *miracles do happen.*

I am grateful to my writing mentor, teacher and poet Max Regan of Hollowdeck Press in Boulder Colorado. Max is a master of many of the 12 Qualities That Matter—particularly compassion, relationship, service, and activism. Since 2008 Max has been my developmental editor and literary midwife, holding my hand and breathing with me, encouraging me to give birth to my creative writing projects even when I doubted I could. Max taught me to write like it matters. His inspiring advice to writers is, "Never let anyone, no matter who they are (even yourself), talk you out of your heartwork."

I would like to thank several professionals at *Foreword Reviews* in Traverse City Michigan: Victoria and Matt Sutherland for their ongoing support of my literary endeavors; Barbara Hodge for her brilliant cover design and skillful layout of this book; and Danielle Ballantyne for content editing.

I am grateful for my three amazing homeborn and homegrown children, Maya, Leah, and Sean, who are at the heart of everything I do. As children and now as adults, they always provide me with inspiration and reasons to love them even more. I am grateful for their wonderful partners, Jake, Joe and Jeff for adding such richness to our family. I adore our granddaughter, Margaret, who is pure joy in a tiny package, and also our new grandchild soon to be born.

And finally, I am grateful for being given the gift, later in life, of Fred Heltenen— an old lover turned new husband—who came with a sailboat, a kind heart, and talent galore. The kismet of sharing the last chapters of our lives together still makes me laugh out loud.

Muchas gracias a todos.

about the author

For nearly forty-five years Geradine Simkins, APRN, CNM, MSN has worked as a midwife practitioner, activist, visionary, leader, author, and consultant. She began as a direct-entry homebirth midwife in 1976 and became a nurse-midwife twenty years later. She provided healthcare for women, infants, and families in a variety of settings: homes, freestanding birth centers, clinics, and hospitals. Among her favorite work has been with migrant farmworkers and Indigenous peoples, with a focus on transforming the current US maternity care system to reflect principles of health equity and social justice.

Geradine has served in key leadership roles regionally, nationally, and internationally. These include: founding member and first President of the Michigan Midwives Association (MMA); Past President and Executive Director of the Midwives Alliance of North American (MANA); President of the Foundation for the Advancement of Midwifery (FAM); member of the Governing Council of the International Confederation of Midwives (ICM); and current member of the Michigan Board of Licensed Midwifery. She is the author/editor of an anthology called *Into These Hands: Wisdom from Midwives* (2011), and editor of her mother's memoir called *Peace, Love, and Harmony Aren't Just Words* (2017). She is owner/operator of Birthways Consulting. For nearly twenty years she has been a lead consultant, trainer and curriculum developer for the Healthy Native Babies Project, which serves American Indian and Alaska Native communities, and is funded by the Eunice Kennedy Shriver National Institute of Child Health and Human Development.

Geradine has three adult children and one grandchild—all born into the hands of midwives. She lives in Northern Michigan with her husband, Fred Heltenen. For fun she sails the Great Lakes, scuba dives in the Caribbean, explores amazing places and cultures around the world, and enjoys her own homeplace on the planet in beautiful Leelanau County.

discussion guide

General Discussion Topics

1. Do you experience the 12 Qualities That Matter identified in The Midwife Matrix as important? Do you have a different understanding of the meaning of these qualities than what has been described in this book?
2. Which of the 12 Qualities resonate with you most? Which come easily or naturally to you? Why is this true?
3. Which of the 12 Qualities would require some work in order for you to acquire or master them?
4. When you are a client or a patient of any provider of healthcare services, which of the 12 Qualities are most important to you? Why?
5. Describe your understanding of how The Midwife Matrix is both a system of ancient wisdom and an avant-garde model for postmodern maternity care.
6. The Midwife Matrix design is modeled after a Celtic knot, which is a circuitry of interrelated loops that has no beginning and no ending. Discuss this design. Why do you think it has been used to illustrate The Midwife Matrix?
7. The Midwife Matrix is described as both *essence* (inherent nature) and *intention* (intended course of action). What does that mean to you?
8. How have you, or someone you know, experienced the maternity care system in the USA? Would you (or they) change anything about the experience? If so, how might The Midwife Matrix help guide those changes?

Topics for Midwives, Educators, and Students

1. In listening to birth stories, what are the most common themes people express? What are the most common positive themes? The most common negative themes?

2. What factors are most likely to disrupt the flow of a normal physiologic birth? What factors are most likely to support the flow of a normal physiologic birth?

3. Midwives, nurses, physicians, doulas, and other healthcare providers have a major impact on the experiences of their patients and clients. What factors within the healthcare environment (context) exert the greatest influence on patient/client wellbeing? On patient/client satisfaction? On patient/client dissatisfaction?

4. How does the model of maternity care (content) impact patients/clients?

5. Discuss the conflict between a maternity care provider's desire to provide services that are based on patient/client needs and preferences (self-determination) juxtaposed with requirements to work within institutional policies, reconcile time constraints, and be cognizant of cost-efficiency (context and content). How do these factors impact the delivery of care?

6. Why do you think 'dehumanization of childbirth' has become a worldwide concern? Discuss what impact the 12 Qualities That Matter could have on 'humanization of childbirth.'

7. Are the key characteristics that identify 'humanization of birth' different for people who have low-risk pregnancies versus those who have high-risk pregnancies? Are they different depending on the childbirth setting?

8. Reproductive justice combines reproductive rights and social justice, which includes the right of women to maintain personal bodily autonomy, have children, not have children, and parent their children in safe, sustainable communities. Discuss the intersecting oppressions of race, gender, sovereignty, and class, and describe how they affect the most marginalized people.

9. Discuss the concepts and practices that underpin efforts to 'decolonize birth.'

10. What are the ways in which you can use (or hope to use) the qualities of The Midwife Matrix in your current circumstances to help women and people with wombs reclaim their bodies, theirs births, and their lives?

references

OPENING
1. Simkins, G (Ed). (2011). *Into these hands: Wisdom from midwives*. Traverse City, MI: Spirituality & Health Books.

THE MIDWIFE MATRIX IS A SOURCE PATTERN
2. Bradfield, Z., Duggan, R., Hauck, Y. & Kelly, M. (2018, April). Midwives being 'with woman': An integrative study. *Women Birth*. 31(2):143-152. Retrieved from https://www.ncbi.nlm.nih.gov/pubmed/28807466.

BIRTH MATTERS
3. Cook, K. (2003, December 23). *Women are the first environment*. Indian Country Today. Retrieved from https://newsmaven.io/indiancountrytoday/archive/cook-women-are-the-first-environment-bZbKXN9CME-UabNOEhKgqg/.
4. National Research Council Division of Behavioral and Social Sciences and Education. (2001). Early childhood development and learning: New knowledge for policy. [Executive Summary]. Washington, DC: *National Academies Press*. Retrieved from https://www.ncbi.nlm.nih.gov/books/NBK223291/.

NOW OR NEVER
5. Peterson-Kaiser Health System Tracker. (2018, December 7). *How does health spending in the U.S. compare to other countries?* [Collaboration between the Kaiser Family Foundation and the United States Bureau of Economic Analysis.] Retrieved from https://www.healthsystemtracker.org/chart-collection/health-spending-u-s-compare-https://www.healthsystemtracker.org/chart-collection/health-spending-u-s-compare-countries/.
6. MacDorman, MF., Declercq, E., Cabral, H. & Morton, C. (2016). Recent increases in the US maternal mortality rate: Disentangling trends from measurement issues. *Obstet Gynecol*. 128(3), 447-55.
7. World Health Organization [WHO]. (2010). *Trends in maternal mortality 1990 to 2008 – estimates developed by WHO, UNICEF, UNFPA, and the World Bank*. Retrieved from http://www.who.int/reproductivehealth/publications/monitoring/9789241500265/en/; Lawson, GW & Keirse, MJNC. (2013). Reflections on the maternal mortality millennium goal. *Birth*. 40(2), 96–102.

8. Rettner, R. (2018, July 27). *Why is the US one of the 'most dangerous' places in the devel-oped world to give birth?* CBS News. Retrieved from https://www.cbsnews.com/news/us-most-dangerous-place-to-give-birth-in-developed-world-usa-today-investigation-finds/.

9. Amnesty International. (2011, May 7). *Deadly delivery: The maternal healthcare crisis in the US*. Retrieved from https://www.amnestyusa.org/wpcontent/uploads/2017/04/deadlydeliveryoneyear.pdf.

10. Vedam, S. et al. (2019, June 11). The Giving Voice to Mothers study: Inequity and mistreat-ment during pregnancy and childbirth in the United States. *Reproductive Health*. 16-77. Retrived from https://doi.org/10.1186/s12978-019-0729-2.

11. Vedam, S. et al. (2019, June 11). The Giving Voice to Mothers study: Inequity and mistreat-ment during pregnancy and childbirth in the United States. *Reproductive Health*. 16-77. Retrived from https://doi.org/10.1186/s12978-019-0729-2.

12. MacDorman, MF. & Mathews, TJ. (National Center for Health Statistics); Mohangoo, AD., (TNO Child Health, Netherlands); & Zeitlin, J., (France). (2014, September 24). International comparisons of infant mortality and related factors: United States and Europe. *Center for Disease Control and Prevention [CDC] National Vital Statistics Report*. Vol 3, Num 5. Retrieved from https://www.ncbi.nlm.nih.gov/pubmed/25252091.

13. MacDorman, MF. & Mathews, TJ. (National Center for Health Statistics); Mohangoo, AD., (TNO Child Health, Netherlands); & Zeitlin, J, (France). (2014, September 24). International comparisons of infant mortality and related factors: United States and Europe. *CDC National Vital Statistics Report*. Vol 3, Num 5. Retrieved from https://www.ncbi.nlm.nih.gov/pubmed/25252091.

14. Institute of Medicine (US) Committee on Understanding and Eliminating Racial and Ethnic Disparities in Health Care. (2003). *Unequal treatment: Confronting racial and ethnic dispar-ities in health care*. Smedley, BD., Stith, AY. & Nelson, AR., Eds. Washington DC: National Academies Press.

15. Davis-Floyd, RE. (1990). The role of obstetrical rituals in the resolution of cultural anomaly. *Social Science and Medicine*. 31(2):175–89; Katz-Rothman, B. (1993). *The tentative pregnancy: How amniocentesis changes the experience of motherhood*. New York, NY: W.W. Norton; Martin, E. (1984). Pregnancy, labor and body image in the United States. *Social Science and Medicine*. 19(11), 1201–6.

16. Davis-Floyd, RE. (1990). The role of obstetrical rituals in the resolution of cultural anomaly. *Social Science and Medicine*. 31(2), 175–89; Katz-Rothman, B. (1993). *The tentative pregnancy: How amniocentesis changes the experience of motherhood*. New York, NY: W.W. Norton.

17. National Partnership for Women and Families. (2018, June). *Blueprint for advancing high quality maternity care through physiologic childbearing*. Washington, DC: National Partnership. Retrieved from http://www.nationalpartnership.org/our-work/resources/health-care/mater-nity/blueprint-for-advancing-high-value-maternity-care.pdf.

18. Wagner, M. (2001, November). Fish can't see water: The need to humanize birth. *International Journal of Gynecology & Obstetrics* 75: S25-S37.

19. Sakala, C. & Corry, M. (2008). *Evidence-based maternity care: What it is and what it can achieve*. New York, NY: Co-publishers Childbirth Connection and Reforming States Group.

20. American College of Nurse-Midwives [ACNM], Midwives Alliance of North America [MANA] & National Association of Certified Professional Midwives [NACPM]. (2013, May 14). Supporting healthy and normal physiologic childbirth: A consensus statement by ACNM, MANA, and NACPM. *J Perinat Educ*. 22(1), 14-8.

21. Wagner, M. (2001, November). Fish can't see water: The need to humanize birth. *International Journal of Gynecology & Obstetrics* 75: S25-S37.

22. Martin, N. (2018, February 22). A larger role for midwives could improve deficient U.S. care for mothers and babies. *ProPublica*. Retrieved from https://www.propublica.org/article/midwives-study-maternal-neonatal-care; Sandall, J., Soltani, H., Gates, S., Shennan, A. & Devane, D. (2016, April 28). Midwife-led continuity models versus other models of care for childbearing women. *Cochrane Database of Systematic Reviews* 2016, Issue 4, Art. No: CD004667. DOI: 10.1002/14651858.CD004667.pub5.

23. Vedam, S., Stoll, K., MacDorman, M., Declercq, E., Cramer, R., Cheyney, M., et al. (2018, February 21). *Mapping integration of midwives across the United States: Impact on access, equity, and outcomes. PLoS ONE* 13(2): e0192523. Retrieved from https://doi.org/10.1371/journal.pone.0192523.

24. Sandall, J., Soltani, H., Gates, S,. Shennan, A. & Devane, D. (2016, April 28). Midwife-led continuity models versus other models of care for childbearing women. *Cochrane Database of Systematic Reviews* 2016, Issue 4, Art. No: CD004667. DOI: 10.1002/14651858.CD004667.pub5.

25. WHO. (2018). *The case for midwifery.* Retrieved from https://www.who.int/maternal_child_adolescent/topics/quality-of-care/midwifery/case-for-midwifery/en/.

26. United Nations Population Fund (UNFPA). (2017). *A safe pregnancy is every woman's right: Midwifery.* Retrieved from https://www.unfpa.org/midwifery.

27. International Federation of Gynecology and Obstetrics [FIGO]. (2015, May 5). *Midwives leading the way with quality care.* Retrieved from https://www.figo.org/news/midwives-key-success-sustainable-development-goals-sdgs-0014938.

28. Stillman, J., Fried, MG., Ross, L., Gutierrez, ER. (2004). *Undivided rights: Woman of color organize for reproductive justice.* Cambridge, MA. South End Press.

29. Ross, L. & Solinger, R. (2017). *Reproductive Justice.* Oakland, CA. University of California Press.

WHAT TIME IS IT ON THE CLOCK OF THE WORLD?

30. Boggs, GL. (2014, Sept 16). What time is it on the clock of the world? The Boggs Blog website. A project of the James and Grace Lee Boggs Center to Nurture Community Leadership. Retrieved from https://conversationsthatyouwillneverfinish.wordpress.com/2014/09/06/what-time-is-it-on-the-clock-of-the-world-by-grace-lee-boggs/.

31. Boggs, GL. (2012). *The next American Revolution: Sustainable activism for the 21st century.* Los Angeles & Berkeley, CA. University of California Press, p. 72.

PART 1: THE MIDWIFE MATRIX

CONTEXT MATTERS

32. Janssen, PA., Henderson, AD., & Vedam, S. (2009, December). The experience of planned home birth: Views of the first 500 women. *Birth,* 36.4, 297-304; Christiaens, W. & Bracke, P. (2009, May 18). Place of birth and satisfaction with childbirth in Belgium and the Netherlands. *Midwifery,* 25.2, e11-e19. Retrieved from https://www.ncbi.nlm.nih.gov/pubmed/17512100; Madi, BC & Crow, R. (2003, December). A qualitative study of information about available options for childbirth venue and pregnant women's preference for a place of delivery. *Midwifery,* 328-36. Retrieved from https://www.ncbi.nlm.nih.gov/pubmed/14623512.

33. Namey, EE. & Drapkin Lyerly, A. (2010, Aug). The meaning of "control" for childbearing women in the US. *Social Science & Medicine,* 71(44): 769-76. Retrieved from https://www.ncbi.nlm.nih.gov/pubmed/20579792.

34. Namey, EE. & Drapkin Lyerly, A. (2010, Aug). The meaning of "control" for childbearing women in the US. *Social Science & Medicine*, 71(44): 769-76. Retrieved from https://www.ncbi.nlm.nih.gov/pubmed/20579792.

35. Pascali-Bonaro, D. (Producer). (2009, January 1). *Orgasmic Birth: The Best Kept Secret*. [Documentary movie.] Retrieved from https://www.orgasmicbirth.com.

36. Johnson, SR. (2019, May 22). Medicaid expansion fills gaps in maternal health coverage leading to healthier mothers and babies. *Georgetown University Health Policy Institute*. Retrieved from https://ccf.georgetown.edu/2019/05/09/medicaid-expansion-fills-gaps-in-maternal-health-coverage-leading-to-healthier-mothers-and-babies/.

CONTENT MATTERS

37. Katz Rothman, B. (1991) *In labor: Women and power in the birthplace*. (2nd ed.) New York, NY: W. W. Norton; Davis-Floyd, R. (1992). *Birth as an American rite of passage*. Berkeley, CA: University of California Press; Davis-Floyd, R. (2001). The technocratic, humanistic, and holistic paradigms of childbirth. *International Journal of Gynecology and Obstetrics*, 75.S1, S5-S23; Bridgman Perkins, B. (2004). *The medical delivery business: Health reform, childbirth, and the economic order*. Piscataway, NJ: Rutgers University Press; Simonds, W., Katz Rothman, B. & Norman, BM. (2007). *Laboring on: Birth in transition in the United States*. New York, NY: Routledge; Boston Women's Health Book Collective. (2008). *Our Bodies, Ourselves: Pregnancy and Birth*. New York, NY: Simon and Schuster.

38. May, M. (2017). *Epiduralized birth and nurse-midwifery: Childbirth in the United States. A Medical Ethnography*. Syracuse, NY: Sampson Book Publishing; Sandall, J., Soltani, H., Gates, S., Shennan, A. & Devane, D. (2016, April 28). Midwife-led continuity models versus other models of care for childbearing women. Cochrane Database of Systematic Reviews 2016, Issue 4, Art. No: CD004667. DOI: 10.1002/14651858.CD004667.pub5; Wernham, E., Gurney, J., Stanley, J., Ellison-Loschmann L. & Sarfati, D. (2016). A comparison of midwife-led and medical-led models of care and their relationship to adverse fetal and neonatal outcomes: A retrospective cohort study in New Zealand. *PLoS Medicine*, 13(9): e1002134. Retrieved from https://doi.org/10.1371/journal.pmed.1002134; de Jonge, A. & Sandall, J. (2016, September 27). Improving research into models of maternity care to inform decision making. PLoS Medicine, vol. 13,9 e1002135. Retrieved from doi:10.1371/journal.pmed.1002135; Simkins, G (Ed). (2011). *Into these hands: Wisdom from midwives*. Traverse City, MI: Spirituality & Health Books.

39. Davis-Floyd, R. (1992). *Birth as an American rite of passage*. Berkeley, CA: University of California Press.

40. ACNM. (2012). Measuring outcomes of midwifery care: The Optimality Index-US. Retrieved from http://www.midwife.org/Optimality-Index-US.

HOLISM MATTERS

41. Jan Christiaan Smuts, JC. (1926). *Holism and evolution*. New York, NY: Macmillan Company.

42. Jordan, B. (1993). *Birth in four cultures: A cross-cultural investigation of childbirth in Yucatan, Holland, Sweden and the United States*. Long Grove, IL: Waveland Press; Davis-Floyd, RE. & Cheyney, M., (Eds.) (2019). *Birth in Eight Cultures*. Long Grove, IL: Waveland Press. 2019.

NATURE MATTERS

43. International Cesarean Awareness Network. (2019). Retrieved from http://www.ican-online.org.

44. Childbirth Connection. (2019). The cascade of intervention. Retrieved from http://www.childbirthconnection.org/maternity-care/cascade-of-intervention/.

45. WHO non-clinical interventions to reduce unnecessary caesarean sections. (2018). World Health Organization. Retrieved from https://www.who.int/reproductivehealth/guidance-to-reduce-unnecessary-caesarean-sections/en/.

46. Harrison, W. & Goodman, D. (2015, September). Epidemiologic trends in neonatal intensive care, 2007-2012. *JAMA Pediatrics,* 169(9):855-862. doi:10.1001/jamapediatrics.2015.1305.

47. Bridgeman Perkins, B. (2004*). The medical delivery business: Health reform, childbirth and the economic order.* Piscataway, NJ: Rutgers University Press.

48. Bridgeman Perkins, B. (2004*). The Medical Delivery Business: Health Reform, Childbirth and the Economic Order.* Piscataway, NJ: Rutgers University Press.

49. Arms, S. (Director.) (2003.) *Birthing the future.* [Documentary movie.] Retrieved from http://www.birthingthefuture.com.

50. *Twilight Sleep.* (2015.) Motherhood Archive. Retrieved from https://vimeo.com/110509071.

51. *Twilight Sleep Promised Painless Birth—But at What Cost?"* (2018, Jan). (Short documentary movie.) Retrieved from https://www.youtube.com/watch?v=oiFRPx7d_eU.

SACRED MATTERS

52. Cook, K. (2003, December 23). Women are the first environment. *Indian Country Today.* Retrieved from https://newsmaven.io/indiancountrytoday/archive/cook-women-are-the-first-environment-bZbKXN9CME-UabNOEhKgqg/.

RELATIONSHIP MATTERS

53. Looking Horse, A., Arden, H., & Horn, P. (2001). *White buffalo teachings from Chief Arvol Looking Horse, 19th generation keeper of the sacred white buffalo pipe of the Lakota, Dakota & Nakota Great Sioux Nation.* Williamsburg, MA: Dreamkeepers Press.

54. Arms, S. (Director.) (2003.) *Birthing the future.* [Documentary movie.] Retrieved from http://www.birthingthefuture.com.

55. Centers for Medicare and Medicaid Services (CMS). (n.d.) Value-based care. Washington DC: US CMS. Retrieved from https://www.cms.gov/medicare/quality-initiatives-patient-assessment-instruments/value-based-programs/value-based-programs.html.

56. Centers for Medicare and Medicaid Services (CMS). (n.d.) Value-based care. Washington DC: US CMS. Retrieved from https://www.cms.gov/medicare/quality-initiatives-patient-assessment-instruments/value-based-programs/value-based-programs.html.

57. Reagan, L. (2018, April 7). Midwife Jennie Joseph: Undermining a deadly maternal health system. [Online interview, Kindred Media.] Retrieved from https://kindredmedia.org/2018/04/midwife-jennie-joseph/.

58. Liberman, MD. (2014). Social: Why our brains are wired to connect. New York, NY: Crown Publishers, Random House.

59. Klaus, M., Kennell, J. & Klaus, P. (1995). *Bonding: Building the foundation for secure attachment and independence.* Reading, PA: Addison-Wesley Publishing Company.

60. Barasch, MI. (2005). *Field notes on the compassionate life: A search for the soul of kindness.* Emmaus, PA: Rodale Press.

COMPASSION MATTERS

61. Kanov, J. M., Maitlis, S., Worline, M. C., Dutton, J. E., Frost, P. & Lilius, J. M. (2004). Compassion in organizational life. *American Behavior Scientist, 47* (6), 808-827.

62. Gallo, S., Netherland Institute for Neuroscience (KNAW). (2018, May 25). Which role does the brain play in prosocial behavior? *Science Daily.* Retrieved from www.sciencedaily.com/releases/2018/05/180525123233.htm.

63. Esch, T. & Stefano, GB. (2011). The neurobiological link between compassion and love. *Medical Science Monitor, 17*(3), RA65-75. doi: 10.12659/MSM.881441.

64. Barasch, MI. (2005). *Field notes on the compassionate life: A search for the soul of kindness.* Emmaus, PA: Rodale Press.

65. McGonigal, K. (2011, Nov 17) What does compassion look like? Stanford Compassion Training. *Psychology Today.* Retrieved from https://www.psychologytoday.com/us/blog/the-science-willpower/201111/what-does-compassion-look.

66. Cosley, B., et al. (2010). Is compassion for others stress buffering? Consequences of compassion and social support for physiological reactivity to stress. *Journal of Experimental Social Psychology* 46.5, 816-823; Kelley, JM., Kraft-Todd, G., Schapria, L., Kossowsky, J. & Riess, H. (2014). The influence of the patient-clinician relationship on healthcare outcomes: A systematic review and meta-analysis of randomized controlled trials. *PLoS One*, 9:4, 1-7; Derksen F., Bensing J., & Lagro-Janssen, A. (2013, January). Effectiveness of empathy in general practice. *British Journal of General Practice*, 63(606), e76-84.doi: 10.3399/bjgp13X660814; Stewart, M., Brown, J., Donner, A., McWhinnery, I., Oates, J., Weston, W. & Jordan, J. (2000, September). The impact of patient-centered care on outcomes. *Journal of Family Practice*, 49(9).

67. Weil, A. (2000) *Spontaneous healing: How to discover and embrace your body's natural ability to maintain and heal itself.* NY, NY: Random House Publishing Group.

68. Kelley, JM., Kraft-Todd, G., Schapria, L., Kossowsky, J., & Riess, H. (2014). The influence of the patient-clinician relationship on healthcare outcomes: A systematic review and meta-analysis of randomized controlled trials. *PLoS One*, 9:4, 1-7.

69. Kelley, JM., Kraft-Todd, G., Schapria, L., Kossowsky, J. & Riess, H. (2014). The influence of the patient-clinician relationship on healthcare outcomes: A systematic review and meta-analysis of randomized controlled trials. *PLoS One*, 9:4, 1-7.

SELF-DETERMINATION MATTERS

70. Young, A., Ungar, L. & Schnaars, C. (2018, July 26). *Deadly deliveries.* Retrieved from https://www.usatoday.com/in-depth/news/investigations/deadly-deliveries/2018/07/26/maternal-mortality-rates-preeclampsia-postpartum-hemorrhage-safety/546889002/.

71. Diaz-Tello, F. (2016, May 24) Invisible wounds: Obstetric violence in the United States. *Reproductive Health Matters, 24*:47, 56-64, DOI: 10.1016/j.rhm.2016.04.004.

72. Bowser, D. & Hill, K. (2010, September 20). *Exploring evidence for disrespect and abuse in facility-based childbirth: Report of a landscape analysis. USAID / TRAction Project.* Retrieved from https://www.ghdonline.org/uploads/Respectful_Care_at_Birth_9-20-101_Final1.pdf; White Ribbon Alliance website. (2019). *Respectful maternity care charter: Universal rights of women and newborns.* Retrieved from https://www.whiteribbonalliance.org/rmctoolkit.

73. United Nations General Assembly. (1993). *Declaration on the elimination of violence against women. UN General Assembly.* Retrieved from https://www.un.org/documents/ga/res/48/a48r104.htm; Windau-Melmer, T. (2013). *A guide for advocating for respectful maternity care.* Washington, DC: Futures Group, Health Policy Project, White Ribbon Alliance & USAID.

74. United Nations General Assembly. (1993). *Declaration on the elimination of violence against women. UN General Assembly.* Retrieved from https://www.un.org/documents/ga/res/48/a48r104.htm; Windau-Melmer, T. (2013). *A guide for advocating for respectful maternity care.* Washington, DC: Futures Group, Health Policy Project, White Ribbon Alliance & USAID.

75. WHO. (2014). *The prevention and elimination of disrespect and abuse during facility-based childbirth.* Retrieved from https://www.who.int/reproductivehealth/topics/maternal_perinatal/statement-childbirth/en/.

76. White Ribbon Alliance website. *Respectful maternity care charter: Universal rights of women and newborns.* Retrieved from https://www.whiteribbonalliance.org/rmctoolkit.

77. Diaz-Tello, F. (2016, May 24) Invisible wounds: Obstetric violence in the United States. *Reproductive Health Matters, 24:47,* 56-64, DOI: 10.1016/j.rhm.2016.04.004.

78. Declercq, E., Sakala, C. & Corry, M. (2014, Winter). Major survey findings of Listening to Mothers III: Pregnancy and birth. *Journal of Perinatal Education.* 23(1), 9–16. doi: 10.1891/1058-1243.23.1.9.

79. Block, J. (2007). *Pushed: The painful truth about childbirth and modern maternity care.* Cambridge, MA: De Capo Press; Savage, V., & Castro, A. (2017). Measuring mistreatment of women during childbirth: A review of terminology and methodological approaches. *Reproductive Health, 14*(1), 138. doi:10.1186/s12978-017-0403-5; Kukura, E. (2017) Obstetric violence. *Georgetown Law Review.* Retrieved from https://georgetownlawjournal.org.

80. Vedam S., Stoll K., Martin K., et al. The mother's autonomy in decision making (MADM) scale: Patient-led development and psychometric testing of a new instrument to evaluate experience of maternity care. *PLoS ONE.* Retrieved from http://dx.doi.org/10.1371/journal.pone.0171804.

81. ACNM. (2016, December). *Shared decision-making in midwifery care.* [Position statement]. Retrieved on 2-25-19 from http://www.midwife.org/ACNM/files/ACNMLibraryData/UPLOADFILENAME/000000000305/Shared-Decision-Making-in-Midwifery-Care-Dec-2016.pdf.

82. ACNM. (2016, December). *Shared Decision-making in midwifery care.* [Position statement]. Retrieved on 2-25-19 from http://www.midwife.org/ACNM/files/ACNMLibraryData/UPLOADFILENAME/000000000305/Shared-Decision-Making-in-Midwifery-Care-Dec-2016.pdf.

83. Attanasio, LB., McPherson, ME. & Kozhimannil, KB. (2014). Positive childbirth experiences in U.S. hospitals: A mixed methods analysis. *Maternal and Child Health Journal, 18*(5), 1280-90.

84. Attanasio, LB., McPherson, ME. & Kozhimannil, KB. (2014). Positive childbirth experiences in U.S. hospitals: A mixed methods analysis. *Maternal and Child Health Journal, 18*(5), 1280-90.

85. Attanasio, LB., McPherson, ME. & Kozhimannil, KB. (2014). Positive childbirth experiences in U.S. hospitals: A mixed methods analysis. *Maternal and Child Health Journal, 18*(5), 1280-90.

86. Ross, L. & Solinger, R. (2017). *Reproductive justice.* Oakland, CA: University of California Press.

87. White Ribbon Alliance website. (2019). *Respectful maternity care charter: Universal rights of women and newborns.* Retrieved from https://www.whiteribbonalliance.org/rmctoolkit.

SERVICE MATTERS

88. Baldwin, LV. (1995). *Toward the beloved community: Martin Luther King Jr. and South Africa.* Cleveland, OH: Pilgrim Press.

89. King, ML. Jr. (1963, April 16, published in 1994). *Letter from the Birmingham Jail.* Birmingham, Alabama: Harper Collins.

ACTIVISM MATTERS

90. Simkins, G (Ed). (2011). *Into these hands: Wisdom from midwives.* Traverse City, MI: Spirituality & Health Books.

91. Consumer Reports. (2018, May 10). Your biggest C-section risk may be your hospital. Retrieved from https://www.consumerreports.org/c-section/biggest-c-section-risk-may-be-your-hospital/.

92. Simkins, G (Ed). (2011). *Into these hands: Wisdom from midwives.* Traverse City, MI: Spirituality & Health Books.

93. Ross, LJ. & Solinger. R. (2017). *Reproductive justice: A new vision for the 21ˢᵗ century.* Oakland, CA: University of California Press.

94. Diaz-Tello, F. (2016, May 24) Invisible wounds: Obstetric violence in the United States. *Reproductive Health Matters,* 24:47, 56-64, DOI: 10.1016/j.rhm.2016.04.004.

95. Beines, W. (2006). *The trouble between us: An uneasy history of white and black women in the feminist movement.* New York, NY: Oxford University Press.

96. Beines, W. (2006). *The trouble between us: An uneasy history of white and black women in the feminist movement.* New York, NY: Oxford University Press; Roth, B. (2004). *Separate roads to feminism: Black, Chicana, and white feminist movements in the second wave.* New York, NY: Cambridge University Press; DiAngelo, R. (2018). *White fragility: Why it's so hard for white people to talk about racism.* Boston, MA: Beacon Press.

97. Beines, W. (2006). *The trouble between us: An uneasy history of white and black women in the feminist movement.* New York, NY: Oxford University Press.

98. Davis, AY. *Women, race and class.* (1983). New York, NY: Random House; Crenshaw, K. (1989, Jan1). Demarginalizing the intersection of race and sex: A black feminist critique of antidiscrimination doctrine, feminist theory, and antiracist policies. *University of Chicago Legal Forum.* Chicago, IL: University of Chicago.

99. Davis, AY. *Women, race and class.* (1983). New York, NY: Random House; Crenshaw, K. (1989, Jan1). Demarginalizing the intersection of race and sex: A black feminist critique of antidiscrimination doctrine, feminist theory, and antiracist policies. *University of Chicago Legal Forum.* Chicago, IL: University of Chicago.

100. Crenshaw, K. (1989, Jan1). Demarginalizing the intersection of race and sex: A black feminist critique of antidiscrimination doctrine, feminist theory, and antiracist policies. *University of Chicago Legal Forum.* Chicago, IL: University of Chicago; Springer, Kimberly (2005). *Living for the revolution: Black feminist organizations, 1968–1980.* Durham, NC: Duke University Press.

101. Crenshaw, K. (1989, Jan1). Demarginalizing the intersection of race and sex: A black feminist critique of antidiscrimination doctrine, feminist theory, and antiracist policies. *University of Chicago Legal Forum.* Chicago, IL: University of Chicago.

102. Davis, AY. *Women, race and class.* (1983). New York, NY: Random House; Springer, Kimberly (2005). *Living for the revolution: Black feminist organizations, 1968–1980.* Durham, NC: Duke University Press; Roth, B. (2004). *Separate roads to feminism: Black, Chicana, and white feminist movements in the second wave.* New York, NY: Cambridge University Press.

103. Wikipedia website. (2019). *Identity politics.* Retrieved from https://en.wikipedia.org/wiki/Identity_politics.

104. Diaz-Tello, F. (2016, May 24) Invisible wounds: Obstetric violence in the United States. *Reproductive Health Matters,* 24:47, 56-64, DOI: 10.1016/j.rhm.2016.04.004; Ross, LJ. & Solinger, R. (2017). *Reproductive justice: A new vision for the 21ˢᵗ century.* Oakland, CA: University of California Press; Roberts, D. (1997, 2ⁿᵈ ed. 2016). *Killing the black body: Race, reproduction, and the meaning of liberty.* New York, NY: Pantheon Books; Oparah, J., Jones, L., Hudson, D., Oseguera, T. & Arega, H. (2018). *Battling over birth: Black women and the maternal health care crisis.* California: Praeclarus Press.

COURAGE MATTERS

105. Whyte, D. (2001). *Crossing the unknown sea: Work as a pilgrimage of identify.* New York, NY: Riverhead Books.

106. Bovbjerg, M., Cheyney, M., Brown, J., Cox, K. & Leeman, L. (2017, September). Perspectives on risk: Assessment of risk profiles and outcomes among women planning community birth in the United States. *Birth*. 2017 Sep;44(3):209-221. doi: 10.1111/birt.12288. Epub 2017 Mar 22.

107. Cheyney, M. & McCullouch, J. (Current). Understanding relative risks in the community birth setting. Retrieved on September 9, 2019 from https://mana.org/blog/understanding-relative-risks-in-the-community-birth-setting-an-interview-with-researcher.

108. Cheyney, M. & McCullouch, J. (Current). Understanding relative risks in the community birth setting. Retrieved on September 9, 2019 from https://mana.org/blog/understanding-relative-risks-in-the-community-birth-setting-an-interview-with-researcher.

109. Bovbjerg, M., Cheyney, M., Brown, J., Cox, K. & Leeman, L. (2017, September). Perspectives on risk: Assessment of risk profiles and outcomes among women planning community birth in the United States. *Birth*. 2017 Sep;44(3):209-221. doi: 10.1111/birt.12288. Epub 2017 Mar 22.

110. McGrath K. (2012). Continuing education module the courage to birth. *The Journal of Perinatal Education, 21*(2), 72–79. Retrieved from doi:10.1891/1058-1243.21.2.72.

111. Campbell, J. Cousineau, P. & Brown, SL. (1990, 2nd ed. 2003). *The hero's journey: Joseph Campbell on his life and work*. San Francisco, CA: Harper & Row.

LINEAGE MATTERS

112. Stearns, FW. (1997). History of the lake states forests: Natural and human impacts. In: Lake States Regional Forest Resources Assessment: Technical Papers. Vasievich, J. & Webster, HH., eds. Gen. Tech. Rep. NC-189. St. Paul, MN: U.S. Department of Agriculture, Forest Service, North Central Forest Experiment Station: 8-29. Retrieved from https://www.ncrs.fs.fed.us/gla/reports/history.htm.

113. Quoi, CQ. (2017, April 26). *Did human ancestor 'Lucy' have a midwife?* Live Science. Retrieved from https://www.livescience.com/58844-did-human-ancestor-lucy-have-midwife.html.

114. Gibson, F. (2015). *The official plan to eliminate the midwife: 1900-1930*. Retrieved from https://collegeofmidwives.org/collegeofmidwives.org/safety_issues01/rosenbl1.htm.

115. Goode, K. (2014, Oct). Birthing, blackness, and the body: Black midwives and experiential continuities of institutional racism. CUNY Academic Works. Retrieved from https://academicworks.cuny.edu/gc_etds/423.

116. Gibson, F. (2015). *The politics of normal childbirth: Helping to end the hundred years war between midwifery and medicine*. A five-part historical series. Retrieved from https://faithgibson.org.

PART 2: WHY MIDWIVES MATTER

JUST THE FACTS

117. WHO. (2012, May). *Maternal Mortality*. [Fact sheet N°348]. Retrieved from https://www.who.int/news-room/fact-sheets/detail/maternal-mortality.

118. MacDorman, MF., Declercq, E., Cabral, H. & Morton, C. (2016, September). Recent increases in the U.S. maternal mortality rate: Disentangling trends from measurement issues. *Obstetricians Gynecol*. 128(3), 447-55.

119. MacDorman, M.F, Declercq, E., Cabral, H. & Morton, C. (2016, September). Recent increases in the U.S. maternal mortality rate: Disentangling trends from measurement issues. *Obstet Gynecol*. 128(3): 447-55.

120. Amnesty International. (2011, May 7). *Deadly delivery: The maternal healthcare crisis in the US*. Retrieved from https://www.amnestyusa.org/wpcontent/uploads/2017/04/deadlydeliveryoneyear.pdf.

121. CDC. (n.d.) *Severe maternal morbidity in the United States.* Retrieved from https://www.cdc.gov/reproductivehealth/maternalinfanthealth/severematernalmorbidity.html.

122. Save the Children Federation. (2015). *State of the world's mothers report.* Retrieved from https://www.savethechildren.org/content/dam/usa/reports/advocacy/sowm/sowm-2015.pdf.

123. Chen, A, Oster, E. & Williams, H. (2016, May). Why is infant mortality higher in the United States than in Europe? *American Economic Journal Economic Policy, 8*(2), 89-124. doi: 10.1257/pol.20140224.

124. Sandall, J., Soltani, H., Gates, S., Shennan, A. & Devane, D. (2016, April 28). Midwife-led continuity models versus other models of care for childbearing women. *Cochrane Database of Systematic Reviews* 2016, Issue 4, Art. No: CD004667. DOI: 10.1002/14651858.CD004667.pub5.

125. World Health Organization. (2016). *Midwives' voices, midwives' realities: Findings from a global consultation on providing quality midwifery care.* Retrieved from https://www.who.int/maternal_child_adolescent/documents/midwives-voices-realities/en/.

126. United Nations. *Millennium development goals report 2013.* New York, NY: United Nations. Retrieved from https://www.un.org/millenniumgoals/pdf/report-2013/mdg-report2013_pr_latin-am-car.pdf.

127. United Nations Population Fund [UNFPA]. *Focus on 5: Women's health and the MDGs.* Retrieved from https://www.unfpa.org/publications/focus-5.

128. United Nations. *Millennium development goals report 2013.* New York, NY: United Nations. Retrieved from https://www.un.org/millenniumgoals/pdf/report-2013/mdg-report2013_pr_latin-am-car.pdf.

129. United Nations. *Millennium development goals report 2013.* New York, NY: United Nations. Retrieved from https://www.un.org/millenniumgoals/pdf/report-2013/mdg-report2013_pr_latin-am-car.pdf.

130. Declercq, E. (2015, January). Midwife-attended births in the United States, 1990-2012: results from revised birth certificate data. *J Midwifery Women's Health, 60(1),10-5.*

131. Diaz-Tello, F. (2016) Invisible wounds: obstetric violence in the United States. *Reproductive Health Matters,* 24:47, 56-64, DOI: 10.1016/j.rhm.2016.04.004.

132. Vedam, S., et al. (2019, June). The giving voice to mothers study: Inequity and mistreatment during pregnancy and childbirth in the United States. *Reproductive Health,* Vol 16, Article number: 77.

133. Schneider, EC., Sarnak, DO., Squires, D., Shah, A. & Doty, MM. (2017, July). Mirror, mirror 2017: International comparison reflects flaws and opportunities for better U.S. health care. *The Commonwealth Fund.* Retrieved from https://interactives.commonwealthfund.org/2017/july/mirror-mirror/.

134. Amnesty International. (2016). *The U.S. maternal health crisis: 14 numbers you need to know.* [U.S. Maternal Health Crisis Facts]. Retrieved from https://www.amnestyusa.org/the-u-s-maternal-health-crisis-14-numbers-you-need-to-know/; Sakala, C. & Corry, M. (2008). *Evidence-based maternity care: What it is and what it can achieve.* New York, NY: Co-publishers Childbirth Connection and Reforming States Group.

135. Sakala, C & Corry, M. (2008). *Evidence-based maternity care: What it is and what it can achieve.* New York, NY: Co-publishers Childbirth Connection and Reforming States Group.

136. Sakala, C & Corry, M. (2008). *Evidence-based maternity care: What it is and what it can achieve.* New York, NY: Co-publishers Childbirth Connection and Reforming States Group.

137. UNFPA. (2011). State of the world's midwifery report: Delivering health, saving lives. Retrieved from https://www.unfpa.org/publications/state-worlds-midwifery-2011.

138. Vedam, S., Stoll, K., MacDorman, M., Declercq, E., Cramer, R,. Cheyney, M., et al. (2018, February 21). *Mapping integration of midwives across the United States: Impact on access, equity, and outcomes. PLoS ONE* 13(2): e0192523. Retrieved from https://doi.org/10.1371/journal.pone.0192523.

139. WHO. (2016). *Midwives' voices, midwives' realities: Findings from a global consultation on providing quality midwifery care.* Retrieved from https://www.who.int/maternal_child_adolescent/documents/midwives-voices-realities/en/.

140. Sandall, J., Soltani, H., Gates, S., Shennan, A. & Devane, D. (2016, April 28). Midwife-led continuity models versus other models of care for childbearing women. *Cochrane Database of Systematic Reviews* 2016, Issue 4, Art. No: CD004667. DOI: 10.1002/14651858.CD004667.pub5.

141. Pew Research. (2018, January). *They're waiting longer, but U.S. women today more likely to have children than a decade ago.* [U.S. Census Data.] Retrieved from http://www.pewsocialtrends.org/2018/01/18/theyre-waiting-longer-but-u-s-women-today-more-likely-to-have-children-than-a-decade-ago/.

142. ACNM. (2012, April). *Midwifery: Evidence-based care. A summary of the research on midwifery practice in the United States.* Retrieved from https://www.midwife.org/ACNM/files/ccLibrary-Files/Filename/000000002128/Midwifery%20Evidence-based%20Practice%20Issue%20Brief%20FINALMAY%202012.pdf.

143. ACNM. (2012, April). *Midwifery: Evidence-based care. A summary of the research on midwifery practice in the United States.* Retrieved from https://www.midwife.org/ACNM/files/ccLibrary-Files/Filename/000000002128/Midwifery%20Evidence-based%20Practice%20Issue%20Brief%20FINALMAY%202012.pdf.

144. Cheyney, M., Bovbjerg, M., Everson, C., Gordon, W., Hannibal, D. & Vedam, S. (2014, January 30). Outcomes of care for 16,924 planned home births in the United States: The Midwives Alliance of North America Statistics Project, 2004 to 2009. *JMidwifery Womens Health*, 59,17–27.

145. Cheyney, M., Bovbjerg, M., Everson, C., Gordon, W., Hannibal, D. & Vedam, S. (2014, January 30). Outcomes of care for 16,924 planned home births in the United States: The Midwives Alliance of North America Statistics Project, 2004 to 2009. *JMidwifery Womens Health*, 59, 17–27.

146. Sakala, C. & Corry, M. (2008). *Evidence-based maternity care: What it is and what it can achieve.* New York, NY: Co-publishers Childbirth Connection and Reforming States Group.

147. UNFPA. (2011). State of the world's midwifery report: Delivering health, saving lives. Retrieved from https://www.unfpa.org/publications/state-worlds-midwifery-2011.

148. New York Times. (2013, June 30). *American way of birth, costliest in the world.* Retrieved from https://www.nytimes.com/2013/07/01/health/american-way-of-birth-costliest-in-the-world.html.

149. New York Times. (2013, June 30). *American way of birth, costliest in the world.* Retrieved from https://www.nytimes.com/2013/07/01/health/american-way-of-birth-costliest-in-the-world.html.

150. Sakala, C. & Corry, M. (2008). *Evidence-based maternity care: What it is and what it can achieve.* New York, NY: Co-publishers Childbirth Connection and Reforming States Group.

DROP DEAD SERIOUS

151. Souza, JP., Cecatti, MA., Parpinelli, MA. & Krupa, F. (2009, May 28). An emerging "Maternal Near-Miss Syndrome": Narratives of women who almost died during pregnancy and childbirth. *Birth*. Vol 36, Issue 2. Retrieved from https://doi.org/10.1111/j.1523-536X.2009.00313.x.

152. Souza, JP., Cecatti, MA., Parpinelli, MA. & Krupa, F. (2009, May 28). An emerging "Maternal Near-Miss Syndrome": Narratives of women who almost died during pregnancy and childbirth. Birth. Vol 36, Issue 2. Retrieved from https://doi.org/10.1111/j.1523-536X.2009.00313.x;

Furuta, M., Sandall, J. & Bick, D. (2012, Nov 10). A systematic review of the relationship between severe maternal morbidity and post-traumatic stress disorder. *BMC Pregnancy Childbirth*, 12, Article No.:125. doi: 10.1186/1471-2393-12-125.

153. Souza, JP., Cecatti, MA., Parpinelli, MA. & Krupa, F. (2009, May 28). An emerging "Maternal Near-Miss Syndrome": Narratives of women who almost died during pregnancy and childbirth. *Birth*. Vol 36, Issue 2. Retrieved from https://doi.org/10.1111/j.1523-536X.2009.00313.x.

154. Block, J. (2019). *Everything below the waist: Why health care needs a feminist revolution*. NY, NY: St Martin's Press.

155. Martin, N. & Montagne, R. (2017, May 12). *The last person you'd expect to die in childbirth*. ProPublica and NPR. Retrieved from https://www.propublica.org/article/die-in-childbirth-maternal-death-rate-health-care-system.

156. Martin, N. & Montagne, R. (2017, May 12). *The last person you'd expect to die in childbirth*. ProPublica and NPR. Retrieved from https://www.propublica.org/article/die-in-childbirth-maternal-death-rate-health-care-system.

157. Young, A., Ungar, L. & Schnaars, C. (2018, July 26). *Deadly deliveries*. USA Today. Retrieved from https://www.usatoday.com/in-depth/news/investigations/deadly-deliveries/2018/07/26/maternal-mortality-rates-preeclampsia-postpartum-hemorrhage-safety/546889002/.

158. Johnson, T. (2019, Jan 11). *Maternity care in crisis: American women are dying from childbirth at a higher rate than in any other developed country*. National Conference of State Legislatures. Retrieved from http://www.ncsl.org/research/health/maternity-care-in-crisis.aspx.

A NEW WAY OF THINKING

159. Wheatley, MJ. (2017). *Who do we choose to be?: Facing reality, claiming leadership, restoring sanity*. Oakland, CA: Berrett-Koehler Publishers.

160. Wheatley, MJ. (2017). *Who do we choose to be?: Facing reality, claiming leadership, restoring sanity*. Oakland, CA: Berrett-Koehler Publishers.

161. Wheatley, MJ. (2017). *Who do we choose to be?: Facing reality, claiming leadership, restoring sanity*. Oakland, CA: Berrett-Koehler Publishers.

162. Drug Policy Alliance website. (2019). *Harm reduction*. Retrieved from http://www.drugpolicy.org/issues/harm-reduction.

STANDING AT A THRESHOLD

163. Center for Ecoliteracy website. (2019, Nov 22). *The Great Turning*. Retrieved from https://www.ecoliteracy.org/article/great-turning.

164. Johanna Macy and Her Work website. (2019, Nov 23). Retrieved from https://www.joannamacy.net/main.

165. Center for Ecoliteracy website. (2019, Nov 22). *The Great Turning*. Retrieved from https://www.ecoliteracy.org/article/great-turning.

166. WHO. (2017, Sept 12). *Nursing and Midwifery in the History of the World Health Organization 1948–2017*. [Nurses and midwives play critical role in meeting the UN Sustainable Development Goals.] Retrieved from https://www.who.int/publications-detail/nursing-and-midwifery-in-the-history-of-the-world-health-organization-(1948–2017).

MIDWIVES ARE CHANGING THE WORLD

167. The Moon Magazine. (2019). *Women are the first environment: An interview with Mohawk elder Katsi Cook*. Retrieved from http://moonmagazine.org/women-first-environment-interview-mohawk-elder-katsi-cook-2018-03-31/.

168. The Moon Magazine. (2019). *Women are the first environment: An interview with*

Mohawk elder Katsi Cook. Retrieved from http://moonmagazine.org/women-first-environment-interview-mohawk-elder-katsi-cook-2018-03-31/.

169. Follett, J. (2005). *Voices of feminism oral history project.* Transcript of video recording October 26-27, 2005. Northampton, MA: Sophia Smith Collection, Smith College.

170. The Moon Magazine. (2019*). Women are the first environment: An interview with Mohawk elder Katsi Cook.* Retrieved from http://moonmagazine.org/women-first-environment-interview-mohawk-elder-katsi-cook-2018-03-31/.

171. Spirit Aligned Leadership Program website. (2019, Oct) *The Spirit Aligned Leadership Program is pleased to announce the selection of its second circle of eight Legacy Leaders.* Retrieved from http://www.spiritaligned.org.

172. Spirit Aligned Leadership Program website. (2019, Oct) *The Spirit Aligned Leadership Program is pleased to announce the selection of its second circle of eight Legacy Leaders.* Retrieved from http://www.spiritaligned.org.

173. National Aboriginal Health Organization. (2008, Dec). *Celebrating birth: Aboriginal midwifery in Canada.* Retrieved from https://www.saintelizabeth.com/getmedia/5b080031-a443-4d71-8a64-2dc429b4d34f/Celebrating_Birth_Aboriginal_Midwifery_Canada_2008.pdf.aspx.

174. Contreras, E. (2009). *Medicina tradicional: Doña Queta y el legado de los habitantes de las nubes.* Aida Guerra Falcón (ed). Oaxaca, MX: ISBN #978-84-935100-0-8.

175. Contreras, E. (2009). *Medicina tradicional: Doña Queta y el legado de los habitantes de las nubes.* Aida Guerra Falcón (ed). Oaxaca, MX: ISBN #978-84-935100-0-8.

176. Návar, MM. (2010). *Mujer Zapoteca de las nubes* (Zapotec woman of the clouds). Austin, TX: Zapotec Press.

177. Návar, MM. (2010). *Mujer Zapoteca de las nubes* (Zapotec woman of the clouds). Austin, TX: Zapotec Press.

178. Jolles, D, et al. (2017). Outcomes of childbearing Medicaid beneficiaries engaged in care at Strong Start birth centers between 2012 and 2014. *Birth,* 44 no 4, p 298-305.

179. Block, J. (2019). *Everything below the waist: Why health care needs a feminist revolution.* NY, NY: St Martin's Press.

180. Consumers Reports website. (2019, released 4-13-16). *Your biggest c-section risk may be your hospital.* Released 4-13-16. Retrieved from https://www.consumerreports.org/search/?query=cesarean%20section.

181. Consumers Reports website. (2019, released April 14). *Your biggest c-section risk may be your hospital.* Released 4-13-16. Retrieved from https://www.consumerreports.org/search/?query=cesarean%20section.

182. Block, J. (2019). *Everything below the waist: Why health care needs a feminist revolution.* NY, NY: St Martin's Press.

183. Allman, J. & Phillipi, J. (2016, Jan 15). Maternal outcomes in birth centers: An integrative review of the literature. *Journal of Midwifery & Women's Health,* Vol 16, Issue1, p 21-51.

184. Block, J. (2019). *Everything below the waist: Why health care needs a feminist revolution.* NY, NY: St Martin's Press.

185. Jolles, D., et al. (2017). Outcomes of childbearing Medicaid beneficiaries engaged in care at Strong Start birth centers between 2012 and 2014. *Birth,* 44 no 4, p 298-305.

186. Block, J. (2019). *Everything below the waist: Why health care needs a feminist revolution.* NY, NY, St Martin's Press.

187. Williamson, M. (Ed.) (2000). *Imagine: What America could be in the 21st century.* New York, NY: Rodale Inc.

188. Collins-Fulea, C. (2009, July-Aug). Models of organizational structure of midwifery practices located in institutions with residency programs. *J Midwifery Women's Health*, 54(4): 287-93. doi:10.1016/j.jmwh.2009.03.007.

189. Smith, DC. (2016). Interprofessional collaboration in perinatal care. *J Perinat Neonat Nurs*, 30(3): 167-173.

190. Smith, DC. (2016). Interprofessional collaboration in perinatal care. *J Perinat Neonat Nurs*, 30(3): 167-173.

191. Kassebaum NJ., Aurora M., Barber RM., Bhutta ZA., Brown J., Carter A., Casey DC., Charlson FJ., Coates MM., Coggeshall M., Cornaby L., Dandona L., Dicker DJ. & Erskine HE. (2016, Oct 8). Global, regional, and national levels of maternal mortality, 1990-2015: A systematic analysis for the Global Burden of Disease Study 2015. *Lancet*. 8;388(10053):1448-1449.

192. Taylor, J., Novoa, C., Hamm, K. & Phadke, S. (2019, May 2). *Eliminating racial disparities in maternal and infant mortality*. Center for American Progress website. Retrieved from https://www.americanprogress.org/issues/women/reports/2019/05/02/469186/eliminating-racial-disparities-maternal-infant-mortality/.

193. Mosaic Midwifery Collective website. (2019). Retrieved from https://www.mosaicmidwifery-collective.com.

194. Centers for Disease Control and Prevention. (2019). *Pregnancy Mortality Surveillance System*. Retrieved from https://www.cdc.gov/reproductivehealth/maternalinfanthealth/pmss.html.

195. Vimeo online video. (2019). *Birth Detroit and Detroit pop-up midwifery clinic*. Retrieved Dec 8, 2019 from https://vimeo.com/341446107.

196. Vimeo online video. (2019). *Birth Detroit and Detroit pop-up midwifery clinic*. Retrieved Dec 8, 2019 from https://vimeo.com/341446107.

PART 3: WILD WISDOM

COLONIZING WOMEN'S BODIES

197. Ross, L. & Solinger, R. (2017). *Reproductive justice*. Oakland, CA: University of California Press.

198. Ross, L. & Solinger, R. (2017). *Reproductive justice*. Oakland, CA: University of California Press.

199. Ross, L. (Ed.) (2007). *Reproductive justice briefing book: A primer on reproductive justice and social change*. Berkeley, CA: University of California, School of Law. Retrieved from https://www.law.berkeley.edu/php-programs/courses/fileDL.php?fID=4051.

200. Ross, L. & Solinger, R. (2017). *Reproductive justice*. Oakland, CA: University of California Press.

201. Decolonize Birth website. (2019). *Decolonize birth conference*. Retrieved from https://www.decolonizingbirthconference.com/about-us.

202. Ancient Song Doula Service website. (2019). Retrieved from https://www.ancientsongdoula-services.com/our-focus.

203. Ancient Song Doula Service website. (2019). Retrieved from https://www.ancientsongdoula-services.com/our-focus.

204. Bey, A., Brill, A., Porchia-Albert, C., Gradilla, M & Strauss, N. (2019, Mar 25). *Advancing birth justice: Community-based doula models as a standard of care for ending racial disparities*. A collaboration of Ancient Song Doula Services, Village Birth International, and Every Mother Counts. Retrieved from https://blackmamasmatter.org/wp-content/uploads/2019/03/Advancing-Birth-Justice-CBD-Models-as-Std-of-Care-3-25-19.pdf.